Also by Emmanuel Carrère

97,196 Words

97,196 Words

ESSAYS

Emmanuel Carrère

Translated from the French by John Lambert

Farrar, Straus and Giroux

New York

Farrar, Straus and Giroux
120 Broadway, New York 10271

Photographs in "The Life of Julie" by Darcy Padilla

Library of Congress Cataloging-in-Publication Data
Names: Carrère, Emmanuel, 1957– author. | Lambert, John, 1960– translator.
Title: 97,196 words : essays / Emmanuel Carrère.
Other titles: Prose works. Selections. English
Description: First American edition. | New York : Farrar, Straus and
  Giroux, 2019. | "Originally published in French in 2016 by P.O.L.,
  France, as Il est avantageux d'avoir où aller."
Identifiers: LCCN 2019019747 | ISBN 9780374178208 (hardcover)
Subjects: LCSH: Carrère, Emmanuel, 1957– | Authors, French—
  20th century—Biography. | Authors, French—21st century—Biography. |
  Literature—History and criticism.
Classification: LCC PQ2663.A7678 A2 2019 | DDC 843/.914 [B]—dc23
LC record available at https://lccn.loc.gov/2019019747

Designed by Jonathan D. Lippincott

www.fsgbooks.com
www.twitter.com/fsgbooks • www.facebook.com/fsgbooks

1   3   5   7   9   10   8   6   4   2

Contents

97,196 Words

Three Crime Stories

1. "I'm Happy My Mother's Alive"

Last 21 and 22 November, a twenty-one-year-old youth, Franck B., appeared before the Melun Criminal Court for having tried to kill Hélène R., his biological mother. Here's their story.

Twenty years earlier, Hélène R. was not yet a *biological* mother. She was just a *single* mother, panicked at what was happening to her. She'd given birth without daring to tell anyone and lost her job as a maid and the room that went with it. She dragged herself from shelter to shelter with her little boy, then with her little boy and her big belly, then with her two little boys because, repetition and hardship going hand in hand, Alexandre was born two years after Franck, to an equally anonymous father. Walled in by silence, fear, and constant rebuffs, Hélène didn't know where to turn for help, or what sort of help she really needed. The Department of Health and Social Services, whose door you knock on in such cases, didn't quite know either if it was better to help her keep her children or to take them away.

No doubt the boys would have suffered less if they'd been given up once and for all, rather than being shunted back and forth from negligent nanny to foster placement, but their mother couldn't resolve herself to sever all ties. She hesitated, then came back to get them right before the cutoff date, so that the separation, which was finally consummated in 1974, took five years. Today she says that she signed the fatal document without understanding what she was doing. She also says that even after signing it, she hoped to see her children again, that she applied to the Department of Health and Social Services for permission. But this time it was too late: they'd been adopted.

All that remained for Hélène to do was cry every night, clam up as she'd always done, and console herself—while turning the knife in the wound—with the idea that somewhere in France her little boys lived with people who loved them and whom they loved.

About which she wasn't wrong. The B.'s, who had adopted both Franck and Alexandre—rebaptized Alain because, unlike his brother, he was young enough not to remember his name—were no doubt good people.

From day one, all parents discover with amazement a sense of fear that will never leave them. Inevitably, this fear is even stronger among adoptive parents. One imagines that the B.'s felt a worried, conscientious love for the boys, considering themselves unworthy at the slightest warning sign. And the warning signs came—from Franck, as one can imagine. He was a difficult, taciturn, rebellious child. The B.'s did all they could to act as if he were really their son, and to be strict but kind. Despite this, or because of it, the typical textbook setbacks came about as the years passed, saddening Mr. B. enough for his wife to prefer not to grieve him any further by showing him what she'd found in Franck's room, and which would later, passing from one hand to the next, send a shiver down his jurors' spines: a printed card with which Mr. B., Mrs. B., and Alain were deeply saddened to announce the death of their son and brother Franck, aged fifteen. The date was left blank.

Franck was fifteen at the time. Two years later, the idea of searching for his natural mother added a new layer to his morose daydreaming. A child who feels misunderstood by his biological parents can always imagine that they're not really his, that his real parents are better looking, more loving, more everything. Such dreams are generally harmless. The problem in the case of an adopted child is that it's not just a dream, and that somewhere in the real world, unknown but real people truly occupy this coveted place, and there is no greater or more heartrending temptation than to try to find them, see what they look like, and throw your love, or your hate, or both, in their faces.

Franck was expecting everything from this reunion: an explanation of his story, and the freedom to live it fully. It seems he had no problem finding his mother: he simply contacted the Department of Health and Social Services and they gave him her name, leaving it up to him to find her address. I say "it seems," as this point was the only bone of contention in a trial where no one disputed the facts: Franck's lawyer condemned the department's shameful irresponsibility, and the department's lawyer did his best to clear its name, without either convincing or even really interesting anyone.

In any event: One fine day in June 1988, the telephone rang at Hélène R.'s place, in a housing project in the suburbs of Melun. Her son Frédéric, aged eight, picked up the phone and told the anonymous caller that he'd go get his mom.

One week later, Hélène R. opened the door to Franck.

He was a big, dark-haired youth, good-looking in a somber, reserved way, and was clearly trying to appear calm. The way he talked, you felt he would rather be silent: he was overly polite and almost pedantically neutral. His voice sounded almost artificial, and he looked a bit like the young zombielike actors in Robert Bresson's films. Hélène R. didn't think any of that, just that this person in front of her was her lost child, that he'd found her, and that was enough.

He called her Madame, then Hélène, but not Mom. He asked

her questions. About his father, but that ground didn't take long to cover because she didn't even know his name: he was a railway worker, just passing through, that's all. About her life, her job: she worked as a housekeeper in a hospital. About the little boy, Frédéric: she'd been able to keep him, at least; her life had become a little less difficult—she was fighting to keep him, in fact, having separated from his father, who wanted custody and who wouldn't get it, she swore. Hearing that, Franck didn't raise an eyebrow. He preferred to ask her about a bump he'd had on his forehead since he was little—he'd often wondered how he got it. She told him that he'd fallen down at his aunt's place; she'd babysat him when he was three.

Hélène gave the best answers she could and hardly asked a thing. For some people, having to put up with events becomes a habit and dulls the mind. You take things as they come and aren't surprised: that's how things are. But as Franck was leaving, Hélène said that if he wanted to come back, the door would be open.

He came back that fall, for Frédéric's birthday, bringing a watch as a present. Then he started coming quite often. His adoptive parents didn't know; he didn't talk to them—or to Alain—about his absences. Hélène furnished a room for him in her little apartment, where he came to sleep from time to time. The contrast between the affluence of the B.'s and his birth mother's world, so bereft of grace, intelligence, scope—of everything—seemed to leave him indifferent. Except as regarded Frédéric, whom Franck would have liked to see get a better education. That his half brother was getting such a poor start in life worried Franck. He loved Frédéric and still does: he approved of his mother's fighting to keep him.

As one can imagine, this reunion didn't bring Franck the clarification or liberation he'd hoped for and only deepened his confusion. His double life, his secret comings and goings, quickly became unbearable. He tried to escape.

He fled to Sweden, under the pretense of doing grade twelve at the French high school in Stockholm. But he returned after just two months, and the back-and-forth started all over again. The B.'s were saddened by his absences and his mood swings. Hélène continued to welcome him with her glum, placid kindness, and her exasperating way of finding such an unbearable situation perfectly normal.

He put up with it for two years, until the day in June when he showed up at her place, without warning, as he often did. He spent the afternoon playing with Frédéric; that evening he went to visit a couple of friends, talking and playing Monopoly until dawn. At eleven in the morning he went back to Hélène's place to take a shower and change, then the two had lunch. During the meal they exchanged a few anodyne words, nothing out of the ordinary. She did the dishes. She found him nervous, tense: standing in the kitchen, he played with one of the knives that she had just washed. She went into the dining room, switched on the television, sat down on the couch, and flipped through the TV guide. Franck stood behind her. She clearly remembers thinking that he was going to come closer, that he was expecting a gesture of tenderness, a hug. It was then that she felt something like a prick in her back. Then another, harder this time, which suddenly caused her a huge amount of pain.

Realizing that her son was stabbing her with the knife, she stood up, shouting, "Franck, what are you doing? Are you nuts?"

He answered, "You abandoned me, my life's the pits" (or "the shits," it's the only difference in their versions). As she fell to the floor, he jumped on her and tried to cut her throat. Struggling and trying to protect herself with her hands as the knife slashed, she shouted, "Franck, I love you!" Then: "Think of Frédéric!" Maybe that's what stayed Franck's arm, maybe not, but starting that moment, both of their memories go blank.

A little later, the phone rang. Franck got up, covered his

mother, whom he presumed dead, with a blue bedspread, then went to wash his hands, determined not to answer. The ringing stopped. Then Hélène moved and gasped that he should call for help. He didn't know what to do. The phone rang again. He picked it up. It was the secretary of the ear, nose, and throat specialist, calling to reschedule an appointment his mother had made. Franck didn't get the irony of the situation, and in any event her bloody throat was hidden by the bedspread that he'd pulled over her face. He merely told the secretary what he'd just done and asked her to send someone as quickly as possible. Fearing that he might be misunderstood or that she'd think he was crazy or a practical joker, he went and knocked on the door of the neighbor across the landing. Having informed her of the situation, he walked downstairs, sat on the front steps, and waited.

According to the policeman who arrested him, Franck was neutral, as if detached from the whole thing, and physically exhausted. He made no bones about what he'd done and even insisted that his acts were premeditated. When asked why he'd called for help if he wanted to kill his mother, he said that he was "being a good citizen." After which nothing else was got out of him for some time.

Hélène was dying when she arrived at the hospital. The knife had slit her throat and basically left her without a chance, and the expert witness at the trial a year and a half later didn't hesitate to say her recovery was a miracle. Because she survived, and even resumed a normal life.

For several months she suffered from an obsessive fear of her son. Each night, before going to bed, she inspected her apartment from top to bottom to make sure he hadn't come back to finish her off. Convinced that he would try again if he was released, she instituted civil proceedings against him.

Then she went to see him in Fleury-Mérogis Prison. When she came back, she withdrew the charges, saying that she alone was responsible for what had happened to her. In a letter to the judge, she asked that Franck be released as soon as possible, "so we can finally get some peace."

Everyone at the trial stressed his or her own responsibility, as if fearing above all to be excluded from this strange circle of love. Hélène first used the meager words at her disposal to say that everything had been her fault from the start. Not wanting to be outdone, the B.'s expressed their regret at having put Franck in a boarding school for a year, thus awakening his fear of being abandoned. Franck insisted that was not the way things were, then contradicted the court psychiatrist and in general rejected all attempts to get him off the hook. He'd known what he was doing, he said: for several weeks he'd been sure that killing his mother was the only way out of his impasse.

Near the end of the trial, presided over by a judge who was generally considered a tough nut but who showed exemplary tact and humanity in this case, Franck was asked if he regretted what he'd done. He thought about it and said, "I'm happy my mother's alive."

A strikingly precise answer. To survive and become a man, Franck B. had to kill Hélène R., his natural mother. A medical miracle allowed this murder to be committed yet annulled. Such grace is rarely accorded: a psychoanalyst or priest would no doubt also see a miracle at work. All that remained was for the jurors, to top things off, to bring about a penal miracle.

Refusing to acquit him—which by negating his crime would have insulted the accused and compromised his return among his fellow men—the court yielded to the arguments of the prosecuting attorney, a young adoptive mother. In her final submissions she gave a personal statement and the most moving of pleas. A prison sentence of three years, of which two were suspended, was handed down. The matricide Franck B., found entirely guilty of his act, left the courthouse free, and perhaps liberated.

Two families, beside themselves with love, were waiting for him at the exit. He would now have to make the best of that.

Published in *L'Événement du jeudi*, January 1990

2. Resilience of an Infanticide

That morning, Marie-Christine was even sadder than usual when she got up. Her last sick leave was coming to an end, she was going to have to go back to the office, and Marie-Christine could no longer stand the office. It hadn't always been like that. Before, she'd been proud of having passed the state exam and becoming a bureaucrat in charge of maintenance in a French ministry, instead of cleaning tiles in city buildings as her mother had done. But then, two years ago, her department had been computerized, coinciding with her maternity leave. When she got back after Guillaume's birth, everything started to go wrong. Her colleagues sniggered behind her back, her superiors bullied her, she spent more and more time on sick leave, and each time it was all the more difficult to come back. This time she couldn't. She preferred to die.

Preferring death to life, at least to hers, wasn't new for Marie-Christine. When she was younger, she'd tried to kill herself two times, and at the start of the previous winter she'd bought a blank pistol over the counter, identical to the Smith & Wesson .22 Long Rifle you see in westerns. She kept it under Guillaume's bed, wrapped as a present so as not to attract her husband's attention.

To say that she loved her son is an understatement, and there was no question of her leaving him alone. So she unwrapped the package and loaded the gun while Guillaume played with the cartridges. Then she pointed the gun at the twenty-month-old's forehead, covered her eyes with her hand, and pulled the trigger.

Then she reloaded, aimed at her own forehead, and fired again. Everything should have stopped at that moment, but it didn't. She just felt a pain between her eyes and saw the child writhing on the bed. Heaven, where she'd imagined they would meet again, didn't look at all as she'd expected. After a quarter of an hour she called an ambulance.

When it arrived, followed by the police, Guillaume was dead. Her face covered in blood, Marie-Christine tried to steal a policeman's gun to finish herself off, but failed. At the hospital she was just as unable to escape the care her state demanded. Fragments from the cartridge remained stuck in her forehead, causing a gnawing pain that woke her up at night and reminded her incessantly of her nightmare. Having survived her son struck her as an atrocious but logical injustice: she'd been dogged by injustice since she was born; it had eaten away at her for her entire life; of course it would end up swallowing her whole.

To a judge's ears, murdered children evoke a familiar litany, and no one at the Nanterre Criminal Court was surprised to learn that Marie-Christine had been abandoned at a young age, that between eleven and fifteen she'd been regularly raped by a brutal, alcoholic stepfather, or that her frightened mother, paralyzed with fear, had preferred to turn a blind eye.

Despite her seemingly uneventful marriage and a social adaptation that was as commendable as it was precarious, no one doubted that the twenty-five years of her life preceding the crime had been twenty-five years of unhappiness, and taking stock of this unhappiness was part and parcel of judicial routine.

What was not part and parcel of judicial routine, by contrast, were the three years that followed the crime. They started normally, if you will: Marie-Christine cried all the time, wanted to die, and no one saw another solution. However, after she'd spent just eleven months in prison, the examining magistrate, impressed by the progress she'd made with the help of her lawyer and the various therapists dedicated to this apparently hopeless case, consented to have her released pending her trial, subject to judicial supervision.

Little by little, with the help of therapy, Marie-Christine came back to life. She went back to work, was transferred to another service, and said she was happy there. She got back together with her husband and, just nine months after getting out of prison, gave birth to a little girl. Another child was to be born in two months' time, so she was pregnant when she appeared before her jurors.

This fact, as well as the witness statements that unanimously praised her newfound psychological balance, and given that she was "feeling much better" about herself, gave a strange twist to the account of Guillaume's murder. A strange and even shocking twist, bearing in mind how hard it is to admit that someone can do such a thing and then pull through. Even harder to admit is the idea that emerged as the trial went on that this act could have been a horrible but necessary stage on life's way—like a child abandoning his security blanket or a swimmer kicking against the bottom of the pool to come back to the surface. In killing her cherished son, one expert stated, Marie-Christine had killed the hated childhood that had prevented her from living.

The ordeal had been terrible, but now the page had been turned and the two were making a fresh start, as her timid, mustached husband confirmed on the witness stand. It was difficult not to look in horror at this man who had had the—the what? The generosity? The madness? The mercy? The love, no doubt, which is all of these together—to get back together with the woman who had killed their firstborn child. What could their life be like? Their conversations, their silences, their joys? Did they think of the child they were now expecting as their second, or their third?

A few weeks earlier I had attended another trial, that of a poor woman who, similarly distressed and confused, had let her baby die. Like Marie-Christine, she was more a victim than a criminal, everyone agreed, in spite of which she'd been given eighteen years. A terrible verdict, but one that was explained not only by the toughness of the jury but also by the fact that the woman was completely destroyed, right down the core, to the point that no development, no project, regardless how much confidence one might have in human resources, seemed imaginable for her.

The court in Nanterre, by contrast, was eager to "let things develop," since—contrary to all expectations and almost contrary to all decency—it seemed that development was possible. Natural morality wants us to be more indulgent with those who suffer the most from their wrongdoings, and to go easy on those who have destroyed themselves. Opposed to this is the harsh and vitalist evangelical law according to which whoever has will be given more, while from the one who has not, even what he has will be taken away. This is the law the jury members followed. Crediting Marie-Christine for her stupefying ability to survive, they gave her back to her loved ones with a five-year prison sentence, of which four years and one month were suspended—the eleven months with no remission covering those she had already served.

To those who would be tempted, as I admit I was, to say that in this case human justice was a little quick in passing the cruel duty to punish on to God or the sinner's conscience, I will simply repeat what Marie-Christine murmured before leaving the stand: "One day I'll have to tell my children."

Published in *L'Événement du jeudi*, February 1990

3. Letter to the Mother of a Murderer

It's with a trembling hand, madame, that you start to read this article. And perhaps, once you've read it to the end, you'll think I would have done better to keep my compassion to myself, rather than splashing your sadness across the sheets of a newspaper. I beg your forgiveness.

Our looks crossed from time to time during those terrible days in the courthouse at Châteauroux. At least I looked at you, a lot: surreptitiously, without daring to come up to you during the breaks to tell you about what I'm now trying to write. I was in the press stand, an amateur legal reporter, a tourist in a way, attracted by the lawyer's reputation and the strange nature of the crime: a forty-five-year-old farmer murdered in his bed, first beaten with a bottle, then stabbed, then shot with a rifle, and finally burned, his charred corpse discovered in his devastated farmhouse. One might think his death was the result of obscure rural strife—clan rivalry, family feuds, hicks doing each other in. Nothing of the sort: the murderer, the son of a Parisian family on vacation in a neighboring village, had no relationship, no common interests, no bone to pick with the victim. No gripes, no motive. A wanton act, one concludes, meaning that the criminal is more or less a monster. And if, madame, you've been coming to this courtroom with your husband for the past weeks—perhaps the way as a student you used to meet your friends after their exams, to see what awaited you—and now hold him in your arms at the front of the gallery, it's because the criminal who "risks life," as the bailiff said, is your son.

It seems to me that when you sense the truth of a cliché, you can say you've learned something. I watched you watch him, this twenty-eight-year-old youth who looked younger, a boy, really, on his face the stubborn look of a dunce whom the teachers have long stopped questioning, in the crested blazer you bought for him so he'd look his best. Watching you watching him—he didn't look at you, or at anyone—I got a better sense of the melodramatic words *the bench of infamy* and *the bane of humanity*. Other words came to me as well, words I'd often heard without paying them much heed, focused as I was on the music with which Pergolesi or Scarlatti had accompanied them: those of the *Stabat Mater*. They were about you.

For two days, following two years of nightmares and insomnia, you had to listen to the endlessly repeated tale of the evening when your son, without a reason and perhaps not knowing what he was doing—no one will ever know, not even he, no doubt—brutally killed a poor farmer whom he hardly knew and who had never done him any harm. The atrocious descriptions of the corpse, which you must have read a hundred times—or made a point of not reading, which amounts to the same thing—accompanied you throughout the trial. First the court clerk recapitulated them at the start of the proceedings, then the medical examiners recited them in detail, and then the prosecuting attorney, who was only doing his job, asked that the most horrible passages be repeated so that the jurors, steeped in horror, would give your son the max.

A crime can have no motive, but it's sure to have a past: that of its author, whose entire life becomes the explanation for, prelude to, and cause of his act. And the younger the author, the more his parents will feel as if they're the ones on the stand. You asked for no more than that: to be found guilty so that your son would be a little less so, to take as much of the burden as you could. You were ready to put up with the cruel paradox so often seen at court, in which the prosecuting attorney explains what exemplary parents your child has so as to hasten his downfall, while the lawyer you're paying to defend him blames you for his neuroses and his crime. Your lawyer was talented—and compassionate—enough to avoid this rhetorical trap and put his client in a humane and poignant light without making his parents look like uncaring monsters or imbeciles, which they clearly are not. It was enough to see you, madame, and to hear you when you testified, to understand that no one, ever, could blame you as much as you have blamed yourself, day and night, rightly or wrongly, for the past two years and more.

If the unexplainable must be explained, you were wrong to entrust your son to a nanny, then to your godmother, for the first five years of his life. Those are the most formative years, the psychologists repeat. But you didn't know, and they were formative years for you as well: for your future, for your marriage, and for your child, you thought. Seeing how hard a time he had at school, you shouldn't have wanted him to succeed like you and your husband succeeded, by dint of hard work alone. You could have prevented—or tried to prevent—his slow slide from a sensitive, fib-prone child to an adolescent plagued by anxieties and fears, then to an immature young man sponging off his parents and his indulgent godmother, spending his time writing unpublishable science fiction novels, watching X-rated videos, and, to stem the panic that threatened to submerge him each night, swilling antidepressants and anxiety pills ten at a time.

You weren't blind, you were worried. But you thought it was a phase he was going through, and that with time, with the love you gave him and the work he would eventually find, this prolonged adolescent crisis would pass: everything would be all right. In most cases, everything is all right; problem adolescents don't become criminals. But your son did; no one will ever know why. Why one day he went ballistic. Why him. Why you.

Because this is really about you; I'm not the only one at court to have seen only you, thought only about you and the atrocious injustice you suffered—to the point of forgetting the victim and his family. Your lawyer spent two hours pressing that point home to the jurors, repeating again and again that if they weren't in your place, it was due to chance and chance alone. That it would take no more than a trifle to tip the scales and turn the worries that all children give their parents into horror—because if there's one thing worse than having a child killed, it's no doubt having one who's a killer.

It's terrible to say, but your being respectable people, who in the normal run of things should not suffer this sort of affliction, must have been a boon to your lawyer. All criminals have parents who care about them and their fate, but it's easier to identify with some parents than it is with others.

Your son was charged with murder—which implies premeditation. He was partially exonerated and found guilty merely of homicide. The prosecuting attorney demanded twenty years, the court decided on fifteen. For you the verdict was unhoped for. At first your relief struck me as preposterous and reminded me of a story I like: An astrophysicist explains that in a billion years there will be no more life on Earth. A guy interrupts him, visibly worried, asks him to repeat himself, then sits down in relief, saying, "You scared me. I thought you said a *million* years!" But I understood that to be bearable, sadness needs degrees, and that this quarter of an eternity skimmed off the sentence and this certificate of *mere* homicide were the first joys you had experienced in the past two years, the first steps on the long path that would take your son back from the bench of infamy to the society of men. Forgive me my indiscretion and inflated tone, madame, but the object of this article is to wish you, from the bottom of my heart, good luck, hope, and courage in accompanying your son on the path he will now follow.

Published in *L'Événement du jeudi*, March 1990

The Romand Case

1. Five Crimes for a Double Life

At dawn on Monday, January 11, 1993, the fire brigade came to put out a fire in a house in Prévessin-Moëns, a small village in France's Ain department, near the Swiss border. They found the partially charred bodies of a woman and two children, and a badly burned man, who was taken to a hospital in a critical state.

The accident hypothesis lasted no more than a couple of hours. The woman had received blows to the head, the children had been shot, and they'd all been dead for almost two days. The man, Dr. Jean-Claude Romand, had tried to poison himself with barbiturates. A cousin went to tell the horrible news to Romand's parents, who lived forty miles away in the Jura department. He found them dead, also shot. Finally, a woman who had been Romand's mistress stated that she had spent Saturday night with him in Paris, and that he had seemed so strange that it had occurred to her that he was going to try to kill her. But she'd stood up to him, she said, and he'd calmed down before heading back home.

The tragic weekend was reconstructed without much difficulty: wife and children murdered on Saturday morning; parents that afternoon; a whirlwind trip to Paris that evening; back to Prévessin in the night; then a twenty-four-hour blank before he poisons himself and lights the fire that was meant to burn the place to the ground.

He went bonkers, as they say. As is often the case when that happens, nothing that was known about him fit in with this five-fold crime: he was thirty-nine but seemed older; calm, collected, cultivated; a doctor who specialized in arteriosclerosis who worked as a researcher for the World Health Organization in Geneva; a considerate father who, their friends said, got along well with his wife; they were a stable and harmonious couple.

In the days that followed there were two surprises. First, Romand didn't die. He got over his poisoning and his burns. Soon he was well enough to be questioned. Then it was discovered that he wasn't a researcher at the WHO, that no one there had ever heard of him, that he wasn't even a doctor. No one in his entourage had so much as suspected him of duplicity, and now it was known to have lasted for eighteen years. It was normal that he hadn't treated patients because he did research, everyone said, normal that he couldn't be reached at his office in Geneva because he traveled a lot. What's more, it was enough to hear him talk with other professionals to see how competent he was in "his" field: he was up-to-date on all the recent research.

Yet all of that was fake. A facade. But what lay behind it? Where did he get the money that had allowed him, year in, year out, to lead the life of the person he was pretending to be? If he wasn't a doctor, what was he? At the start of the investigation the newspapers had the time of their lives, evoking espionage, money laundering, organ trafficking, and a huge international scam. But it quickly became clear that such leads went nowhere. Romand had led a double life, but the hidden part of this life seemed to have taken place without either accomplices or witnesses, and to have had no other goal than backing up, day after day, the official version. He spent exactly as much energy pretending to be that person as it would have taken to really be him.

Before setting the house on fire he'd scrawled a confused note on the back of an envelope, which the police later found in his car. It mentioned an "injustice," and a "banal accident" that could "drive you mad." No one knows what injustice he was referring to, but the banal accident—a fractured wrist—took place in September 1975, and that's when, without anyone knowing, Jean-Claude Romand's life headed off in two separate directions that only met up eighteen years later in blood and flames.

Winding back the clock, then, twenty years earlier he's in second-year med school in Lyon. How to describe his life up to that point? The only child of a forest-ranger couple from the Jura region, he grew up close to nature, a little solitary perhaps but surrounded by love and, according to everyone, affectionate and good-natured. And he's a good student, too: the pride of his parents, who are delighted to see him becoming a doctor. For some time he's had a half-sensible, half-passionate relationship with a distant cousin, Florence, also a medical student: a beautiful girl, and a good girl. Their future is laid out for them. The only glitch: he failed his spring-term exams, but he only needs to pass the makeup exam to be readmitted in September.

That's when he falls down the stairs. Fractured wrist. Whether it was subconsciously deliberate is anybody's guess. He doesn't write the makeup exam. He could have chosen to dictate his answers, that's possible, but he doesn't. When the results are posted, he says he passed, perhaps because he's afraid to disappoint his parents and Florence. They're happy, if not particularly surprised. A minor, childish fib that he doesn't know will seal his fate, and the fates of his parents, his future wife, and their still-unborn children.

At what moment did it become impossible for him to go back on his lie? No one knows; all that's known is that he couldn't. His life starts to take place on two levels, with a fiction that everyone takes for reality, and with the reality that isn't real for anyone, not even for him.

He does brilliantly at medical school, all the while enrolling again and again in second year. He announces his success in exams he doesn't write, and no one suspects a thing as the years go by, no one gets the idea of looking for his name on the lists of exam results. He studies, too, attending courses and spending hours in the library. Florence—who's dropped out of medical school, lowered her sights, and gone into pharmacology without too many regrets—helps him study for his final exams. He doesn't say anything, because on top of everything else he's modest, but everyone—goodness only knows how or why—firmly believes he finishes fifth in his class.

In 1980, he and Florence are wedded (that's true), and he accepts a position as researcher at the WHO (that's false). To be closer to Geneva, where he'll now be working, the couple move to Ferney-Voltaire and quickly settle into the community of international functionaries who inhabit this border region, befriending a lot of doctors and researchers. Two children are born, Caroline in 1985 and Antoine in 1987. They'll be beautiful children, healthy and happy, and outgoing. Everyone likes the family. Their friends think Florence and Jean-Claude complement each other perfectly: She's tall and beautiful, athletic, extroverted, always in a good mood, even a bit of a joker, and at the same time a model of propriety. He's more reserved, calmer, but without seeming cold or arrogant. On the contrary, he's appreciated for his discretion: he doesn't brag but he could, because scientifically speaking he's a brain, he's got huge responsibilities, he goes out to dinner with former ministers and prime ministers, and his name has been put forward for director of the National Health and Medical Research Institute. Again, he's not the one to let the cat out of the bag, that's not his style, but word gets out . . . Physically he's tall and well built, with a receding hairline, handsome gray-blue eyes, and a soft-mannered smile that inspires confidence.

Romand's professional life was an illusion, but his family life wasn't. Everything suggests that his wife and children were happy with him, that he loved them fondly and that they loved him, and that the affection and the tenderness that everyone saw weren't just a charade. Their house was open to visitors, there was no hidden chamber of horrors. This transparency makes it all the more astonishing that Florence never suspected a thing, that year in, year out, it never occurred to her to go visit him at his office, that she accepted his silence regarding his work, his comings and goings, his hours that were so irregular that she joked innocently in front of everyone that one day she'd find out he was a KGB spy. Hearing that, he'd smile indulgently and take her lovingly by the hand, and everyone present was amazed at how well they got along.

Then what did he do all day? What did he do with the empty hours after he'd dropped the kids off at school, without any role to play, when he was no longer anything at all? He spent them reading in his office—in his car, that is. He read huge amounts: first the newspapers, then scientific texts to keep himself up-to-date, then philosophical and theological works. During his last year of high school he'd written a test on "What's the truth?" and the question kept nagging at him. Depending on his mood, he spent his time in Geneva or Lyon, or he went walking in the forests of the Jura region, where he'd spent his childhood. Sometimes he'd treat himself to a massage: it was his only human contact in these days of absolute solitude. In the evening he returned to what had become real life for him, the life where he was Dr. Jean-Claude Romand. Then it was the other, secret life that seemed like a dream.

And money? During his studies, his parents had paid for his expenses and bought him a small studio apartment in Lyon. But after that? After that he lived from the confidence he inspired. Since he'd started working for the WHO, his family and his wife's family were well aware that his status as an international civil servant opened up sound investment opportunities. So, quite naturally, if his relatives sold their home, received a small inheritance or a retirement gratuity, they came to see their son-in-law or brother-in-law Jean-Claude, who invested the money in Switzerland, where—if the tragedy hadn't happened—everyone would have continued to believe it was peacefully yielding a tidy profit. There was so little talk of anyone asking for it back, its owners seemed so satisfied to know it was in a safe place, that he had almost no qualms about spending it to support himself and his family.

As absurdly simple as it seems, this system worked for more than ten years without a hitch, and in the automatic pilot of his double life, it seems that Romand ruled out as an almost abstract risk the possibility that one day one of his relations would ask to have his or her savings back. In the same way Romand ruled out the possibility of a tax audit (now in his thirties, he continued to declare an income of zero francs as a second-year medical student), or that he or one of his children could fall ill and oblige him to have recourse to the social security system. It would have been enough for someone to ask him for a pay slip, or even to try to reach him at the WHO (and all things considered, it's incredible that no one did), for him, with one thing leading to another, to be tried for breach of trust, and for five deaths to be avoided. Seen from the outside, his deception would have seemed harmless, a little like someone who uses his ambassador's physique to mingle with heads of state at international summits. But only from the outside, because to him the truth about his life would have devastated his loved ones literally to the point of killing them, and that was to be avoided at all costs.

This idea must have started to weigh on him more and more in the last year, when his system started to go haywire. He gets involved with a woman named Chantal, although it's not quite clear whether they're really in a relationship or if it's more of a loving friendship. But one thing is for sure: adding marital infidelity to his social duplicity troubles him a lot: a double life squared.

Chantal has just broken up with her husband and left Ferney-Voltaire, where she met Romand, for Paris, and sold her dental office, which brought her nine hundred thousand francs. Jean-Claude, her lover and confidant, is immediately tasked with investing it in Switzerland and, although he must know she'll want it back before long, squanders it all the quicker because he wants to look good in her eyes. Suddenly things start happening fast. For years he's known abstractly that he's heading for an abyss, but now he's on the brink.

As expected, Chantal asks for her money. She needs it to buy a new practice in Paris. He puts it off, hems and haws, comes up with pretexts that she swallows without smelling a rat, but he knows the game is up. He could make himself scarce. Or accept going to prison. Or even kill himself and leave behind a moving note, telling his close ones that he loves them, that he did everything he did because he loved them. But once again the thought of Florence, the children, and his parents finding out that he wasn't who they thought he was is unbearable to him. He's sure it would be just as unbearable to them, that it would kill them to discover the truth. They don't deserve to die like that. At the least they should die without suffering, that is, without knowing.

Christmas comes and goes, followed by New Year's, in the warmth of family celebrations. Then the last week begins. He buys ammo for the rifle, barbiturates, jerricans full of gas, everything he needs to die together with his loved ones. He watches himself do it in an incredulous stupor. He becomes a murderer the way he became an impostor, knowing all the while that it's not true, not possible, and at the same time that there's no turning back. A dreadful logic locks him in his future crime the way it locked him in his lies. On Friday evening the family goes to a nearby shopping center to buy a present for a friend of Antoine's who'll celebrate his birthday the next day. They have dinner in a restaurant, talk about school, joke, laugh, then go home early to have time to wrap the LEGO set before going to bed.

The next morning, Jean-Claude watches his wife sleeping. Everything goes blank for a moment, then he's standing over the bed with a bloody rolling pin in his hand, and she's dead, her head cracked open. He goes downstairs where his children are watching a video of *The Three Little Pigs*. He sits down beside them on the couch, hugs them for a moment: they love a good hug, and so does he. Then he gets them to go up to their room and invents a game that allows him to shoot them, one after the next, without giving them the time to suspect a thing—and how could they, until the sudden but infinitely surprising moment when the bullets hit their bodies? He leaves the house and goes to have lunch at his parents' place, where he gets them to go upstairs one by one and kills them, too. They don't expect anything either, don't understand a thing. He even kills the dog, whom he loved and whose photo he always kept in his wallet.

He drives to Paris, where he's arranged to take Chantal to dinner at the house of a friend of his, Minister of Health Bernard Kouchner, in the elegant suburb of Fontainebleau. The episode is as sinister as it is absurd: Jean-Claude doesn't know Bernard Kouchner, who doesn't live in Fontainebleau. They drive for hours through the forest in search of an address that they don't find, until Chantal loses her temper and he tries to kill her, too. But she doesn't let him, and no doubt he thinks confusedly to himself that it doesn't matter, that there's no harm in her living even if she knows the truth about him, and that there's no harm in his dying even though he knows she knows. So he lets it drop, says he lost his head for a moment, that he's sick. He apologizes, drives her home, and takes the highway in the opposite direction. He arrives on Sunday morning, locks himself up in his house with the bodies of his wife and children. He remains there, listless, for almost twenty-four hours. Then, early on Monday morning, he figures the time has come, prepares a cocktail of barbiturates, douses the house with gas, and sets it on fire.

Three and a half years later he's still alive. The trial will start on June 24 at the criminal court of the department of Ain. The facts are established and acknowledged by all. The verdict won't fail to be harsh. Eight days have been set aside, not to lessen the sentence but to understand the story of a man who wandered between two realities for so long and now resides in only one, perfectly uninhabitable one.

Published in Le Nouvel Observateur, June 20, 1996

2. At the Ain Criminal Court

He sees himself sitting beside his wife on the living room couch on Friday night. She's upset over a phone call with her mother, and he's trying to console her. Then there's a blank, a hole in his memory. They may have argued, she may have guessed the truth and asked him to explain. He doesn't deny it: it could be that, it could be anything, but he can't remember a thing. The next image is the blood-covered rolling pin in his hands on Saturday morning, and Florence's lifeless body on the bed. Then his children wake up, and it pains him to remember how he shot them, but he remembers, he even gives details before bursting into tears in the box.

Then he goes to buy the newspapers—the local daily *Le Dauphiné libéré* and the sports paper *L'Équipe*, according to the vendor, but he puts in, "Couldn't have been *L'Équipe*, I never bought it"—gets the mail from the mailbox, takes the car, and drives to his parents' place, forty miles away in the Jura department. Once again he sees his father opening the gate, then once again there's a blank until he kills him, and his mother after him. Then he drives to Paris, meets his former mistress to take her to dinner at the home of the minister of health at the time, Bernard Kouchner—another lie—and no one knows if during this absurd evening spent driving aimlessly through the forest of

Fontainebleau he was aware that he had killed his wife, children, and parents just a couple of hours earlier, or if he had deleted this unbearable reality and behaved as if nothing had happened.

On Sunday morning, he's back at his place, and only at dawn on Monday does he try to poison himself and set the house on fire. Did he eat, did he sleep, did he cry over his family's bodies during this final, twenty-hour blank? No one will ever know because he himself doesn't know. The investigation into the case, however, has established that he watched television. He even put a tape into the VCR and recorded 240 minutes of anything and everything: snippets of popular music of the sort all the channels air on Sunday afternoon, broken up by frequent zapping, a second of this, two seconds of that, the whole thing forming a series of disorderly flashes, a dismal, unwatchable kaleidoscope. Since the cassette wasn't blank, one imagines—and true to his habit he doesn't deny it—that he recorded all of this to erase its contents: images of the children, birthdays, trips to the mountains, memories of the happy family life that, as he alone knew from the beginning, was entirely based on a lie.

At the courthouse in Bourg-en-Bresse, watching and listening to Jean-Claude Romand, who faked being a doctor for eighteen years and then murdered his family when it became clear his deception would be discovered, you can't help thinking about the two layers of this cassette. Most of the time the man in the box, gaunt and dressed in black, still looks like what Dr. Jean-Claude Romand looked like—or at least appeared to look like. Like him, he speaks clearly and precisely. He reasons more than he feels; familiar with his file, he explains details, corrects himself, and you're ready to believe that this composed murderer is in full control of his mental faculties and therefore responsible for his acts.

But at other, not necessarily spectacular, moments, the good cassette breaks in places, and an incoherent chaos of reflexes, suppressed groans, and devastated memories shows through. All of a sudden the man becomes fissured, and it's as if you were standing on the brink of an abyss. At that moment you sense with certainty that the silence that has grown in him since his childhood was nothing more and nothing less than hell. It doesn't last long, then the abyss closes back up, Jean-Claude Romand picks up where he left off, but we in the audience have had ample time to wonder, from the height of our clinical ignorance and flying in the face of four psychiatric experts, if he really belonged in a criminal court, and if what you felt on your nape wasn't the cold wind of psychosis.

In such cases the court looks for whys. Why didn't he write the exam that he was practically certain he'd pass? Why did he say he had passed? Why did he marry a woman he loved only to lie to her the whole time, and why did he never try to tell her the truth? Why did he swindle those who trusted him? He's the only one who can answer these questions, but all he says is that he asks them, too. That he never stopped asking them during the years of deception and never stops turning them over in his head today. In vain. No doubt he wants to understand just as much as we do. But perhaps he's even less able to than we are and really is denied access to a whole part of himself: the one that lied, killed, and seems as strange and monstrous to him as it does to us.

Weary of speculation, one turns to the hows, the advantage being that at least you can talk about them to other people than him. He alone can say why he lied, and he doesn't know. But how others believed his lies is a question that concerns his entire entourage. His wife, whose blindness is the most troubling, is no longer there to answer. But his friends are. All doctors, pharmacists, or dentists, they lived within five miles of the WHO, where he said he worked, and seem never to have asked themselves any questions. The same goes for the medical school, where he enrolled in second year for twelve consecutive years, and the tax authorities, to whom he continued to declare zero income although he was pushing forty.

One day, however, the man he considered his best friend, also a doctor, did have a doubt. He never thought Jean-Claude was an impostor, but something about his professional life *was* strange. The friend got the idea of looking him up in the directory of the WHO, which he'd placed on his desk. He went to open it, and this gesture, if he'd gone through with it, could have been the first in an inquiry that could have saved five lives. But all of a sudden he felt bad about harboring such suspicions about his old friend. He put the directory back on the shelf. Now, in court, he says that for the past three years this story has haunted him. Although he keeps turning it over in his mind, he admits that he still doesn't understand it. But he says that he doesn't understand other things in life, and that he's decided to accept them because that's the way things are. Behind his glass enclosure, Romand listens, expressionless. No one knows what he's thinking, not even him.

Published in *Le Nouvel Observateur*, July 4, 1996

Philip K. Dick

When I started reading him around 1975, I wore little round glasses, an Afghan vest, and a pair of beat-up Clarks on my feet, and I went around saying he was the Dostoyevsky of our time; in a word, the man who'd grasped the bigger picture. For me his books *Ubik*, *The Three Stigmata of Palmer Eldritch*, and *A Scanner Darkly* were as prophetic as *The Possessed*.

Some went even further: Around exactly the same time (but I found that out much later, when I was working on Dick's biography), one of his French editors explained very seriously to Philip K. Dick that his novel *Ubik* was one of the five greatest books ever written. Not one of the five greatest books of science fiction, the editor insisted to Dick's amazement. No, one of the greatest books of all time, along with the Bible, the *I Ching*, the *Bardo Thodol*, and I forget what the fifth one was. One of the books to which people turn, and will always turn, to catch a glimpse of the secret of their condition, the meaning of meaning, ultimate knowledge, et cetera.

Twenty-five years later, things haven't changed. I recently participated in one of those book-fair debates, which are usually horribly boring. But this one wasn't boring at all because it was about Dick, and talking about Dick—just talking about him, exchanging views about him—can suddenly become like taking a tab of acid: quickly you're a long way from where you started. Participating in the talk were people who'd known him and other people such as me who'd read him when they were young and never gotten over it. We got excited, yelled at one another, agreed and then disagreed again. We had the impression that we were in one of his novels, where everyone's private universe threatens at any moment to invade and devour that of his neighbor, the way the cryogenized child in *Ubik* invades and devours the minds of his half-life companions. To give an idea, the host, at his wit's end, made this remark, which I think of often: "I think it would be good if we could agree on what we mean by reality, *at least among ourselves.*"

What everyone agreed on, nevertheless, is that with Dick you're dealing with something other than a great science fiction writer, or even a great writer *tout court*. Something else, okay, but what?

One of his first novels, *Time out of Joint*, tells the story of a guy living in a small American town in the 1950s who ekes out a living by answering questions in a contest organized by the local newspaper: "Where will the little green man be next?" The answer sheets are in the form of grids, and the little green man is under one of the hundreds of squares on the grid. Every day he changes his square, and every day Ragle Gumm (that's the protagonist's name) tries to guess where he'll be. In a way that's hard to explain, his intuition proves right just about every time, and this series of successes gives him a distinct place in the community: part artist and part freak, a bit of an oddball.

One day he has a strange experience: Coming into the bathroom, he feels for the light cord to the left of the door—and doesn't find it. Taking a look, he sees no cord, but a switch is on the right. Clearly this switch has always been there. Nevertheless,

Ragle, who's been living in this house for the past twenty years, felt around for a cord and knew where to find it. His gesture was a reflex, perfectly integrated into his subcortical routine. Where can this reflex come from? he wonders.

Most people who have this type of experience will just say, "That's strange," and move on. But Ragle belongs to the category of people who don't move on, who look for an explanation for things that might not have one, an answer to something it's already going a long way to call a question. He starts to investigate. He's nagged by strange impressions of being out of step. He hears radio messages about himself. He senses that those around him are plotting, hiding something. Finally he discovers the truth.

The truth is that it's not 1959 but 1997, and that war is raging between Earth and rebel lunar colonists, who bomb Earth non-stop. Luckily, the leader of Earth's defenses is a strategic genius, Ragle Gumm, who by dint of reflection, experience, and above all his sixth sense almost always predicts where the next missiles will fall, so that the targeted cities can be evacuated before the catastrophe. One day, unfortunately, the crushing weight of responsibility got the better of his psychological resistance. He cracked and took refuge in a tranquil delusion: the carefree 1950s of his childhood. Withdrawal syndrome, the psychiatrists diagnosed; no way to rouse him out of it. The terrestrial authorities then adapted his environment to his psychosis and re-created the world where he feels safe. In an ultrasecret military zone they constructed a prewar American city, just like in a film studio; they inhabited this city with actors and gave Ragle a hobby that allowed him to make use of his talent in spite of everything. While thinking he was solving banal puzzles in the newspaper about the whereabouts of the little green man, he was in fact locating the missiles' points of impact and continuing to protect the world's population. Until the day when he had a doubt and

started to recover his memory through a series of tiny incidents.
The lamp cord triggered it.

This novel dates from the fifties, like many of the stories in
this book. In them, again and again to the point of obsession, is
repeated the motif of the guy who, thanks initially to a tiny detail,
becomes aware that something is wrong, that reality isn't reality.
When he wrote them, Dick saw himself as a poor wretch, an ill-
starred, working-class writer condemned to earning his living—
badly—by banging out stories about little green men that stopped
him from writing the work of literature he was counting on to
leave his mark on the sands of time. However, he sensed that this
appraisal only imperfectly summarized reality; that unbeknownst
to him, he was doing something else altogether. Something else,
okay, but what?

•

Over the years he came up with a lot of different answers to this
question. Since he was very cultivated in his own way, he knew
and cited pedantically the earlier versions of the intuition he was
developing from book to book: Plato's cave, the cosmologies of
the Alexandrian gnostics; the dream of Zhuangzi, who, four centuries before our era, asked himself if he was a Chinese philosopher dreaming he was a butterfly or a butterfly dreaming he was
a Chinese philosopher; and the most menacing version of this
question, asked in 1641 by René Descartes: "How do I know that
I'm not being fooled by an infinitely powerful malignant demon
who wants to force me to believe in the existence of the external
world—and of my body?" In the California of the 1970s, these
vertiginous doubts that had become Dick's trademark encountered drugs. Timothy Leary maintained that in the second half
of the twentieth century it was just as absurd to live a religious
life without LSD as it was to study astronomy without using a
telescope. Because that was really what it was all about: religion,

that is, accessing reality, for which *God* is nothing but the oldest code name. Dick, who indulged in all possible and imaginable chemical substances, only took acid once. But that one time was enough. He found himself in the nightmarish and fleeting world of his books ("My friends," he must have said to those around him, "I was in hell and it took me a thousand years to crawl out"), and from that he deduced what he had long suspected: that these very books, under the cover of fiction—and, it must be said, of a type of fiction that was at first glance as far as possible from daily experience—literally told the truth. That the whole time when he had naively thought he was writing works of the imagination, he had never written anything but *reports*.

•

His last period is hardly represented in the present collection because he no longer wrote short stories, and because it arouses embarrassment even among his most fervent admirers. Still, I'd like to say a few words about it.

In 1974 he had a mystic experience that he later defined as an invasion of his mind by something else, another mind that had taken control of his motor centers and did his acting and thinking for him. "This rational mind was not human," he notes. "On Thursdays and Saturdays I would think it was God, on Tuesdays and Wednesdays I would think it was extraterrestrial, and sometimes I would think it was the Soviet Union Academy of Sciences trying out their psychotronic microwave telepathic transmitter. It was equipped with tremendous technical knowledge. It had memories dating back more than two thousand years, it spoke Greek, Hebrew, Sanskrit, there wasn't anything it didn't seem to know."

The only thing that is for sure is that this experience obsessed Dick for the last eight years of his life. A wealth of information, for the most part religious, poured into him through the portal of his dreams, or by means of the minor coincidences that he put all of his brilliantly twisted mind into interpreting. He earnestly believed, for example, that the Roman Empire never ended, and that twentieth-century America was nothing but a vast hologram in which this cruel, deceptive empire obliged its subjects to live. He thought that Richard Nixon was the heir to the Caesars, that is the Antichrist, and that he, Dick, under his Californian freak's clothing, was the head of an underground Christian movement bent on awakening humanity from this illusion and leading them into the light. Right up until his death he never stopped jotting down fragments of this revelation in a document stretching to more than several thousand pages, which he called his *Exegesis*, and which by his own admission permanently oscillates between prophetic inspiration and paranoid delirium ("assuming," as he himself says, "there's a difference between the two").

In *A Scanner Darkly*, one of his most beautiful novels, there's a strange character: a narcotics officer who's also a junkie when he's off work. Thanks to a narrative invention that is too long to explain here, it's precisely this junkie that the narcotics officer is charged with investigating. A similar personality split is at the heart of *VALIS*, in which Dick, recasting his *Exegesis* as a novel, gives himself two roles: that of Philip K. Dick the science fiction writer, and that of his friend and alter ego Horselover Fat (Philip means "he who loves horses" in Greek, and Dick means "fat" in German).

God, or someone he calls God for the sake of convenience, speaks to Horselover Fat. That makes Horselover Fat a prophet— in the original sense of the term: not someone who predicts the future, but someone who reveals a hidden truth about the present.

Everyone thinks Fat is crazy, and for good reason, it must be said, because above and beyond the craziness expressed in the syncretic mishmash he spouts, he has a long history as a drug addict and paranoiac. What's more, that's exactly what he thinks as well, and this opinion is shared by his friend Phil Dick, who looks on with curiosity and compassion in the final mental odyssey that *VALIS* traces.

The result is a document unique in the history of psychic investigation: superimposed onto the report of an experience that can only be understood as a divine revelation or a delirious system (with a strong presumption in favor of the second) is a critique of this experience conducted by a witness who passes in review all of the possible reactions to such raw mysticism, more or less as if Sigmund Freud and Daniel Paul Schreber—the paranoid schizophrenic whose sickness Freud commented on—had been one and the same person.

Psychological denial: "An encounter with God is to mental illness what death is to cancer: the logical outcome of a deteriorating illness process."

Sociological denial: "The time of drugs was over and the whole world was looking for a new trip. For Fat as for many others, that was religion. You can say that the drugs consumed in the 1960s were the marinade in which his brain steeped in the 70s." (Or, as Harlan Ellison said with harsh concision, "Took drugs; saw God: big fucking deal.")

But also something like uncertainty, indecision, a principle of indiscernibility: "Maybe Horselover Fat didn't meet God, but what I believe no matter what is that he met something."

Something, but what?

•

One thing has struck me in the last couple of years. When films such as *The Matrix, The Truman Show,* or *eXistenZ* come out, not only do their authors not refer to Dick; the critics and audiences don't either. Apart from the circle of his longtime aficionados, it's rare if anyone mentions him at all. On the one hand you can say with Baudelaire that true genius is to create a commonplace, and what Dick imagined now belongs to everyone. But you can also put it a bit differently and say that we're now living in Dick's world, this virtual reality that was a fiction in the past, the invention of a sort of wild gnostic that has become reality, the only reality. He's won; like the protagonist in *The Three Stigmata of Palmer Eldritch*, he's swallowed us all. We're in his books, and his books don't have an author.

•

I don't quite know how to conclude; with Dick there isn't any way to conclude. So to wind up I'll copy the quote I used as an epigraph in my book about him. It's taken from the mythical speech he made in Metz in 1977. He thought that this speech, a condensation of the *Exegesis*, equaled the prophesies of Isaiah or Jeremy and was perhaps even their completion. For the honest French leftists in the audience it was like the ranting of a madman—which didn't bother them, as madness was looked upon well in those days—doubled with those of a religious zealot, which went over a lot less well. Here:

"I'm sure you don't believe me, and don't even believe I believe what I'm saying. Nevertheless it's true. You are free to believe me or disbelieve me, but please take my word on it that I am not joking; this is very serious; a matter of importance. I am sure that at the very least you will agree that for me even to claim this is in itself amazing. Often people claim to remember past lives; I claim to remember a different, very different, present life. I know of no one who has ever made this claim before, but I rather suspect that my experience is not unique. What perhaps is unique is the fact that I am willing to talk about it."

Preface to *Nouvelles*, the French edition
of the collected stories of Philip K. Dick (Denoël, 2000)

The Lost Hungarian

1

Nyíregyháza, in the east of Hungary, is a large, tranquil town surrounded by a multitude of green villages. It's to one of these that the last prisoner of the Second World War, András Toma, is to return today after fifty-six years of absence. It's 10:00 a.m.; he's not expected before noon. We've just arrived from Budapest and wander at random through the streets, greeted by prattling from the courtyards. We're not too worried: the first villager we meet will no doubt be able to tell us where the homecoming will take place.

The first villager we meet is an old woman. Leaning on her cane, she's taking in the sun in front of her gate. Does she know where the Toma family's house is? Of course she does. And András Toma himself, might she have known him, too, before he left for the war?

A pretty, fresh smile, a girl's smile almost: "Know him? He gave me my first kiss, when I was sixteen."

Even when you're only *writing* a report and you hear something like that, you can hardly believe it's just happened. Then you pull yourself together and pick up the thread of the conversation. A television report is different: once the bomb has fallen, it's fallen, what you didn't get on film at the right moment isn't going to happen again, meaning that a dream sentence such as that, dropped when you're not on your guard, is a minor catastrophe. When Geza, our interpreter, translated what the old woman had just said, Alain and Jean-Marie looked at each other, then blurted out, "Stop, stop, stop, ask her to stop." Then they ran to open the trunk of the car and, thirty seconds later, camera and microphone in hand, asked if the old woman would repeat what she'd just said. This first comment is the only thing in our whole report that needed two takes, like in a feature film.

Erzebet turned out to be a willing actress. Since she was being filmed, she took off her head scarf, shook her beautiful white hair, and said her line again with a little laugh that was even more fresh and mischievous, if that was possible. After which she invited us in for a coffee and above all for a glass of *pálinka*, the fruit brandy that is proposed to you—or rather imposed on you—good-heartedly in the Hungarian countryside as early as nine in the morning. While serving us *pálinka* in large mustard glasses, which she ordered us to knock back so she could fill them up again, she told us the story of the wedding in the fall of 1944 when she met András Toma. She was sixteen, he was nineteen. He was handsome and danced beautifully. Since it was forbidden to use the lights once night had fallen, everyone had gone outside to dance in the darkness. Someone was playing a muted trumpet. That's when he kissed her.

Three days later, as he was coming back from the village where he worked as an apprentice boilermaker, the Germans recruited him by force. The Red Army had just entered Hungary and the Wehrmacht was retreating northward, taking with them as they went the last Hungarian soldiers who would fight in the final battles of the war in Poland. András Toma was in one of these contingents, along with other youths from the village. Many of them were captured by the Russians and imprisoned in camps. Those who didn't die went home in 1945 or 1946.

Not him. He was mourned, then forgotten. Erzebet married one of the former prisoners of war, who became the president of the village cooperative—so that even today she's respectfully called "Mrs. President." She had children, and they had children in turn. She's a widow now, she lives alone, but you only need to spend a quarter of an hour with her to understand that she doesn't let life get her down: she still loves to sing and dance, and she downs her *pálinka* with the best of them.

Two months ago, along with everyone else, she heard the story of this Hungarian who'd been discovered quite by accident, rotting away in a psychiatric hospital in deepest Russia. He'd been there since 1947, he didn't speak Russian, he'd become completely autistic. He was repatriated; the televisions of the entire world showed images of his return: the glass doors at Budapest Airport opening for a wheelchair in which a poor, terrified old man was huddled up under a plaid blanket. The flashes from the cameras blinded him; elderly women pushed and shoved around the car he was escorted to, flailing their arms and shouting different names: "Sándor!" "Ferenc!" "András!" In the weeks that followed, dozens of families claimed him as their own: he was their lost brother, uncle, granduncle. A small group of psychiatrists and army personnel were charged to look into the case. They got him to talk, to the extent that was possible with a man who'd lived beyond the pale of communication for so long, a blend of Tarzan and Kaspar Hauser. Little by little they awakened his memories and collected, among the snippets of incoherent sentences, the names of places and people that focused their search on Nyíregyháza and a certain Toma family, who, certain to be his true relatives, were patiently waiting for the authorities to come to them. DNA tests confirmed that Ana Toma was indeed the lost soldier's sister, and János Toma his brother. The two want nothing better than to welcome him with open arms, and so after two months of psychiatric observation in Budapest, he returns home to his family, in this corner of the country that he left fifty-six years ago.

Erzebet followed the developments with mounting emotion. She found a photo of the famous wedding in which, a few hours before the kiss, the two of them pose on the square in front of the church. She thought of the past, of her life. It was a good, full life; she wasn't the type to spend her time remembering a dead man. But this unexpected return awakens in her something both sweet and cruel, which makes her heart beat faster. What was doubtless no more than the promise of a passing romance becomes the phantom of her youth. As she putters around her kitchen taking out mountains of poppy seed cake, she shows us with a total lack of inhibition, behind her wrinkles, the face of the young girl in love who she once was, and who, resuscitated today, thinks of nothing other than hurrying with her cane to a meeting from which she expects everything in the world.

All of this may sound overly sentimental, but Jean-Marie, Alain, and I have just come back from Russia, from the city where for fifty-three years poor Toma lived without anyone talking to him, touching him, or looking at him like a human being, deprived of all desire, tenderness, and warmth, and it's balm to our souls. To be frank it brings tears to our eyes to hear this old peasant woman's astonishingly clear, youthful voice as she sings us the song she's prepared for his return: a beautiful, popular melody that could have been by Schubert or Brahms, about a handsome youth who goes on a long trip in the spring and promises his beloved that he'll return when the white flowers of the acacia fall. The flowers of the acacia fall fifty times, and then one autumn an old man with white hair returns to the village. He says, "You see, my love"—she's become old and gray as well—"I kept my promise, I returned when the white flowers of the acacia fall."

Erzebet is planning to welcome her love who's returned from

the dead by singing him the song of the acacia, but she isn't
invited to the party. András's brother János, who like her lives
in the village, has nothing but respect and admiration for Mrs.
President. But Ana, his sister, who lives in the center of town and
in whose house András will be staying, snubs her. Erzebet is
proud: it breaks her heart, but if she's not invited, she won't go.
Well then, since we're not invited either, how about if we all
go together? Erzebet may be proud, but she doesn't play hard to
get: she claps her hands and asks for just enough time to put on
her best clothes; while waiting, we should finish off the *pálinka*,
she says.

2

"We're in Hungary, you can get out!" the young psychiatrist who
looks like John Lennon repeats. But the old man sits rooted in the
minibus. He's not at all sure that this is Hungary. Since his return, his caretakers have had to reassure him nonstop. Back in
Russia he was told that Hungary no longer existed, that it had
been wiped off the map. So who are these people talking to him
in a dead language, acting as if they knew him, giving him flowers
and blowing him kisses? Is it all a new trap?

Underneath his cap, his face is a wreck. It's the face of a *zek*,
as the prisoners of the Soviet Gulag called themselves, the face
of the sort of inmates whose ruined lives Solzhenitsyn and Shal-
amov described. He's only got one leg; the attendants help him up
and hold out his crutches. It takes him a good five minutes to put
his foot on the ground. He doesn't have any teeth, either, so he
spits a lot. "Soviet culture . . . ," a member of the family murmurs
to us in sad disgust.

How much of what's happening does he understand? These
journalists hustling all around him, pointing machines full of

black reflections at him, what could it all mean to him? Does it bother him like a light that's too bright, or an insect buzzing around him when he wants to go sleep? Does it frighten him? A lot of clichés come to mind: "a look like a hunted animal's," "peered at like a strange beast." All of that suits him to a T.

There was a meal with speeches and expressions of sincere, touching affection, all of which probably horrified him. Everyone was amazed at how much he looked like his father. János, a mild-mannered farmer in his Sunday best who was still a child when András left for the war, wanted to ask his brother some questions, no doubt to show us that he was capable of answering. János cited names from bygone days: Sándor Benkö, the schoolteacher . . . Smolar, the neighbor with the combine harvester . . . Meanwhile, under his cap, his brother spat, turned his head, mumbled indistinct phrases that the affable János did his best to interpret as the right answers.

Not feeling entirely welcome, Mrs. President remained on the doorstep in her beautiful embroidered dress. She watched him, devoured him with her eyes, but he didn't see her. She didn't sing her song. She didn't open the bottle of champagne she'd insisted on buying for him on the way. We decided to take her home. There were too many people, too many journalists—who would soon be leaving since they'd just come to film a few minutes for the evening news. We were going to stay, we had all the time in the world.

We invited Erzebet to have dinner with us, in the restaurant at our hotel. We were sad, she was, too, like after a missed date. We'd just seen a man in whom all of the conditions of humanity had been destroyed. He was gutted. Dead. We told Erzebet that ten days earlier we'd been in Kotelnich, the place where he'd lived this death.

3

Captured in Poland at the end of the war, he spent a year in a camp near Leningrad, then was transported a thousand miles farther east. The likely destination: Siberia. According to his patchy account it seems that during the train trip quite a few of his fellow prisoners died of hunger, cold, and fatigue. He survived, but cracked, which led to his being transferred from a transit camp to the psychiatric hospital in the closest city: Kotelnich.

In the last century Kotelnich must have been the kind of place where Chekhov's characters sighed "To Moscow! To Moscow!" while watching trains they'd never take leaving the station. Today it's a gray, muddy backwater where for the past ten years not a single house has had hot water and where the inhabitants refer matter-of-factly to these past ten years—that is, since the end of communism—as a historic catastrophe: we didn't live well in the past but at least we had heating, we had work, above all we were more or less all in the same boat. Now Moscow and Saint Petersburg look like Manhattan, ads on TV depict them as luxurious, hectic science-fiction metropolises, so in a word you feel permanently left behind.

Arriving at the hospital fifty-three years after András Toma, we vaguely hoped to find some people who'd been there since the first days of his stay: an aged nurse, for example, whose memories we'd revive with swigs of vodka. But the first thing Dr. Petukhov, the head doctor, explained to us is that no one, patient or staff, went back that far. So there were no witnesses.

Yet there was one. The day Toma arrived, a medical file was opened bearing the name Toma, Adrian Adrianovich; nationality: Hungarian; age: twenty-two; diagnosis: schizophrenia. His entire history is written up in this file, which we were allowed to consult, and in which, every two weeks for half a century, the psychiatrists noted their observations.

It's an impressive document: an entire life, and with it an unrelenting process of destruction, is cut up into little, lifeless, neutral, repetitive phrases. Some examples:

January 15, 1947: The patient speaks neither Russian nor German. He is passive during examinations, he tries to explain something in Hungarian.

October 30, 1947: The patient doesn't want to work. When forced to go outside, he shouts and runs in all directions. He hides his gloves and bread under his pillow. He wraps himself in rags. He only speaks Hungarian.

October 15, 1948: The patient has a sex drive. He laughs on his bed. He does not obey hospital rules. He flirts with Nurse Guilichina. Patient Boltus is jealous. He hit Toma.

March 30, 1950: The patient is completely withdrawn. He remains on his bed. He looks out the window.

March 15, 1951: The patient has taken pencils from the nurses. He writes in Hungarian on the walls, doors, and windows.

February 15, 1953: The patient is dirty, irascible. He collects garbage. He sleeps in inappropriate places: in the hallway, on a bench, under his bed. He bothers his neighbors. He only speaks Hungarian.

September 30, 1954: The patient is idiotic and negative. He only speaks Hungarian.

It goes on like that page after page. Reading it, you have to ask yourself some questions. Clearly, since the beginning of his captivity and above all since the terrible episode on the train, something

wasn't right in András Toma's head. It's all very well to say that
in the depths of Stalinism, the first mission of Soviet psychiatry
was not to cure the mentally ill. Nevertheless, it's clear that this
was not a political imprisonment and that Toma needed help.
He received none. Nowhere in his file is there any mention of
medicine, let alone therapy. It's true, at the time there was no
medication for schizophrenia. That was only discovered in the
1960s, and even then it's unlikely that it got as far as Kotelnich.
But was he really schizophrenic, or had he simply unhinged after
a major trauma? This young man was clearly shocked, walled up
in terror, and no one ever tried to talk to him, to listen to him.
When Dr. Petukhov is asked why, he shrugs and says as if it
goes without saying that the patient only spoke Hungarian, and
no one spoke Hungarian at the hospital. As the pages progress
that becomes a litany: "The patient speaks Hungarian." It's his
symptom. And in fact it is one. Someone who insists on speaking his own language, which no one understands, year after year,
and refuses to learn the language that everyone all around him is
speaking certainly has a major adaptation problem. Was he trying
to protect himself, seeking refuge in an impenetrable fortress like
an autistic child? Was it a form of resistance, like that of some
of Kafka's heroes, or of Melville's Bartleby? What is certain is
that no psychiatrist tried to communicate with Toma in any way
whatsoever.

There's something poignant about this file. For the first ten
years, András Toma was a fiery, violent, rebellious patient. A burly
young guy who got into fights, swore at his guards, and wrote
on the walls the way you'd toss a bottle into the ocean. A tough
nut. Toward the end of the 1950s he changed, and this change
coincided with something that happened back in his hometown,
Nyíregyháza.

4

Life had gone back to normal. The prisoners of war had come home one after the next. Those who didn't come home had to be accepted as dead. It's a painful but psychologically necessary act: someone who's disappeared is a ghost, the source of a nameless dread that can poison a family for several generations, whereas the dead you can mourn, weep over, and forget. On December 11, 1954, ten years after his departure, András Toma's death certificate was delivered to his family. He didn't know it, but strangely everything happened as if he did. He was dead; he no longer existed. And so he gave up.

He became a docile patient. He was still walled up inside himself, he didn't mix with anyone, he muttered to himself in Hungarian, but he was calm. Hardworking. "Stabilized," as his file says. He was transferred from the ward of the agitated patients to the ward of the calm. Dr. Petukhov allowed us to visit and film this ward as much as we wanted—or almost as much: after three days he was a bit surprised to see us still there and let us know that we should start wrapping things up.

With a blend of naivete and voyeuristic pleasure, we'd imagined this psychiatric hospital in a little Russian city as something out of Dante's *Inferno*: a particularly remote circle of hell. And that's what it is, only no more so than many of its Western European equivalents. The metal grate opens onto a wet highway, and the courtyard resembles a wasteland, in the middle of which an old army truck rusts away. Goodness only knows how it got there. The buildings are sad and decrepit, but clean. Posters of Polynesian lagoons do what they can to brighten the piss-colored walls. Life is spent waiting for meals, which are invariably composed of the same gruel, carted around by the nurses in large enamel pails. The radio plays soothing music all day. When we first arrived, it was a fantasia by Mozart, one of those mysteriously harrowing pieces that pierce your heart without even seeming to touch it. Alain recorded it while Jean-Marie filmed the corridor, the yellow light, an old patient sitting on a bench and tapping out the beat, and for all three of us it was as if these images together with this music, the slam of a metal door, the muted sound of a telephone in the background and slippers dragging across the floor, were from beyond the grave. We also thought, but that's another problem, that these sounds only made sense if they were recorded live and if the viewer knew, or at least sensed, that this music had really sounded in this yellow corridor, whereas if we'd shot the images and then searched around for the right music to accompany them—"Hey, how about Mozart?"—this overwhelming match would have been a pure obscenity. But anyway.

Two months before our visit, András Toma was still living in this ward. He slept in this bed in the corner of the room, and his neighbor was this guy we call the stiff, because he lies stretched out on his bed all day long, immobile, his fingers crossed on his chest, with his face fixed in a scowl that has no doubt long been void of meaning. Others seem less in a bad way. They pace up and down; some even read. They've all wound up here because life outside was too hard, the alcohol was too strong, their heads were too full of menacing voices, but now they, too, are "stabilized." They're not dangerous, hardly agitated at all. No doubt the hospital would like to send them back home, but they don't have a home, so they stay. They're not really cared for, they're hardly spoken to, but they're kept. It's not much, but it's not nothing either.

They kept András Toma. He did have a family, however, and a country he could have been sent home to. At least in theory it wasn't impossible to inform the Hungarian consulate in Moscow of his whereabouts, but it never occurred to anyone: Moscow is so far away—to say nothing of Hungary. So he stayed there, like an uncollected parcel, and little by little any hope of his ever leaving faded and died. After the years of revolt, his file only registers one other burst of energy.

February 15, 1965: The patient has become attached to the hospital dentist. He follows her around, begging her to pull out his healthy teeth. The dentist refuses. The patient smashes his jaw with a hammer.

That was his only violent outbreak in all these petrified years—and the only time he reached out to another human being. Every two weeks the psychiatrists write in his file, "The patient's state remains unchanged."

That said, these psychiatrists weren't bad people. The one who led us around on Dr. Petukhov's orders is a smiling, doleful fellow, a real figure from a Chekhov play, who, when asked about the quality of life in the town, shrugged his shoulders and said, "We don't live here, we survive"—a sentence we'll hear again, in exactly the same words, from at least two other residents. He speaks about Toma with tenderness, shows us the carpentry workshop where this solitary and seemingly autistic patient spent his days assembling rattraps and miniature gas pumps. Toma was nice provided he was left alone, so he was left alone. He wasn't crazy, he was just lost, stranded, far from home. Since he was permitted to leave the premises, he was sent on shopping errands with someone who spoke Russian. He got to know the muddy streets of Kotelnich, its poorly stocked market. He lived through the gray Soviet era and the post-Soviet breakdown without understanding a thing about them. In the summer months he went out to work the fields on the edge of town, on a farm owned by the hospital. He came back loaded with cabbages, which he distributed to his wardmates in silence. In 1996, thirty years after the episode with the dentist, something else happened to him. To quote his file:

June 11, 1996: The patient complains of pains in his right foot. Diagnosis: arthritis. The patient's family must be consulted regarding amputation. The patient has no family.

June 28, 1996: The patient's right leg is amputated above the knee. No complications.

July 22, 1996: The patient does not complain. He smokes a lot. He has started to walk with crutches. In the morning his pillow is wet from tears.

As a rule, arthritis appears symmetrically, and when Toma arrived in Budapest, the medical examination revealed no trace of it in his other leg. One can't help thinking his leg might have been amputated for nothing . . . Out of consideration for their Russian colleagues, the Hungarian doctors don't say it officially. Some even prefer the less awful alternative of saying that to some extent the amputation served a purpose, that it helped make his carers aware of his emotions, maybe even of his suffering, and that, with one thing leading to another, it led to his deliverance. Unfortunately, such wishful thinking is wrong. Three and a half more years went by without anyone taking any interest in his fate, until the day in December 1999 when a bigwig from the Health Ministry came to visit the hospital. Leading his guest around the wards, Dr. Petukhov passed in front of the old, one-legged man and introduced him as the most senior of his patients. I imagine him tweaking his ear affectionately, like Napoléon with his veteran soldiers: "A peaceful old guy who only speaks Hungarian. Imagine that!" Dr. Petukhov told what little he knew about Toma's past. A local journalist was covering the event, and as the story wasn't exactly a scoop, she concentrated on this angle: "The last prisoner of World War II is in our midst." The news was out. Moscow newspapers picked up on it, and the media descended on the hospital. Quite pleased with himself, Dr. Petukhov started giving interviews and collecting visiting cards from *Izvestia*, CNN, Reuters, and today it's one from *Télérama* . . . The Hungarian consul alerted his government, which organized the

rescue of the lost countryman. Six months later, without understanding a thing about what was happening to him, András
Toma was back in Hungary.

5

Three days after he arrived in the village, it was Mrs. President's
saint's day, Saint Erzebet, which she invited us to come celebrate
with her. For the past three days we'd been scouring the countryside in search of witnesses and hadn't been back to see Toma.
She hadn't either. She didn't talk about it, but we sensed that
the missed rendezvous and the song she hadn't been able to sing
pained her. Nevertheless, she wanted to celebrate; she'd baked
bread, put some *pálinka* in the fridge, and covered the table
with salami, sausages, and jellies. Just as we were about to clink
glasses, we heard a car park in front of the house. Alain looked out
the window and said:

"It's . . . it's him!"

The next moment Erzebet was outside. We ran after her and
only caught up to her at the car, where she was bending over
the open door. She'd taken András by the hand and was already
singing the song. At the third verse, when the man with gray hair
returns under the acacia tree whose white flowers have fallen
fifty times, her voice cracked. We were hardly doing any better ourselves. She made it through to the end, albeit in tears. Huddled
up in the back of the car, he watched without understanding as
this old woman touched his hand, stroked his cheek, kissed his
hand and then his cheek, and started to talk to him while both
laughing and crying, calling him András, my little András. "You
don't remember me, my little András? Erzebet, the girl you kissed
at the wedding, you have to remember, you will remember . . ."
The young people who'd brought him, and who'd been introduced

to us at the party as the children of his brother János, smiled in embarrassment.

"Do you know this woman's name, Uncle András?" the niece asked nicely. "Er . . . Erz . . ."

He shook his head and muttered, "I don't know." After a pause he said, "I miss my leg." Five minutes later when the car drove off, Erzebet blew kisses and followed it with her eyes.

She was disappointed that he hadn't recognized her, but happy to have seen him, to have spoken to him, to be free of her song, and we shared her joy, thrilled that what we were sure was the last scene of our documentary was in the can. That had to be celebrated, and the meal on Saint Erzebet's Day turned into quite the binge. We put back glass after glass of *pálinka* and danced with Mrs. President to old Hungarian melodies until dusk fell, so that we were sorely hungover the next morning when, believing that our job was done and the story was in the bag, we went to take leave of András Toma and his sister.

We weren't expecting much from this second and last visit. We were sure no more was to be gotten out of him than the snippets we'd already recorded, and we were also a bit embarrassed because yesterday's reunion had been organized behind the back of Toma's sister, who for obscure village reasons doesn't like Mrs. President. From what we'd been able to gather, Ana Toma's nephew and niece had gone to get András on the pretext of taking him for a ride in the countryside and had taken him to see his old love on the sly.

We'd brought a bottle of whiskey so as not to arrive empty-handed, which was gutsy considering the shape we were in. We said cheers and drank. Toma tasted it, made a face, but reached out his glass for more. Apart from that, he remained huddled up in his corner, spitting and occasionally grumbling to himself. His sister was talking about him, for him, affectionately but as if he weren't there. After an hour we got up to leave and packed the equipment in the trunk of the car. Then, as we were standing on the doorstep, something happened. He started talking. The grunts became sentences, and for almost an hour he didn't stop. Jean-Marie and Alain ran to get the camera and the microphone, Geza translated off-the-cuff what he could understand, which was not much. We who didn't speak Hungarian were completely at a loss, but Geza, too, didn't understand half of what this toothless mouth was going on about, and Toma's sister didn't understand any more. Back in Paris, it took several days and three Hungarian interpreters, each one exhausted in turn, to decipher just half of what remained of these verbal hieroglyphics. Be that as it may, Toma was talking, and not to himself. After fifty years of autistic rumination he was now talking to someone else, and it was as moving as the first words spoken by the "wild child" in François Truffaut's eponymous film, or by Kaspar Hauser in the movie by Werner Herzog.

I reread the notebooks in which I jotted down our various attempts at transcribing what Toma said. Higgledy-piggledy it deals with Siberia, Hungarian battalions in a potato storehouse, his leg, which a Hungarian blacksmith might be able to weld back on, the frozen soil that was so hard you couldn't bury the dead, the cold and the sun, crossing the Dnieper, Hungarian crutches and Russian crutches—which are junk—cigarettes, cabbage, trains, and Adolf Hitler. Some sentences stand out among the rest and are almost worthy of Marguerite Duras: "The snow stripped me of my force, now I have no more. They take your strength away, then you can't go anywhere." Memories of the harrowing Russian exile blend with those of his youth in Hungary. It's hard to follow the thread, but there is one.

Delighted with his sudden desire to communicate, his sister wanted him to sing a Hungarian song. For the first time he smiled, and his *zek*'s face took on a wily, childish gleam.

"A Hungarian song?" he said. "I know one." And he started to croon, "'I came back when the acacia flowers were falling' . . . A woman sang that to me yesterday."

"A woman? Yesterday?" his sister repeated in surprise.

"It's a woman's song. She was there, yesterday, near the car. She sang it for me."

His sister chuckled. She didn't understand, so she thought there was nothing to understand. But we, who had been there yesterday and had witnessed this minuscule fragment of his past, understood. Most of his life had taken place without witnesses, in an almost unimaginable solitude, and that's why no one will ever understand all of what he says. Still he tries to say it. Back from his silent abyss, he is once more in contact with his language and so with speech, with something that resembles an exchange. He's seventy-five years old, his life was stolen from him, but he's alive. It does us a world of good, before leaving, to go back to Erzebet's place to tell her that he remembered the song of the acacia.

Published in *Télérama*, March 2001

This article accompanied a fifty-two-minute documentary report that I made for the TV program Envoyé spécial *(Special Envoy). Jean-Marie Lequertier was the cameraman, Alain Kropinger the sound technician. No sooner had I finished this double testimony, in words and images, than I started to long to return to Kotelnich—in an insistent, mysterious way, without knowing why I was so attracted to this unattractive little Russian city.*

I did go back. Over a period of two years I shot a film there that didn't have a subject at the start and then got one as it went along: a terrible tragedy. Retour à Kotelnitch *(Return to Kotelnich) came out in 2003, but I still hadn't finished with the city. The next four years I spent first unable to write, then, finally, writing,* My Life as a Russian Novel. *This book is at once the novelization of my documentary, a public psychoanalysis, and the last stage in this cycle that took shape in an unpremeditated way, in groping loyalty to life's twists and turns and the demands of the unconscious.*

Nine Columns for
an Italian Magazine

1

At one point over dinner, between the soup and the sushi, there was a moment of silence. Not unpleasant, not embarrassing: the sort of silence you could use to look at each other a little more intensely, or maybe to come closer over the table. At a moment like that you have the choice between saying something like "I really want to kiss you" or simply doing it, without feeling obliged to announce it. For a long time I'd belonged to the first school, and for the past couple of years more to the second. That's one of the advantages of getting older: you're more direct. But that's not the situation tonight, or not quite, so we smile, enjoying the mild feeling of discomfort—which is very mild indeed, and even enjoyable, since it's shared—and I bring up this column that I have to write over the weekend for an Italian magazine. "On what?" she asks.

"That's just the thing, I don't know. The idea is that it should be a male take on the female world, or, if you like, something about the relations between men and women, but written by a man and read first and foremost by women. At least that's how I understood what the editor in chief said. Ideas?"

"You don't have to look too far: Why not talk about our dinner?"

That's what we start doing. We have dinner, eat our sushi, and talk about it. That is, we experience the situation while at the same time describing it to each other. It's a bit caricaturally postmodern: a commentary on reality that takes the place of reality. At the same time it's like when you tell your lover what you're doing in bed while you're doing it. I'm someone who finds that exciting, and so is she apparently. This is the situation: Friday evening, Japanese restaurant in Paris, blind date. We didn't meet through the Internet, but through a mutual friend who'd said, "You know what? You two should meet." Right now both of us are single—well, not really single, but available, and happy to agree on the word. Both of us are in our early forties, divorced, with two children. I write, she's a painter; our mutual friend told her that I was seductive and me that she was seductive, and we seem to be pretty much in agreement. The purpose of our meeting being clear, there's no way we can pretend it didn't occur to us, as is strangely the case with so much interaction between men and women: you think about nothing else, you both know it, but it's as if it were something to be ashamed of, as if admitting it would make you weak, or laughable, or the butt of cynicism. I spent my youth getting all wound up over dinner dates that skirted around the question of seduction. I remember I envied the gays, for whom things seemed more simple and direct. Their desire seemed easier to express, whereas we heteros seemed to have come no further than Montaigne, who asked, "What has rendered genital action—an act so natural, so necessary, and so just—a thing not to be spoken of without blushing?" (Isn't that perfectly put?) Tonight, then, in this Japanese restaurant, we examine the possibility of having sex, I won't say with detachment, but with a sort of lightness accentuated by the resolve we've just made, pretexting the needs of this column, to say and comment on what usually remains unsaid. What are we hoping for, deep down, what are we after? Let's be honest: true love, real love, love that will last. *Him* for her. *Her* for me. We're more or less halfway through life, we've divorced, loved and stopped loving, left and been left, but we continue to believe, to want to believe, not just that it exists, but that it hasn't really happened yet, that it's ahead of us, that at one unpredictable, unexpected moment it will be there and we'll recognize it without hesitation, without the shadow of a doubt. The idea that in fact it's behind us, that perhaps it already happened and we weren't able to hold on to it, is too sad, and we reject it with all our might. As for me, I have to admit something: as I'm inclined to believe in it, I believe in it a little too easily. They say you can't be wrong about something like that, but that's just the thing: I can. Then I snap out of it, and that can hurt the other person. I'm just coming out of such a situation: the two of us head over heels in love, absolutely certain, three ecstatic months telling each other that we're so lucky, that what everyone dreams of happened to us, that we'll never part, that we'll grow old together . . . Of course I was being sincere, but you can be sincere and be wrong, or in any case you can persuade yourself that you're wrong as sincerely as you persuaded yourself of the contrary. The result: a turning away that's as massive as my commitment had been, and she doesn't understand, she's suffering and says with a look of astonishment, "It's incredible: I'm devastated, and you're just a little put out." And it's true. I've just spent part of the afternoon with that woman who used to be the love of my life and who still thinks of me as hers; I was tender, half out of a real sense of tenderness, half so as not to think of myself as a bastard, and in the evening here I am, telling the story a bit complacently to another woman whom I don't know, and who listens to me in such a way as to make me think that the story isn't new to her, that she's suffered as my ex-lover is suffering, that she got over it as my ex-lover will get over it, and that she doesn't mind hearing it from the man's point of view because this time it's not happening to her. Then it's her turn to tell me about her situation, with a guy she loves but who lives far away, in California. So he comes to France, or she goes there, it's complicated . . . She loves him, fine, but is it *him*? She thinks, no, no doubt it's not *him*. Anyway, if she has to think about it, that proves it's not *him*. And if she's here with me tonight . . . We've finished the sushi, we're drinking green tea, we don't know each other, but we talk freely, seduction is in the air but there's no obligation, and since the game is to tell each other everything, nothing's at stake. It's a human, friendly, relaxing way of getting along, we feel, both civilized and a little vain. A small respite in the war between the sexes, like a cigarette shared on the trench floor. We tell each other everything, apart from one thing that we both know full well, namely that at our age a man's fate is far more enviable than a woman's, and that while he can look forward to a procession of young and attractive women, what awaits her is a dwindling number of married, elusive men. It's terribly unjust, but it's the truth. Aloud, now, we ask if we're going to sleep together. By mutual consent we decide that, in any event, not tonight. We'll see each other again, we'll call. I pay and take her back home on my scooter. As we part, we say we had a nice evening, and it's true. Riding back to my place, I wonder, just what does that mean, *by mutual consent*?

2

She's a Kierkegaard specialist. And what, I ask you, is sexier than a sexy Kierkegaard specialist? I've known her for several years, I've always found her extremely attractive, but I was with someone, so was she, and it had on occasion happened that we'd said to each other half in jest that the day when we were both free, we should get together. Then the day comes: I'm free, she is, too— more or less, but more than less, she implies. I propose that we sleep together and more if we hit it off, and I strongly sense that we will. What a good idea, she says with a radiant smile. The only problem is that she's leaving early the next morning so the time isn't right—that's what she says—despite which we kiss like adolescents on the street in front of her place, and I go home almost happy with this setback that leaves me ten days to savor being a little in love and to wait for her return. In her absence I try to reach her on her cell phone and can't get through, but since she's in Colombia, I put this silence down to a technical glitch. The day she's due back I send her a huge bouquet of flowers. A couple of hours later I get a text message: she dreams of seeing me as soon as possible. Fine, it's a dream that's easy to fulfill, I want nothing better. I call. Both her phones are always on answering mode. I leave messages, send text messages and e-mails. Nothing. After a couple of days, again by SMS, she announces that she's leaving on another trip, and that we'll meet up as soon as she gets back. When she gets back, it's the same thing. She closes all the channels through which I try to get in touch with her. A wall, thwarting all of my demands for an explanation. Because the situation isn't only frustrating, it's inexplicable. You'll say there's a simple explanation, very simple even: she's not attracted to me. That's possible, very possible even, but I don't believe it. First of all because if that were the case, it would be easy for her to tell me—or to tell me she loves someone else, or that she doesn't want to ruin our beautiful friendship . . . Secondly, because if it were true, a woman who doesn't say it one way or another would be a ridiculous tease, and this woman is anything but a ridiculous tease. Finally—this might make you laugh after what I've just said—because I'm certain she's attracted to me. Not that I think I'm irresistible, not at all, but in her case I'm certain, otherwise I wouldn't insist like that. I know that this conviction leads me dangerously close to an interpretation along the lines of she's avoiding me because she loves me, and from there straight to denying reality the way Belise does in Molière's *Learned Women*,

explaining the silence of her imaginary suitors with the words
"They have, up to the present time, respected me so much that they
have never spoken to me of their love." I'm aware of all of that, but
I insist nonetheless. I continue to wait for a sign, and to while away
the time I read Kierkegaard's correspondence, which she translated into French. The key to this correspondence is the story of
Regine, the young girl who was engaged to the philosopher before
he broke off the engagement, perhaps because he believed his
melancholy would prevent him from being a good husband, perhaps for another reason; he never said and no one will ever know.
What we do know is that he was passionately in love with her,
that he remained in love with her for the rest of his life, but that,
one fine morning, without a word of explanation, he broke off all
ties. From that moment on, he did his best to be as odious as possible, both so that Copenhagen's fashionable society would blame
him and feel sorry for Regine, and also so that Regine would have
good reason to hate him. He thought that the hatred and disdain
she would feel for him would make her an accomplished woman,
and that by mistreating her like that he was secretly doing her a
service. These letters, in which he tasks his best friend with spy-
ing on Regine and gauging her progress along the path of frustration, of resentment, and, at the same time, of self-consciousness,
are rather delirious, but for me, looking as I am for information
not about the author but about his translator, they're also food for
thought. Since everything was preferable to what was unfortunately the most plausible hypothesis—she had better things to
do than answer my messages—I identified her with the devious
Kierkegaard and myself with the innocent Regine, who finally
got over the separation but nevertheless spent a good part of her
life waiting in vain for an explanation, as I do. Not understanding is the cruelest thing, and not explaining the most indelicate.
With that in mind I keep reading and come across this sentence,
which floors me: "In every love relationship that reaches an im-

passe, delicacy is in the end the most offensive behavior." (Except that here, I immediately say to myself, there is no love relationship, and so no impasse—and so I keep trying.)

3

She's my best friend. We used to be lovers, there's no saying we won't be lovers again one day, and for the more than twenty years that we've known each other, we've always gotten together just the two of us—we don't have any mutual friends. We tell each other everything, confide in each other completely, laugh a lot, and sometimes even cry. This loving friendship is one of the most precious things in my life, in hers, too, I think, and I'm counting on it to show on Judgment Day that I wasn't a complete washout. She doesn't need to prove anything because God spits out the lukewarm, and she's anything but lukewarm. Everything she does, she does with passion, starting with passion, without which she can't breathe. She loves her husband with a familiar, stubborn passion, her children with a concerned passion, her lover with an all-out passion, and her project now is to put an end to their liaison before this passion turns into grief. That's what they've resolved to do, they dream of a breakup that's as sizzling hot as their affair; they feel the time has come, but they can't go through with it. "I did it," she said to me the last time we met. "I broke up with him." But today: "I saw him again, it's started up again, I can't do without him, and he can't do without me."

"So why try?" I ask.

"Because it's driving me up the wall: the meetings, waiting for the meetings, the pain each time we say goodbye, thinking about him all the time, even when I'm with my kids—and my patients [she's a psychiatrist]. I want out, I want to take a deep breath, I want a bit of calm. Calm, you know?" She's lost weight, she smokes a lot, her eyes shine. I think to myself that calmness will never be her strength, and I think that I envy her a bit. All the more so because today I don't feel that proud. A little while ago I told her about these columns I'm writing and gave her the first one to read, a story about a blind date with no conclusion. She found it amusing and a little sad. What saddened her the most was when I say that past forty, men are better off than women on the love front. "You're going to get irate letters," she warned me.

She was right, I've received one already, which I show her. "I'm forty years old," the woman writes. "I'm beautiful, lucky in love, and I plan on remaining that way. And you, you're nothing but a loser. I wouldn't give you the time of day."

"The thing is," my friend tells me, "I could have written that. I mean, did you mean what you wrote?"

I hesitate. The funny thing is that I wrote it after talking with a woman who had lucidly—and bitterly—defended that very point of view while I'd defended the opposite, and that in defending her ideas I thought I was expressing a woman's point of view. After all, many women denounce it as a crying injustice, more social than biological, true, but as blatant as the reverse injustice in life expectancy: six or seven years less for men. Only, they say, at fifty men stand a better chance of being with a woman of twenty-five than a woman of fifty has of being with a man of twenty-five, that's how it is.

"That's how it is," my friend acknowledges, "but on the one hand women care far less about bolstering their egos with younger partners, and on the other hand this is a purely sociological phenomenon with which your reader is right to take issue. She talks about desire, you don't. She talks about uniqueness and you talk about generalities, and that makes all the difference. It's like the difference between eroticism—which thrives on experience, free choice, and the entire history of the body—and pornography—which is neutral, afraid to choose, and subject to the authority of the interchangeable. In that sense your cynical little sentence is on the side of pornography. And it's not surprising, considering the state you were in two months ago when we saw each other last. Remember: you weren't in love, you weren't attracted to anyone, when you met women all you thought about was what they were after, so as to avoid thinking about what you yourself were after. In pretending to put yourself in their shoes, you projected miserable magazine clichés onto them. Luckily, you've fallen in love since then. And to compound the irony it's with the woman you'd just split up with, when you realized that she could leave you, too. You know what you should do? Use your column to answer this woman. Tell her that, yes, what you wrote was stupid, even if there is a grain of truth to what you said. Only it's such a mediocre truth that it backfires on the person who says it. And say you're sorry she wouldn't give you the time of day. You don't deserve that, I can assure her of that. Hey, that reminds me of a definition I read in the crosswords. Four letters: 'young psychopath from the Carpathians.' You give up? 'Love.' Because as Carmen says—and she should know—'Love is a gypsy's child. It has never, ever, known a law . . .' So there you go: no age, no law, no generalities, that's love. Or in any case, that's desire."

4

Today, as usual, we'll talk about love—or about what counts as love—but also about movies. I've got a reason for that, namely that if everything goes well, I'll shoot a movie at the end of the summer. I say if everything goes well because in this trade I discover that nothing is certain until the first day of shooting: an actor can drop out at the last minute, you can run out of money, as soon as you've fitted two pieces together on one side of the puzzle, a third that you were sure was rock-solid comes loose on the other. If you want to work in the business, it's good not to have a heart condition. After months of stressing because the shooting might not go ahead, I'm now stressed because there's a good chance it will. I wonder if that's not worse; in any case I'm terrified: a rabbit caught in the lights of a car. The screenplay is a more or less fantastic tale, but above all it's the story of a couple, and one day last week as we were reading it over, the lead actor said to me, "You know, you're getting ready to film two people who talk, cross paths, avoid each other, and tear each other apart in the confined space of an apartment; you should really take another look at Jean-Luc Godard's *Contempt*. There's no film that does a better job of showing all that." I'd seen *Contempt* long ago; I remembered that it was beautiful, but I'd forgotten just how beautiful it is. Beautiful and terrible. Absolutely terrible. Rent it and watch it with the person you love. You risk a bad case of the blues, but it's a truly overwhelming experience. It's based on a book by Alberto Moravia and takes place at Cinecittà film studios at the start of the 1960s. A French screenwriter, played by Michel Piccoli, works together with the filmmaker Fritz Lang, played by Fritz Lang, on an adaptation of *The Odyssey*. To that end the screenwriter goes with his wife, played by Brigitte Bardot, first to Rome and then to the villa that Curzio Malaparte had built on the island of Capri. The producer, played by Jack Palance, notices that the screenwriter's wife is beautiful, which isn't difficult, and offers to drive her to his villa, where he's invited the crew to join him. She shoots a look at her husband, hoping he'll say, no, that's out of the question, she's coming with me. But her husband, who's a bit of a coward and wants to get in good with the producer, says, of course, sure, why not, go on, honey, I'll grab a taxi. She doesn't say a thing, she just looks at him and it's over, or at least it's the beginning of the end, and the whole film shows the stages of torment that love goes through when it dies. A little later comes the scene that the actor said I

should see. It lasts thirty-five minutes. Thirty-five minutes of two
people together in an apartment. They go from one room to another, they pour a bath that they get into one after the other, he
with his hat and cigar like Dean Martin in Vincente Minnelli's
Some Came Running, while she sits on the toilet in a black wig
and smokes a cigarette. They get dressed, set the table for a meal
they won't eat, punch a bronze statue that makes different sounds
depending on whether you hit the stomach or the breasts, and
while doing all of that the way you do things in a place you share
with someone else, they exchange banal, atrocious remarks. He
understands that she's annoyed with him but still doesn't know
why, or doesn't want to know, and she refuses to tell him because
there's already no point. She says she wants to sleep alone from
now on.

He says, "You don't want to make love?"

She smiles. "Listen to the jerk . . ."

Since he hasn't given up all hope, he asks, "Is that a mocking
smile or a tender smile?"

"A tender smile."

It's clear that it's not true, and he knows it, too, and from that
moment on it's like quicksand. He no longer stands a chance, he's
lost. Whatever he does, whether he's ironic or brutal or implor-
ing, he's pathetic, he'll never be anything but pathetic, because a
man who's no longer loved is pathetic, that's just the way it is. I
watched all of that with the woman whom I'd started to love again
and who'd started to love me again, despite which—or because
of which—our relationship hadn't really improved. And even if
it had, it would have been the same: teary eyes, goose bumps,
something that gets you right in the gut, something that, in addition to its beauty—because it's one of the most beautiful scenes
ever shot—has to do with pure terror, no matter which of the two
characters you identify with. Because falling out of love—the
moment when the other person stops loving you and when you

know that it's hopeless, irrevocable, relentless, that you're no longer anything at all, that you're nothing in the person's eyes, or in
the eyes of the world, or even in the eyes of God, if you're a
believer—is the most terrible thing of all. It's what everyone
dreads the most, what they'll do anything to avoid or put off, because it's bound to happen one day. I think it happens in every
life at one time or another, and that everyone is condemned to
play one role or the other, one role *and* the other, and that the role
of the person who no longer loves isn't any more enviable than the
role of the person who's no longer loved.

(What I'm writing here isn't upbeat, but who said love was
upbeat?

Who? You. And me sometimes. I'll try to remember that in the
next column.)

5

A couple of months ago, not long after I met Hélène, I took her
to dinner at François and Emmanuelle's place. A couple of years
ago, not long after I met Emmanuelle, I'd taken her to dinner at
François's place. The three of us spent a lot of time together. Emmanuelle and I were very much in love; we lived together for a
year, then our love faded. We broke up, sad but not bitter, and
not long after that Emmanuelle went to live with François. The
months that followed were a bit embarrassing, then we became
close friends again, with Emmanuelle's now being with François
and not with me not changing our affection: it was as if we'd
simply traded places at the kitchen table where we'd spent so
many evenings drinking wine, smoking joints, and swapping stories. François and Emmanuelle are my best friends, the people I
go see when I'm lonely and down in the dumps. At any hour of
the day or night I'm sure to find comfort, a bed if necessary, and

an ideally tolerant friendship. I know the difficulties they've had as a couple; they know—Emmanuelle firsthand—the difficulties I have just *being* in a couple. Once we've drunk a bit, we ritually pat one another on the back for our three-way bond. You could find it all a bit twisted, regressive, vaguely incestuous even, but I like it and so do they, and I have a hard time imagining being together with a woman who doesn't meet them sooner or later. For me that's clear, but not necessarily for the woman in question, and Hélène wondered just what this presentation—which, as she said on the way home, reminded her of some kind of entrance exam—was all about. That she passed it with flying colors didn't change that. What was the idea, to show her to Emmanuelle? To show Emmanuelle to her? To obtain the consent of both? Did I want each to find the other seductive, and to be flattered to have me in common? And did I want to pride myself on being that lucky man? "The problem when you meet past girlfriends of the man you love," Hélène said, "is that either you like them, in which case jealousy isn't far off, or you don't, in which case your idea of the other person suffers. Of course the first case is preferable by far. It's like that Jewish joke: Moshe and his wife, Rachel, are at a party. There are a lot of people and Moshe first points out his colleague Aaron, then Aaron's wife, and then—he lowers his voice—that girl over there is Aaron's mistress. Rachel takes a good look at Aaron's mistress, then says to Moshe, 'Ours is better.' I liked Emmanuelle, I found her beautiful and intelligent, I like the fact that she likes you so much, and I think she's sexy. But what I didn't like is your way of showing me all that, the message you're confusedly trying to get across. It's as if you were telling me, 'Look what a great ex-lover I am.' As if you couldn't wait for it to be over between us, for us to have put behind us the passion and fury [the fury would make its first appearance that night] so that we can settle into a peaceful, loving friendship. Well, let me tell you: that's not how it's going to be with me. When it's over, it'll be over. When we no longer love each other, we're not going to be friends."

A couple of days ago I reminded Hélène of this conversation, and she laughed. Because right now we're in a strange situation. To sum up the previous episodes, some of which I've described in these columns: Our encounter last winter. Both of us totally in love. Three months in a tub of ecstasy. We make plans to move in together. No sooner do we start looking for an apartment than I panic. I want nothing better than to live with someone in general and her in particular, but at the same time I'm petrified. I can no longer get an erection, I no longer see her, all I see is my own panic. I know, all this isn't exactly glorious, but I'm supposed to be *Flair*'s special envoy to the male heart, and the male heart can be a pretty weird place. She's hurt, becomes afraid in turn, we split up. We both drift around on our own, taking care to suffer as little as possible by knowing as little as possible about what the other is doing, while doing all we can to find out. Jealousy, fear of loss, horror at the idea that stupidity and neurosis prevented us from getting what we'd always longed for, what we wanted the most. A timid reunion. Then? Then we're careful not to talk of love, knowing that brings bad luck, at least to us. We don't make plans together because we've broken up. We're ex-lovers, friends and only friends, a promise is a promise, let's let sleeping dogs lie. So we make love as friends, sleep at each other's place as friends, go on holiday together as friends. It's not out of the question that we'll end up sharing an apartment in a friendly spirit, like Sherlock Holmes and Dr. Watson. It's like that story where everything you ask for is granted on one condition: that you don't say a certain word. You can think about it all you like; as long as you don't say it, all's well. The only problem now is, how long can we go without saying it?

6

This column makes me a bit nervous because I have to write it
in advance. Of course I always write them in advance, a month
or so before they're published, but here, because of the summer,
the upcoming holidays, the film I'll shoot in August, the gap is
longer. I'm writing in July something you'll read in October, and
I can't help thinking about everything that could happen in the
meantime. It's like when you prerecord a radio or TV program
that's supposed to be happening live, and the host reminds you
that you have to say "good evening" although it's ten in the morning, and that you shouldn't say anything about what's happening
in the news because all of that will be long out-of-date the day
the show is aired, and there's no way of knowing what'll be in the
news then. All you can hope for if talk comes around to geopoli-
tics, for example, is that nothing like 9/11 will happen in the meantime. I felt that particularly strongly two years ago when I wrote a
piece for the major French newspaper *Le Monde*, which publishes
a story by a more or less well-known writer every week in the
summer. I had carte blanche to write about what I pleased; the
only restrictions were the length, the date of publication—mid-
July—and the deadline in May. I took the job on in April, spent a
couple of weeks wondering what I could write, then got an idea
that struck me as funny. In mid-July, precisely, my girlfriend was
planning to come visit me on the Isle of Ré, off the west coast
of France. I decided to organize things in such a way that she'd
take the train precisely on the day my story would be published,
and that she'd read it on the train. Then I sat down and wrote the
story, which was explicitly addressed to her and took the form of
instructions: You're in the train going from Paris to La Rochelle.
It's July 20, 2002, 4:15 p.m. You read these lines, I tell you to do
this, I tell you to do that—and this and that involved indulging in
sexual fantasies and then going to masturbate in the toilet. So in

short it was a pornographic letter whose distinctive feature was that it was to be read not just by the person it was addressed to, but also by the 1 million people who read *Le Monde*, some of whom would no doubt be sitting in the same train. Of course I didn't tell my girlfriend, everything depended on surprise, and I was terrifically amused—and aroused—by the idea of concocting this thing that was simultaneously an erotic game, a joyful hijacking of the most respectable French newspaper, and a literary performance that was to my mind unprecedented. That said, my excitement was accompanied by a slight apprehension. Because between the moment in May when I would submit the text to *Le Monde* and the day in July when I'd welcome my girlfriend, wild with passion and gratitude, on the platform of the station in La Rochelle—when the operation could be considered a success—anything could happen, from the most minor setback to the most irremediable disaster: she could miss the train, the train could go off the tracks, she could no longer love me or I could no longer love her. And that was only what I imagined, whereas you can count on the gods to be even craftier than that when it comes to punishing smart alecks who dare to defy them by presuming, as I was doing, to control a future event. I was right in believing the gods could thwart my plans. The story caused a minor scandal in France (you can read it, and what happened next, in my book *My Life as a Russian Novel*, which gave the editor in chief of this magazine the idea of asking me to write these columns), but I didn't care, caught up as I was with my own private 9/11 that resulted in things not at all turning out as I'd planned: I broke up with my girlfriend, what should have been funny and lighthearted turned out to be horribly sad, and I told myself that never again would I get mixed up in trying to control reality.

Why am I writing about this disaster? Because it has to do, I believe, with the fear of commitment that many men suffer from, many women complain about, and of which I, unfortunately, am a typical example. This fear is founded on a lucid and even wise apprehension of reality: the knowledge of the transience of things and feelings, of our inability to master them, of the risk that we may no longer be tomorrow who we are today, which also goes for the other person. But such lucidity and wisdom are paralyzing: if you listened to them, you wouldn't say yes to anything, neither projects, nor children, nor erotic stories. I'm not saying my erotic story is a supreme human achievement, but even if I bungled the whole thing up, I don't regret having written it, quite the contrary. To do something, to experience something, you have to agree not to anticipate, not to calculate, not to worry about suffering or causing others to suffer—and in writing this sentence I think that's the most difficult thing, and I don't think I'm speaking only for myself. Deep down we can accept being hurt without too much concern. But what many of us fear the most is hurting others; that's what we have the hardest time accepting, and consequently it's what's the most necessary to accept. Sorry, I'm sounding a little pedantic here, but it seems to me that I've just understood this, not only in this column but in my life. Run the risk of hurting the other person, run the risk that today will be betrayed by tomorrow: take the plunge and swim. As General de Gaulle said when someone cried out "Death to idiots!": "Vast program."

7

"Yesterday at the beach I ran into a guy I used to know," Hélène said. "We hadn't seen each other for years and told each other what we were up to. His wife was playing with their two small children a little way off. The whole time we were talking she never approached, all she did was give a little wave at one point to say hi. She's pretty, slim, Japanese, a little enigmatic the way Japanese women often are. She's a novelist, her husband told me. She lives with him in France, she learned French and they speak French with their children, but she continues to write in Japanese. Her books appear in Japan, they're not translated into any other languages, and he doesn't understand Japanese. That's strange, don't you think? To live with an author and not be able to read what she writes? But the strangest thing is that her books are autobiographical and, it seems, erotic, if not pornographic."

"How does he know that if he can't read them?" I objected.

"She told him, and it's also what their Japanese friends say when he asks about them. They look so embarrassed he thinks they must be pretty steamy."

For me it sounded like the start of a novel, a Japanese novel in fact. A little perverse, a little chic, with just one weak point in the plotline; namely, that if he really wanted to read what his wife wrote, he could easily get it translated, just for himself. "That's what I said to him," Hélène said, "and he said that, yes, of course he could, that he thought about it often, but that in all the years he'd been thinking about it, he still hadn't gone ahead and done it; a little because he was afraid, no doubt, and a lot because the situation excited him." Fifty yards away the children were building a sandcastle with their mother. They were laughing, and Hélène wondered if they would read their mother's books when they got older. There was a silence, then Hélène added in an offhand way, "Would you like me to read the columns you write for that Italian magazine, or would it bother you?"

The question took me by surprise. "Would you like to?"

"Let's say I would. Would you let me read them?"

I said yes, what else could I say? And that evening at my computer I opened the French versions of the six columns I'd already written. I reread them, trying to put myself in the place of Hélène, the leading lady. It started with a breakup, followed by brief encounters, then a cautious, once-burned-twice-shy reunion, and most recently a loving friendship. The column I'd just sent off was a fastidious examination of this voluntarily precarious situation, blended with thoughts about my fears of no longer feeling tomorrow the sentiments I feel today, and so of hurting the other person, and so of committing myself . . . It's a familiar, depressing theme, which depressed me all the more as I printed up the texts; there are better presents you can give a woman, that's for sure.

At that point I looked at my e-mail and found a message from Fiona, the editor in chief of this magazine. She's the one who recruited me, and our correspondence had been purely formal—I sent the text, she published it—until the day a month ago when, both because I was swamped with work and because I was quickly running out of ideas, I announced that I was stopping. From northern India, where she was on vacation, Fiona called me and told me that, no, I was not stopping. She knew perfectly well that she couldn't force me to go on, she said, and that I was as free to leave as she was to fire me if my articles no longer suited her. However, in hiring me she'd given a commitment to her readers, and in accepting I'd given a commitment to her, so I wasn't going to stop, period. Fine, fine, I said, and from that moment our relationship became affectionately sadomasochistic, without a clear distribution of roles. In her e-mail now, Fiona acknowledged receipt of my new column, informing me that something was definitely wrong. The worst thing was that it wasn't my prose, but my life. My entire life, everything what I was: a complete disaster. I quote: "Emmanuel, do you really think I can publish a phenomenology of fear in a column signed by you as the special envoy to the male heart? I understand that, like Moses before the burning bush, you're tempted to say, 'Why me? Why was I chosen for this? Why is this woman hounding me to write about the depths of my soul while it's so warm outside and I have so many other things to do?' I understand all of that, Emmanuel. But, come on, is there nothing else in your life? No other sentiment that you feel for a woman? Something beautiful or painful, some passion, jealousy, tenderness, rage? Anything, in fact, other than this urge to flee, which you say is your chief characteristic? Don't you get tired of that after a while?"

No doubt you're starting to catch on that there's no standing up to Fiona. She asked me to rewrite the text, I was going to have to do it, and as well as pleasing her, I wanted it to please my new reader: Hélène. I tried to imagine how the Japanese writer would feel if she decided one morning to let her husband read six years' worth of porn novels dedicated to their married life. As for us, in the eight months that we'd known each other, we'd come as far as a sexual friendship. It's a delightful state, but one that, in my mind, couldn't last if we said a certain word. While I'd been burning to say that word for some time, I was afraid to pronounce it, terribly afraid even, for all of the reasons listed in the column that Fiona so disliked. It's as if this woman whom I didn't know, this editor in chief of a women's magazine to which I contributed without reading it (I can't read Italian), had morphed into a sort of Jiminy Cricket, an apostle of fearless love, who, perched on my shoulder, repeated, "Come on, you jerk, if you want to tell her you love her, tell her!" Okay, Fiona. I told her.

8

"Why not add a little sex next time?" asked Fiona. Good question. Why not? I thought back to my previous columns and said to myself that for someone who'd been hired on the basis of his reputation as an amiable pornographer, I'd been remarkably chaste up to now. Flirts with no tomorrow, lame blind dates, ruminations about the fear of commitment; lucky that in the meantime I'd fallen in love or, to be more precise, fallen back in love with the woman I left six months ago. She loves not only to make love but also to talk about it, two things that conventional wisdom deems contradictory (the more you talk about it, the less you do it), but on this point as on many others I distrust conventional wisdom. On the contrary, I believe that sex and talking go exceedingly well together. I like it when a woman tells me about her sex life, the ways she desired the men she desired, what she did to them, what they did to her, what their cocks were like. You can say an element of homosexuality is in all of that, I won't take offense: I agree completely. As the time for writing this article was approaching, I consulted my lover: a thousand words, give or take a few, with a little sex thrown in. Any ideas? She had several, enough to fill a couple of columns. Here's one:

"I was at a disco once, with some friends. There were a lot of people, it was dark, the place was packed. I'd been dancing for a long time and had come back to talk with a friend at the bar—well, talk: I mean form words with my mouth that the music and noise prevented her from hearing—and laugh with her because we couldn't understand a thing. I'd drunk a bit, I was wearing a skirt and standing sideways at the bar, other bodies pressed up against mine but it didn't last long, just in passing. Then something that must have been a hand settled on my butt and stayed there. I moved, shifted my weight a little, but the hand kept up its pressure. I analyzed the situation: a guy's got his hand on my ass. Even without any whole-hog feminism it's a gesture you associate with a lousy come-on, one that merits a rebuff or even a slap in the face. Normally you send a guy who puts his hand on your ass packing without much further ado. But this hand had—how to put it?—something friendly about it. It was firm but not clumsy, insistent but not indiscreet. It was warm; in fact I was happy it stayed put and wasn't discouraged by my faked twitches

of annoyance. I was also happy not to know who it belonged to.
I continued to talk, and the hand that I had done nothing to dis-
courage felt encouraged, the fingers slipped under my skirt from
the waist, first the fingers, then the whole palm. Sure, everyone was squeezed together, still I wondered if anyone could see
what was going on: a hand had slipped inside my skirt and now
was rubbing against my panties. I moved to ease its way, and
in any case from where it was the hand couldn't fail to grasp
that I was excited. It started caressing me—very well—and the
whole time I kept talking to my friend, wondering if you could
see on my face that an unknown hand was making me come.
The funniest thing is that since she was standing in front of me,
she must have seen the man or woman behind me who was fin-
gering me so well."

"What do you mean, the man or woman? You mean there's a
doubt in your mind?"

"Sure there is. I think it was probably a man, but who knows?"

"Come on, between a man's hand and a woman's hand caressing you, you should know the difference."

"Really? You said the same thing when I blindfolded you the
other day and defied you to say whether I was taking you in my
mouth, my pussy, or my ass; you said it was too easy, that you'd tell
from the first contact. And you were wrong, remember? Let's say it
was a man. Actually, I also think it was a man. To finish the story:
He made me come, he felt me come from inside, he remained
there for a bit, as if to calm me down, and then he took his hand
out. I kept talking, pretending nothing was happening, and then a
couple of minutes later I turned around. Some people were talking, drinking, and smoking behind me; the person closest to me
was a man, neither good-looking nor ugly. The key thing is that
if it was him—but maybe it wasn't, maybe he'd already left—he
didn't give me the slightest sign. That's what I like about this
story: to have been jerked off in a public place by stranger, fine,

but above all that this stranger remained a stranger, that that's all he did, that he didn't try to chat me up. It must have been enough for him to make me come, he didn't ask for anything in return. It was a gift with no strings attached: the exact opposite of rape. You know, I was young when that happened, twenty or so, and it gave me a lot of confidence: in sex, in men, in men's potential generosity, to the point where each time I met one who would ·count for me I imagined for a moment that it was him: the man who liked to make women come without asking anything in return, the man who loved their pleasure. I thought that about you, the first night. I wondered, not if it was you of course, but if you would have been able to do that. If you'd have liked to do that. I think you would. The men I like are the men I can think that about."

9

It must be said: for men, there aren't many things in the world that are more mysterious—and fascinating—than women's orgasms. Just like men's orgasms for women, I suppose, although I suppose it partly for reasons of symmetry, and almost of equity, because despite everything male orgasm is simpler, more mechanical—although it becomes subtler as soon as you dissociate orgasm from ejaculation, but if you like, we'll talk about that another time. Today I want to use this column as a sort of chat room, to generate comments and gather reactions to a particular sexual trait. I don't know if it's rare or widespread, if it's thought of highly or vaguely rejected, or even if it has a name, either scientific or informal. Two times in my life I've met women who ejaculated when they came. When I say ejaculated, I don't mean the type of vaginal secretions we're all familiar with, but a copious spurt of dense liquid that fills your mouth—because as far as

I know it only happens with clitoral orgasms brought on by oral stimulation. The first time it happened to me I must have been around twenty. I didn't understand what was happening, and I thought my partner was pissing. Although we were already pretty close, I couldn't help thinking that pissing in your lover's mouth like that without warning was pretty cavalier. A huge stain was on the sheet, the liquid tasted acidic and had a sour smell, but it wasn't urine. What was it then? What had come out of her, together with her pleasure? I didn't dare ask her; she seemed as troubled as I was by what had just happened: I got the feeling it didn't happen to her every day. But it happened again with us. Not every time I licked her, but often, and was associated with the most violent orgasms, so that I came to consider these deluges as an indication of maximum satisfaction, which I did my best to bring about. It was as if my tongue were boring away at a dam, and I loved the moment when the dam finally gave way. It happened often during the time we spent together. I think that, seeing my pleasure when she came like that, she stopped trying to keep the floodgates closed, but we never spoke about it. We were young: maybe neither of us dared to admit our inexperience, so we both acted as if it happened all the time. It couldn't have been that common, however, or I just missed out, because in the twenty-five years that followed no other woman gushed into my mouth like that. Until I met the woman I now love, and whom I hope to love for a long time to come. She was also troubled when it happened to her with me, but one of the advantages of being older is no doubt that it's easier to talk with your lover, and she described it from her point of view. The first time it happened she must have been the same age as my girlfriend was back then, and not only did she not understand what was going on, she also felt horribly ashamed. She knew full well that it wasn't urine, but it was similar, and the idea of pissing when you come is enough to inhibit even the most free-spirited of girls.

That's what she was, too; she loved making love, she loved men's desire, their hands, their cocks, their tongues, but despite all that she was always a bit afraid of their tongues on her clitoris; it was the only thing she let happen without giving herself up to it, with a perpetual reluctance, always careful not to let herself go: she didn't want to squirt like that again, or to be ashamed, or not to know what was going on. That was the real problem: not knowing. Not knowing if it was normal or abnormal, clean or dirty, possibly exciting or definitely disgusting. She tried to find out: she asked her gynecologist, read sexology books. In vain, or almost. Some women do that when they come: they're known as fountain women. But what is *that*? What's the real term? And why do *some* women do it and not others? What percentage of the female population: one, ten? Is it more like having green eyes or having an extra toe? Is it a talent that only a few privileged women cultivate, or a disability? "It's funny to have a sexual tic that no one talks about although it seems that everything is talked about nowadays," says the woman I love. "You can't open a women's magazine without coming across some kind of test: Are you vaginal or clitoral? Followed by a comparison of different lubricants. In fact it's a little as if I didn't know that all women have periods and had spent my entire adult life keeping quiet about this mysterious thing that happens every month to me and only me. Why don't you talk about that in your Italian magazine? Who knows? Maybe it'll come as a liberation to a whole bunch of women like me, who've always felt a bit strange. You'll get letters, we'll read them together, it'll become a big social debate, and in the next elections to the European Parliament we'll look on in pride as the party of the fountain women and the men who love to lick them makes tremendous strides. Fountain Pride: That's quite the program, no?"

Published in *Flair*, December 2003–August 2004

This last column disgusted Fiona so much that she ended my collaboration with Flair. And more or less consciously, that's why I wrote it: I'd had enough. After that I discovered that such female ejaculations, listed on porn sites under the heading "squirt," are the delight of a large number of fans—myself included on occasion.

Death in Sri Lanka

(with Hélène Devynck)

Later, during one of those strange, post-catastrophe conversations, they told us that they'd been amused to hear one of our children order spaghetti Bolognese. We'd just arrived at Tangalle, after six hours of driving to cover the 125 miles from Colombo; we were having lunch under the veranda of this dreamlike hotel, the Eva Lanka, perched on a hill above the sea. They were at the next table, a French couple in their thirties: he was tall and dark haired, she was blond and pretty, with a little girl as blond and pretty as her mother, and an older man whose hooked nose and salt-and-pepper curls made him look strikingly like the actor Pierre Richard. They were more like residents than tourists. In any case they looked as if they knew the lay of the land, and we thought it would be good to see them again: they seemed nice and were sure to have good tips to share with us.

We did see them again, on the afternoon of December 26. Of the disaster itself we neither heard nor saw a thing. We didn't even know the word *tsunami*. Hesitating that morning between the pool and the beach below the hotel, we were lazy and chose the pool. Only when the hotel staff, ordinarily rather sluggish, started rushing around in panic did we understand that something had happened. Two hours later the hotel was full of half-naked, wounded, distraught Westerners. Among these survivors, some lucky ones had just lost all their belongings, their passports, money, and plane tickets, while others were searching for their wives, their husbands, their children. And some were no longer searching, because they knew.

Philippe, the man who looked like Pierre Richard, was in a bathing suit, feverishly talking and talking. The wave had surprised him in front of his bungalow, where, while his daughter Delphine—the pretty blond—and his son-in-law Jérôme went to the market in the village, he had stayed behind to babysit little Juliette and her best friend, Osandy, the daughter of their Sri Lankan friend M.H. The little girls were playing inside the bungalow; he'd tried to get them out, but the flood had swept him away, and he'd clung to a tree. Just when he was about to let go, he'd been saved by a board that pinned him against the trunk. When he found Delphine and Jérôme unharmed, he knew already, almost for certain, that Juliette and Osandy were dead. The three adults had gone to the hospital in Tangalle, where the bodies were starting to rush in. Juliette was there, in her red dress, and so was Osandy, and Osandy's father, and other villagers—most of whom they'd gotten to know in the ten years they'd been coming there.

They didn't cry. Philippe talked. Delphine was silent, Jérôme looked at her, then, little by little, he started to talk as well, and even to joke around. This black humor without a trace of hysteria left us speechless on the first evening. Then we understood: they couldn't yet afford the luxury of going to pieces. They still had something to do: recover Juliette's body and bring it home. In all the chaos they would have to soldier on until that was done.

The next day, we left Delphine with our children at the hotel—yes, with our children, whom she did her best to entertain by showing them hummingbirds, carnivorous plants, and a huge tortoise at the bottom of a well—and went with Jérôme and Philippe to Tangalle. At the hospital, right after the catastrophe, Jérôme had been given a slip of paper on which three words had been scribbled in Sinhalese, which must have meant something like "little white girl, four years old, blond, red dress." He had nothing more official and feared above all that his daughter might be added to one of the groups of non-identified corpses that were now being cremated for fear of an epidemic.

"Finding the hospital is easy," he joked when we arrived in the village, "just follow the flies." Even from a distance the odor was suffocating. Coffins were coming in and out, for the dead who'd been recognized by their families. The others were loaded onto pickups, and inside, dozens were lying on the floor. A small group of Westerners had gathered in the vacant lot surrounding the main building, those who didn't want to leave without having found the person they were looking for, dead or alive. Their clothes were in tatters, they were covered in wounds that had been hastily rubbed with a purplish disinfectant, their eyes were wide with horror.

Juliette was no longer at the hospital. The corpses of the Western victims had been transferred in the night, some to Colombo, others to Matara, that's all they could tell us. Matara is roughly twenty-five miles from Tangalle, but no vehicles could take us there because there was no gas. In the best of cases we would have to wait until the next day. To while away the time and keep fear at bay, we wandered through the devastated village. On the beach strewn with boats we saw the ruins of the bungalow where Juliette and Osandy had died. There were still some bits of the wall on which Delphine had painted—with real talent—a fresco of palm trees and hummingbirds. Farther off we saw the old Sinhalese house that Philippe had bought two months earlier, which the family had been planning to move into in January

when the work was done. With every step we took through the
mud and debris, villagers stopped Philippe and gave him a big
hug. Whereas just the day before he thought he'd never return
to Sri Lanka, now he was already vowing he'd be back soon. He
couldn't leave them like that. They were his friends. They'd lost
everything, he had to help them, the way a fisherman, seeing him
wandering half-naked in the streets, had tried to help him the
day before, insisting that he accept a thousand rupees—maybe a
quarter of what he makes in a month. For the past twenty years
Sri Lanka had been part of Philippe's life, and in the thick of the
catastrophe it was touching to hear him stress the inhabitants'
moral qualities and solidarity: "You saw the old guy in front of
M.H.'s house? That's his father-in-law, he's from Colombo. Don't
ask me how he got here: the roads are cut off, you can't get gas
anywhere, and he was already here on the first night."

At the Eva Lanka, the Garden of Eden was looking more
and more like the Raft of the Medusa. All the foreigners who
had been stranded along the coast had gathered there, both for
safety in case the tsunami struck again and because there they
were given food, shelter, and clothing. The Italian owners performed this task without departing from their lymphatic, icy
courtesy; nevertheless such efficiency was worth far more than
more exuberant demonstrations of sympathy. The staff were
as respectful to the victims as they were to the paying guests.
Like us unharmed by the disaster, these guests did what they
could to help, with the notable exception of a group of German
Swiss who were taking a course in Ayurvedic medicine, and
who, dressed in loose-fitting robes and strange caps, continued
to care for their bodies and souls as if nothing had happened.
In the evening, when the generator was running and we could
recharge our cell phones—in the rare moments when calls
could get through, these were the only means of contacting care-
worn families, assistance services, and overworked embassies—

everyone gathered around the television to take stock of the growing extent of the disaster.

With the passing hours, the increasingly frugal—although still ceremonious—meals, and the chain-smoked cigarettes, a friendship was born. We spoke of our lives, so very different: we were stressed-out Parisians, they were pleasure-loving Bordeaux residents from Saint-Émilion, fond of vintage wines, good food, and the outdoors. The children fell in love with Philippe, who never stopped joking with them. We also talked about Juliette, how she was born the day her parents got married, the four years of her life, and all of that without pathos, without lowering our voices as if we were in church. They continued to soldier on. They impressed us. We grew close to them.

At the hospital in Matara, the next day, it was worse than at the one in Tangalle. A medical examiner pulled the corpses' entrails out by the handful, and the cold room had only six drawers, which Jérôme had opened one after the other. Juliette wasn't there. Like everyone, Jérôme had come in with a mask over his nose and mouth, but he'd taken it off right away: "I'm a wine merchant, my nose is my tool. I've registered and classified that odor alongside wood violet and flint, it no longer has any effect on me." Transformed into a machine for finding his daughter, this nonchalant joker had become a terminator. He still had one hope: a police photographer had taken shots of all the dead before they were evacuated, and the images were being shown over and over on a computer screen. Cutting through the crowd that was thronging around the monitor, Jérôme took the mouse from the policeman and clicked and clicked until the photo of two young white girls lying head to toe appeared; one of whom, like Juliette, had a Band-Aid on her leg. The next picture showed her face: blond, pretty, not yet ravaged. Jérôme insisted until a kind officer—and they were all kind, even if they weren't all efficient—assured him that Juliette had been transferred to the police morgue in Colombo. We decided to leave for Colombo the next day; with or without a vehicle we'd find a way: nothing short of death would stop Jérôme.

That night, talking about Juliette's repatriation with his medical assistance company, Jérôme discovered that she could only be brought back to France in a lead-lined coffin, that they wouldn't be able to open it when it arrived because of the health risk, and that consequently they'd have to bury their daughter, instead of cremating her. This cremation meant a lot to them. "Have you ever seen a funeral with a child's coffin?" Jérôme asked me. "I have, and I'm sure of one thing: I never want to see it again." But it was either that or leave without Juliette. Jérôme took Delphine in his arms, something he didn't often do. An overwhelming tenderness emanated from this couple, but they avoided tenderness the way they avoided everything that ran the risk of making them go to pieces. Softly he said that it was her decision.

No one spoke at the start of dinner. Delphine was in shock, her face blank and her chin trembling slightly. Then, after fifteen minutes, she lifted her head and said, "Juliette will stay here. She'll be cremated here." This decision bowled us over. The self-evidence, the lucidity, the complete lack of procrastination or regret. We were all on the verge of tears, and then in no time we all started to laugh and talk about the fantastic bottles we'd open when we came to Saint-Émilion, the rare Rolling Stones albums Philippe would play for the children, and the Ayurvedic clowns in their swimming caps who were chewing away impassively at their brown rice just a few yards away—it did us good to be a little catty, it was only human, and we had a terrible need to be human.

At the Alliance Française in Colombo we were found tickets on a plane leaving at dawn the next morning. Before that, Jérôme faced one last ordeal. He went to the morgue, alone, to see his daughter for the last time—he thought—and to order her cremation according to Buddhist rites. He came back with an impassive look on his face, told Delphine that Juliette was still beautiful, told us it wasn't true, and knocked back a big glass of whiskey.

At this point Nigel, a chunky, jovial—and to judge by his car, wealthy—thirtysomething Sri Lankan, appeared on the scene. He asked us how we'd fared in the catastrophe. Jérôme answered naturally that they'd lost their daughter. Nigel merely said, "Sorry," then asked just as naturally about the situation: Had we found her? Where was her body? . . . Jérôme explained, telling him about the cremation planned for the next morning. "It's a good thing you're telling me," Nigel said. "I'll go there myself and make sure things are done right." We were starting to understand that when Nigel makes sure things are done right, they are. He took us to a splendid restaurant, where he announced straight off that the bill was on him, then left again, leaving us to drink, eat, smoke 850 cigarettes, and marvel at this encounter. It didn't surprise Philippe, who remembered the thousand-rupee note he'd been given by a poor fisherman: all Sri Lankans, from the top to the bottom of the social ladder, are like that, he said. Delphine was overwhelmed but happy: what had just happened confirmed that she'd made the right decision. This ceremony, taken charge of by a complete stranger, was fate, and, in the midst of tragedy, a sort of perfect manifestation of human kindness.

Near the end of dinner Nigel came back with his wife, a beautiful neurosurgeon, whom he proudly presented to us. Then he took Jérôme and Philippe for a short walk, saying they wouldn't be long. They went to a boutique, the most luxurious one Nigel could find, where he bought the most sumptuous girl's dress they had. From there they went to the morgue, where they dressed Juliette and prepared her for the ceremony. Nigel assured them that by the time our plane had landed, everything would be done and the ashes transferred to Kandy, the former capital in the hills, where he would scatter them himself in the Botanical Gardens. Delphine loves gardens passionately, and in all of Sri Lanka the

Botanical Gardens at Kandy are the place she loves the most. At this precise moment, when Jérôme told her that, she understood that the period of mourning had commenced, and that she could start to cry.

Published in *Paris Match*, January 2005

As things panned out, this Nigel, whom we had considered the very embodiment of kindness, did none of what he said he'd do. Nevertheless, Juliette was cremated, and a few weeks later her ashes were strewn by Philippe in the Botanical Gardens at Kandy.

Room 304, Hôtel du Midi
in Pont-Évêque, Isère

On the table in front of me are four sheets of paper ripped from a spiral pad and covered on both sides with notes written—or rather scribbled—with a black felt pen. These notes were to help me give a detailed description of room 304 of the Hôtel du Midi in Pont-Évêque, in the Isère department. I wrote them down on the night of June 12, 2005, at the end of which Hélène's sister Juliette died.

Her cancer had been diagnosed four months earlier. The prognosis was poor, as they say, but no one thought things would happen that quickly. One day before the night in question, Hélène called me in tears to tell me that Juliette was dying, that it was just a matter of hours, and that she was going take the next train from the Gare de Lyon without coming home first. I met her there, and the whole journey all I could do was take her hand, say her name now and then, and tell her I loved her. She stared straight in front of her. Sometimes she closed her eyes.

Juliette lived near Vienne, not far from Lyon. The whole family was there, both Juliette's side and the side of her husband, Patrice. I knew Juliette's side a bit, Patrice's not at all. Hélène and I had only been living together since the start of the year; I was the latest of the new additions to the family. What I knew about Juliette had made me like her, but I'd only seen her once before. This was not my mourning: I was there for Hélène. Late on the evening of our arrival we went to the intensive care unit at the hospital. Juliette was weak, but it was understood that, barring any accidents, she would not die that night. The doctors believed they could keep her alive until the following evening at least, and in agreement with her husband she had planned to spend this last day bidding farewell to her loved ones. To that end she had asked for help to be in the best condition possible, meaning conscious, not suffering too much, and physically presentable, above all for her three girls and the image they would retain of her.

That Saturday was also the day of the school's end-of-year party. The two eldest daughters, Amélie, seven, and Clara, four, had roles in the play. Two days earlier they'd still thought both their parents would come to see them perform. The next day their father had had to tell them that it wasn't sure Mommy would be home from the hospital. Now he had to tell them that not only was she not going to be home, but that after the show they'd go to see her for the last time.

I was, and still am, a screenwriter. One of my trades consists of constructing dramatic situations, and one of the rules of this trade is that you must not be afraid of overdoing it or being too melodramatic. Still, I think I wouldn't have allowed myself to write such a blatant tearjerker as the parallel montage of little girls dancing and singing in their school play and the agony of their mother dying in the hospital. What made things even more heart-wrenching, if that's possible, is that the play was great. Really. I have two boys, aged eighteen and fourteen, and so I've seen quite a few year-end performances, at their kindergarten or elementary school, with plays, songs, and pantomimes. They're always sweet, but they're also invariably awkward, rough-hewn, and slipshod, so if there's one thing the more indulgent parents are thankful for, it's that the teachers who put so much effort into organizing these shows keep them short. The play that Clara and Amélie were in wasn't short, but it wasn't overly long either. The little ballets and sketches had a precise quality that could only have been achieved with much work and care.

Their grandparents had brought the girls to the hospital, together with little Diane, just a year and a half old. I wondered what she could be feeling and how, later, she'd try to put it all together. Late in the day our turn came. I accompanied Hélène. Juliette had lost consciousness. She'd done everything that remained for her to do. Patrice was lying on the bed, holding her in his arms and talking to her in a low voice. It was up to him, and him alone, to remain with her until the end. Just before leaving, as night was falling, Hélène left her cell phone number with the night nurse, asking that she be called when it was over.

After that there was a dinner back at the house, in the garden. It was a warm June evening, the neighbors were barbecuing outside, we could hear children splashing in inflatable pools. Hélène and I went home early, to the Hôtel du Midi in Pont-Évêque, where we'd already spent the previous night. Smoking was forbidden in the room, there were no ashtrays, so we used a plastic tooth glass with a bit of water in it to prevent it from melting, making for a disgusting concoction at the bottom of the glass. The window looked out over the parking lot, and we'd left it wide open. Far off we could hear gravel crunching under tires, car doors slamming, a few words being exchanged: the sounds of a summer night. Lying on the bed with the sheets thrown back, we couldn't sleep or make love, and Hélène was too tied in knots to cry. Speaking was difficult enough.

I said I was going to cancel my trip to Yokohama, scheduled for the following week. Yokohama hosts a festival of French cinema; I'd been invited to present a film I'd just made. I'd never been to Japan and was delighted—and flattered—by the invitation, but I wasn't going to let Hélène bury her sister alone. What bothered me, I said half-jokingly, was that I'd planned to write a text when I was there for the anthology of stories written by friends of my fellow writer Olivier Rolin. I'd already told Hélène about it, but only vaguely. She knew Olivier a bit, but not much. Both of them, for reasons that are a mystery to me, were more or less convinced that the other didn't like him or her—Hélène thinking that Olivier thought of her as a frivolous, stuck-up bimbo,* Olivier that Hélène thought of him as a bombastic drunk—and each time they met, they had to have a few drinks to dispel the misunderstanding. I told her about the idea behind the book—a collection of texts describing hotel rooms all over the world—and my hesitations about the choice of room. The tone of the project called for a sophisticated, exotic establishment, for example the People's Friendship Hotel in Magadan, in eastern Siberia. I said Magadan both because Hélène was just reading the moving memoir of Yevgenia Ginzburg, and because it seemed to me that Olivier's book started there. In fact it doesn't, I just checked, it starts at the Polar Hotel (Zapolyarye Gostinitsa) in Khatanga. In this glacial, seedy, twilit register I had in reserve the Hotel Vyatka in Kotelnich, Kirov Oblast, a perfect example of a Brezhnevian-type establishment that's slowly going to seed, where not a lightbulb must have been changed since it opened, and where, if I put my stays together, I had spent almost two months. On the other end of the spectrum, the only other hotel I could boast I'd lived in, for several weeks that is, was the sumptuous InterContinental Hong Kong. The film I shot there has a scene in a room with the most impressive view of the bay, and that was my room. Hélène came and stayed with me. When we met up in the lobby, or when we walked up and down the stairs, we felt as if we were in *Lost in Translation*. The hotel awaiting me in Yokohama must have been like that, I imagined, and I'd promised myself the enjoyable holi-

---

*No. (Note by Olivier Rolin.)

day homework assignment of describing my room down to the last detail. To this description I would graft memories of other rooms and, all going well, the outline of a story in which Tahar Tagoul played a role.

"Who's Tahar Tagoul?" Hélène asked.

I explained. Two years earlier, I'd spent several days in the summer at Olivier's place in Brittany; we'd sailed a bit in his boat *Maline*, and for a couple of hours, in the crackle of messages coming over the boat's radio, an anonymous voice had tried to contact a certain Tahar Tagoul. We loved the name, and Olivier, who was writing *Suite à l'hôtel Crystal* at the time, vowed to include Tahar Tagoul: he'd be perfectly at home in this gallery of dodgy characters, Olivier said. He didn't do it, I don't know why,* but I was resolved to make up for that. Tahar Tagoul in Yokohama: that was the task I'd set for myself.

I went on talking and talking, in the hopes of distracting Hélène as much as I could. We were lying beside each other in this room that was too hot, thinking about Juliette dying at the hospital, about Patrice holding her in his arms, about Juliette and Hélène's parents, who, three doors down the hall, must have been thinking about the same things, about the little girls in their little girls' beds, with their little girls' lives that would be torn apart for good tonight, and to fill the silence I reeled off my memories of luxurious and sordid hotels, of Olivier on his boat and Tahar Tagoul. Hélène listened and smiled occasionally; what else could she do?

I think it was she who said to me, "If you don't go to Yokohama, you can describe this room. We can do it now, it'll give us something to do."

I took out my notebook and a black felt pen and wrote down under her dictation that the room had an area of around 130

---

*I was given to understand that it would be better not to. (Note by Olivier Rolin.)

square feet and was completely papered—including the ceiling—in yellow. Not with yellow-colored wallpaper, she insisted; with wallpaper that must originally have been white and had then been painted over *in* yellow, with an embossed design imitating coarsely woven fabric. After that we moved on to the paneling, the door-frames, the window frames, the baseboard and headboard of the bed, which were painted in a deeper yellow. All things considered, the room was very yellow, with touches of pink and green pastels on the sheets and curtains, which were reflected in the two lithographic reproductions hanging over and across from the bed. Both of them, put out in 1994 by Nouvelles Images SA, seemed equally influenced by Matisse and Yugoslav naive painting. Propping myself up on one elbow, I hastily jotted down everything that Hélène pointed out. She was now walking around the room, counting the wall sockets and trying to get a handle on the multiway switches controlling the lights. She was naked, and as she moved back and forth like that, I was starting to get turned on. But now she had the bit between her teeth and wanted to finish our inventory. I'll skip the details: it was a banal room in a banal, although well-kept and friendly, hotel. The only thing a little out of the ordinary—and which was the most difficult to describe—was in the little entranceway. According to my notes: "It's a cupboard with two doors, one of which opens inward, into the entranceway, and the other, at a right angle, which opens outward into the corridor. It's like a serving hatch with two shelves, the top one reserved for linen and the bottom one for the breakfast trays, as is clearly indicated by pictograms engraved in the two little peep windows on each shelf, which both indicate what goes where and let you see if it's there or not." I don't know if that's entirely clear; too bad. We wondered if this sort of cupboard, which is quite uncommon, had a name that could make such a laborious description super-fluous. Some people have a mind for that sort of detail and can tell you the name of everything in every situation—or at least in many situations. Olivier can; so can his brother Jean. Not me. Hélène can a bit. For example, the expression *peep window* in the lines I just quoted comes from her. I also know that among the many other reasons I loved her that night, I also loved her for knowing the phrase *peep window* and using it astutely.

Dawn came. We'd finished our inventory and Hélène's phone hadn't rung. She started to be afraid. Afraid of futile medical treatment, afraid that her sister was being kept alive although she was ready to die, afraid that she would miss the right moment to die. I tried to reassure Hélène, although I wasn't so sure myself. We closed the curtains, pulled the sheet over us, slept poorly but a bit, snuggled up together like spoons. The phone woke us at nine. Juliette had died at four in the morning. She was thirty-three.

Five days later we returned to the Hôtel du Midi for the funeral. We stayed in the same room. There was a wedding that day; cars decorated with white ribbon pulled up loudly in the parking lot. All summer, I kept my four pages of notes in a drawer. When I thought about them, I told myself that this bundle of sadness wouldn't fit in with a group of fanciful, spirited texts and that I'd have to write something else, but I didn't come up with anything. That's the hotel room I described, and that's what happened there. I don't know where all of this is taking me, but all I can write is what happened.

Published in *Rooms* by Olivier Rolin and other authors
(Les Éditions du Seuil, 2006)

The Invisible

This is a synopsis, or statement of intent, for a film whose idea I developed around 2005 or 2006 in the hope of getting around the trouble I was having writing My Life as a Russian Novel. *I later dropped it, without excluding the idea of coming back to it: I know from experience that most abandoned projects resurface in some form. Finally this embryonic story appeared in a magazine dedicated to intimate writing. Does it belong there? I wondered. All things considered, I think it does.*

•

The boy is eight years old. He's on vacation. His cousins, a little older than he is, tell him mysteriously that they've found a way to become invisible. You have to drink a potion; it's not very good. They pass him the glass and dare him to drink. The boy's a bit afraid, he hesitates, then drinks it to the last drop. It's true, it doesn't taste good. In fact it's soapy water, but they'll only tell him that later. In the meantime, it works: he's become invisible. His cousins call his name, they look for him, stretch out their arms in what they think is his direction, only he's changed places. He moves around the room, walks between them, brushes up against them as if they were playing blindman's buff and their eyes were blindfolded, but their eyes aren't blindfolded, it's just that they no longer see him. He can stand right in front of his cousin, within his reach, make faces: his cousin looks right through him. It's frightening, and exhilarating.

Intoxicated by his power, the boy goes out onto the terrace where the parents are just finishing lunch. He shouts, "I'm invisible!" Everyone turns and smiles sweetly, the way you smile at a boy who's playing. The parents weren't in on the secret, and the cousins who followed him onto the terrace burst out laughing, delighted with their joke.

•

Because it was a joke. The boy was terribly disappointed, and terribly hurt. Still, for five minutes he'd felt what it was like to be invisible.

I want to make a film to explore this sensation, and to stretch these five minutes of ecstasy and torment over an entire life. I want to imagine what the life of a man who had this power would be like.

•

This power. This talent. This gift. The man who inherits all of this, without reason or justice, is a king, but also a rat. He is chosen, but also excluded. This above all is what I want to deal with: how a gift can enhance but also devastate a life.

I imagine this film narrated in voice-over by the protagonist.

To a woman.

To her he will explain what this power that is now leaving him has done to his life.

•

It's not like in the movies, or the way his cousins imagined it. There's no need for a potion, it's a lot simpler than that: all he has to do—or had to do—was want to disappear, and he would vanish from people's vision—and minds—at the drop of a hat. No need to get naked either, to avoid having people see a suit topped by a hat and preceded by a pipe with smoke trailing from it. Adaptations of H. G. Wells's foundational novel have popularized such arresting images. When you talk about the "invisible man" in the movies, that's generally what comes to mind. But he doesn't have such logistical problems; he can disappear together with his belongings. Whenever he wants, people can look in his direction and see nothing. It's as if he weren't there.

He's not bodiless, however. He's not a draft of air you can walk through. The people he brushes up against can feel him. He can touch and be touched. If he decides to get into a two-door car with a couple he's followed along the street, for example, it takes a good deal of ingenuity—and dexterity—for him to slide into the back seat without their suspecting anything. He's not altogether beyond reach.

•

What did he do with this fabulous power? And what about us, what would we do with it? Would we linger in rooms when everyone thought we'd left, to hear what our friends say about us? Would we go around to the other side of the till at the bank, wander over to the safe, and fill our pockets with big bills? Would we try to right wrongs, punish the wicked, rescue hostages in Iraq? Would we side with the profiteers or with the selfless? Would we involve ourselves in the affairs of the world or stick to our own?

I don't see the man in the film as some kind of Superman. What interests him isn't influencing the world, but possessing it in secret; that is, by watching what other people do when they don't know they're being watched. When they believe they're alone. He's obsessed by people's privacy, and in particular by the privacy of women.

•

I imagine a scene near the start of the film (near the end should be another that functions along similar lines, but with a different outcome). The man in the film is interested in a woman. It's someone he knows, but not intimately. Maybe she's a colleague, if he works in an office, and in that case they might have lunch together from time to time. Maybe she tells him about her love life. It's child's play for him to fish her keys out of her purse and have them duplicated; he doesn't even need to be invisible for that. He has plenty of time to check out her flat and get to know the tight spots. When she gets home, he's waiting for her and precedes or follows her in. He stays close to her; ever since that summer day when his cousins made him drink the glass of soapy water, he's never tired of this heady game that consists of getting as close as you can to the other person, without touching them or being touched. He stays by her side, close, when she gets undressed, when she goes to the toilet. Some people close the bathroom door when they're inside, even when they're at home alone. As these rooms are often quite cramped, it's an art to get inside at the right time. Later, when she's taking her bath, he crouches by the side of the tub. Right up close. He can smell her breath; she could smell his if he weren't holding it.

Later, he watches her sleep.

•

Maybe he doesn't just spend one evening invisible in this woman's apartment. Maybe he lives with her for several days without her knowing. I'd like to film these scenes using a simple rule, but one that runs counter to other films that deal with the subject, or at least to the films I know. In them you don't see the invisible man, just the visible results of his actions. The cushion on the armchair squishes under his weight, the curtains part on their own, the cigarette burns and moves around in thin air. By contrast, I'd like him to be visible to the spectator, but invisible to the other

characters. Rather than using special effects, I'd like to film a bal-
let performed by two or more bodies in space: with one person
seeing the other—or others—and them not seeing him. There
would have to be a contrast between the "normal" scenes and
those in which the man is invisible; the first would be choppy,
with a lot of fixed and reverse shots; the second, sinuous, with a
series of enveloping long takes. For these scenes, rather than working with a special effects artist, it would be good to get the help
of a choreographer.

·

He hasn't always been this rambling man, this Peeping Tom.
Other women were in his life than these women he gazes at in
silence.

Women with whom he had love relationships as a visible person. But they didn't work, there's no way they could. Each time
one such relation started, he swore he wouldn't use his power, and
then finally he'd wind up ceding to temptation. A woman who's
been watched when she thought she was alone can't put words
to this experience, but somehow or other she knows. Something
alerts her in the look, no matter how tender, of the man who lies
in her bed and holds her in his arms. Sooner or later she winds up
telling him that she doesn't know why, but she finds him strange,
that while she can pin nothing precise on him, he makes her uneasy, she feels she can't trust him.

One of these women, perhaps, guessed the truth. And she
hated him.

In any case, he's alone.

·

The person with such a remarkable talent is alone.

But is he the only one with such a talent? Not necessarily.

There are other invisibles, and even if they don't hunt in a pack, they do form a sort of secret society. They get together in the city, in bars, bookstores, or department stores, recognize one another, and watch one another rub shoulders with normal people. They dare one another to do things, playful or cruel. Being invisible is a childhood dream, and the invisible play children's games—but those of children who aren't like others, children who are often cruel.

They live their condition in different ways. For a while the man in the film was fascinated by a friend with a rational, cynical, absolutely uninhibited way of using his power: a financial genius, he engaged in insider trading and carried out fast-paced, targeted raids. He was rich and famous, universally admired. And no one except for the man in the film ever knew the truth about him. Other, more timid, less talented people had to renounce their gift to live normal lives, letting it atrophy for lack of use or stifling it by force—like someone who's victimized by his own sexual desires and who wears himself out just trying to fight them. Still others have almost completely gone over to the other side: they're almost never visible, perhaps they're no longer even able to be visible. They're outlaws, phantoms, derelicts, and those who've managed to integrate are terribly afraid of them: that's what they could become, that's what they're up against.

Some seek contact with those like them, others shun it.

For me, the man in the film is between the two. For a moment he's attracted by this parallel society, then he distances himself from it. He had that flamboyant friend. He loved an invisible woman. Together they shared their secret, relishing the glory and the shame, reveling in their superiority over normal people, playing tricks on them, taking risks. Little by little the perpetual one-upmanship became like a drug; he understood that with her he, too, would go over to the other side and forever cease to be visible, and he didn't want that.

Sometimes he runs into her. No one sees her but him. She dares him to join her in her ghostly world. He lowers his eyes.

•

An invisible doesn't need to work. Money and goods circulate; all he has to do is help himself. But he didn't go over to the world of those who are never seen again, and since he still has a social existence, he still has to work. For now I don't know what job he'll have. What's certain is that there's no prestige in it, and unlike his trader friend he has no desire to make a career of it. He's considered the failure of his family. If he wanted, he could also use his gift to scam his way into fame and fortune, but that doesn't interest him. What really interests him is the magic realm where he can see without being seen.

He's an anonymous sort of guy, with no particular sparkle to him. A man of the crowd who waits on the subway platform dressed in old sweatpants and a secondhand coat, the frames of his glasses mended with duct tape. Who pushes his cart in the supermarket and fills it with frozen food for a depressive bachelor. Who watches his clothes spin behind the bubble window at the laundromat.

He's a king, but a secret one.

He alone knows it.

•

When the film starts, he's losing his gift.

•

His gift disappears.

No doubt this takes place progressively, unpredictably. Things start going wrong. What he once did without effort, the way you breathe, becomes problematic. One day he wants to become invisible and can't. Another, he wants to become visible again and he's unable to. Or he becomes visible at the wrong moment, with all the embarrassment one can imagine.

It's like getting old: there are things you could once do, things you liked to do, that you now have a hard time doing, and you sense that soon you won't be able to do them at all.

It's trite, it's terrible.

It's even more terrible when it's not *things* but a single thing, and that single thing abandons you.

The invisible man in the film has nothing but his invisibility.

Those who have a gift, a talent, often have only that.

Often that's all they are: a secret realm, and the immense misery that accompanies it.

And this misery is what they cling to above all: it's their neurosis.

•

If he's no longer invisible, if he no longer secretly rules over other people's secrets, over women's pleasure, he's nothing.

•

And if he's nothing, he can become a man.

He can finally become visible for a woman—the woman to whom he tells his story.

He can stand before her, deposed, wrung dry, and she can say, "You're here."

Published in *Les Moments littéraires*, spring 2010

Capote, Romand, and Me

In January 1993, Jean-Claude Romand killed his wife, his children, his parents, and his dog, and tried unsuccessfully to kill himself. In the days that followed, it came out that he wasn't either a doctor or a researcher at the World Health Organization, as everyone thought, and that everything that was known about his life was untrue. While still a student, he claimed he'd passed a medical exam that he didn't even take. From that point on he told lie after lie for eighteen years, and against all likelihood he was never caught. He wasn't a doctor, but he wasn't anything else either: neither a spy, nor an arms dealer, nor an organ trafficker, as people had initially believed and hoped—preferring anything to admitting that someone could be nothing at all. He spent his days in his car, at highway rest stops. And when he realized that people were finally starting to get suspicious, he preferred to kill his family rather than face their disappointment.

I remember the first articles on the case, by Florence Aubenas in *Libération*. I remember immediately thinking I'd write a book about it. I remember rereading *In Cold Blood*, whose shadow necessarily stretches over all projects in this genre, as well as a book of interviews with Truman Capote, in which he says, "If I had ever known what I was going to have to endure over those six years, I never would have started the book."

(The warning didn't fall on deaf ears: I would do seven years myself.)

•

In 1960 Capote was a celebrated novelist, but he felt that he'd reached the end of his tether and was looking for a way to put the lie to F. Scott Fitzgerald, who'd said that there are no second acts in the lives of American writers. Capote had developed a theory on what he called the nonfiction novel and was on the lookout for a subject that could illustrate it. Something that would normally go under the heading of reporting and that he would make into a work of art. One day in *The New York Times* he came across a short dispatch about a farming family who'd been murdered by unknown assailants in Kansas. He thought to himself, A crime, deep in the Midwest, why not? He headed off and took up residence in Holcomb, where it happened. He met the sheriff who was conducting the investigation and started to talk with people. The diminutive Capote, with his squeaky voice and eccentric manners, was viewed askance by the local rednecks. Everyone thought he'd get tired of it after a while, but no: he settled right in.

•

At first I thought I'd do the same: go to the Gex region near Geneva where Romand committed his crimes and settle in as Capote did. Have a drink with the police officers, stick my foot in the doors that traumatized families would try to slam in my face, spend time with the people crime articles call "close sources." Nevertheless this case was very different from the atrocious, banal murder Capote wrote about. The latter was a random, savage attack by two unknown thugs, who burst in on a family of hardworking farmers one night and killed them for nothing, for fifty dollars. The former that of a man whose life was devoured over eighteen years by the gangrene of lies. For me the main thing was to have access to this man. So I wrote to him and told him that I wanted to understand, to correspond, to talk with him. He didn't answer. I dropped it. Then I started a book of fiction, *Class Trip*, which on the face of it had nothing to do with the Romand case, yet which dealt with exactly the same thing: a murdering father, a child caught up in lies, steps in the whiteness, emptiness and absence. When the book came out, something happened: Romand read it in prison. He was moved by it because it reminded him of his own childhood, and two years after my first letter he answered: now he was ready to meet me. The project I thought I'd escaped—not without relief—now caught me by the sleeve.

•

Initially, Capote set out to investigate an unsolved murder. Everything changed for him when the murderers were arrested and he met them face-to-face. It was no longer a matter of reconstituting life in a little town in Kansas around this shock wave, but of contending with these two men, one of whom, Perry Smith, Capote got to be on close terms with, like a sort of monstrous brother: "It's as if," he said, "Perry and I grew up in the same house and one day he stood up and went out the back door, while I went out the front." The two men were soon tried and convicted, and Capote understood he would have to accompany them until the day they died in order to write his book. At this point the story told in *In Cold Blood* and the writing of *In Cold Blood* start to diverge in a fascinating way, resulting in one of the most vicious literary situations I know of.

Perry called Capote "amigo," thought of him as his only friend, and expected him to plead his case, find him better lawyers, help him appeal his sentence and at least put off his execution. From 1960 to 1965, Capote lived an insoluble moral dilemma in appalling dread. He passionately wanted to finish and publish his book, which everyone was waiting for and which he knew would be his crowning achievement. But to finish it, the story itself had to end; that is, the two men who thought of him as their benefactor had to be hanged. His future, his fulfillment as a writer, hung on their deaths. So all the while comforting Perry and Dick, and assuring them of a friendship that was sincere at least toward Perry, Capote prayed—and asked his friends and family to pray—that the two men's appeals would be rejected and that the noose would finally tighten around their necks.

•

As the death penalty no longer exists in France, I didn't go through such torment—no doubt the most gruesome a writer could experience. Romand's trial, which I attended, had practically no impact on the sentence. The facts were established and acknowledged, and life imprisonment had been agreed on in advance. The only room for discrepancy had to do with the time to be served before parole could be granted, which was set at twenty-two years. But then, first by letter and then in the visiting room, I learned more about what the private life of a murderer who trusts you despite everything is like. I say "despite everything" because I always stressed to Romand that I was not his advocate and that I would not write his version of the story. But which version would I write? I then did the investigative work that I hadn't done right after the crimes. I crisscrossed the Gex region in Romand's footsteps, with his words and maps as a guide. I met his acquaintances. He agreed that I should have access to the case file: it's a stack of boxes twice my height, and even as I write, they're still in my closet, ready to be returned to Romand when he gets out of prison. I took hundreds of pages of notes, wrote snippets of stories from different points of view, and spent something like five years in this quagmire of paper, not knowing how to get started. Once a year at least I reread *In Cold Blood*, each time more impressed than the last by the strength of the construction and the crystalline limpidity of Capote's prose. I tried to imitate his deliberately impersonal approach, without clearly seeing what's strange about this masterpiece: that it's based on duplicity.

•

Capote loved Gustave Flaubert above all other writers. Capote had vowed to write a book where, like God, the author is everywhere and nowhere, and in this book he accomplished the magnificent tour de force of erasing his own cumbersome presence from the story altogether. In doing that, however, he told another story and betrayed his second aesthetic ideal: to be scrupulously faithful to the truth. He tells everything that happened to Perry and Dick from their arrest to their hanging, but says nothing about how, during their five years in prison, he was the most important person in their lives, which he changed considerably. He chose to ignore the paradox that is well-known in scientific experimentation: that the presence of the observer invariably modifies the observed phenomenon—and in this case he was far more than an observer; he was one of the key players. And I think that he did this not only for aesthetic reasons, out of a desire for self-effacement, or because he hated the first person, but also because the story of his relations with his characters was too atrocious for him to admit.

•

I, meanwhile, persisted in wanting to emulate *In Cold Blood*, and to tell Jean-Claude Romand's life from the outside, based on the case file and my own investigation, and I think that I never consciously asked myself whether I should write in the first person. I cross-referenced the points of view, ceaselessly asked myself which version I should tell, from what angle, and simply never considered my own. And if I didn't think about it, I suppose it's because I was afraid of it. I was stuck in a rut, caught up in a terrible depression, and for the second time I decided to abandon the project. That decision did me a world of good. I felt liberated, relieved to put behind me the mass of work I'd invested to no avail. No more Romand, no more nightmare. Then, a few days after this return to life, I said to myself that it would be good to write a report on what this story had meant to me, for my own personal use and not with an eye to having it published. That would allow me, I thought, to wrap things up and get them out of my system. I searched out my old datebooks and, for the first time in years without wracking my brains, I wrote the first sentence: "On the Saturday morning of January 9, 1993, while Jean-Claude Romand was killing his wife and children, I was with mine in a parent-teacher meeting at the school attended by Gabriel, our eldest son." I went on like that, and only after several pages did I realize that I had finally started to write the book that had eluded me for so long. In saying yes to the first person, in occupying my place and none other, that is, in breaking with Capote's model, I had found the first sentence, and the rest came—I won't say easily, but in one go, naturally.

Six years have passed since then. It's a cliché to speak of a work that won't let you rest, but I'm not afraid of clichés. Along with the pride of having seen through to the end something that was worth it—and no matter if it seems pretentious, I'm certain of that—I can't shake the fear of having done something bad despite all my scruples. I've done other things since: I've made films, started books and given them up again—a real project graveyard. And a familiar shiver ran down my spine when I read the final credits of the film *Capote*, reminding viewers that after *In Cold Blood* Capote never finished another book, and that the epigraph he chose for his last, unfinished work was this sentence by Saint Teresa of Ávila: "More tears are shed over answered prayers than unanswered ones."

Published in *Télérama*, March 2006

The Last of the Possessed

1

I knew Limonov in Paris, where he arrived in 1980, preceded by the scandalous success of his first novel, *It's Me, Eddie*. Expelled from the Soviet Union, he'd spent five years in New York, in a hardship that he tells vividly: odd jobs, living from day to day in a sordid hotel or on the street, flings with both men and women, drunken benders, robberies and brawls. In its violence and rage, it was faintly reminiscent of the life of the urban drifter played by Robert De Niro in *Taxi Driver*; in its vigor, of the novels of Henry Miller—whose tough skin and cannibal's composure Limonov shared. The book wasn't half-bad, and those who met its author weren't disappointed. In those days we were used to Soviet dissidents being bearded, grave, and poorly dressed, living in small apartments filled with books and icons, where they would spend all night talking about how Orthodoxy would save the world. And here was this sexy, sly, funny guy, a cross between a sailor on leave and a minor rock star. We were in the midst of the punk era; his proclaimed hero was Johnny Rotten, the lead singer of the Sex Pistols; he didn't think twice about calling Solzhenitsyn an old fart. This new-wave dissidence was refreshing, and when he arrived in Paris, Limonov was the darling of the small literary world.

This favor could have lasted just one season, but the charming ruffian had more than one trick up his sleeve, and year in, year out, working with several editors to off-load his production, he lived from his pen for a decade. He wasn't a novelist—all he could write about was his life—but his life was captivating, and he told its story well in a simple, unadorned style, with all the energy of a Russian Jack London. From book to book we read about his childhood in the suburbs of Kharkov in Ukraine, his time as a juvenile delinquent, and his life as an avant-garde poet in Moscow under Brezhnev. He talked of this era and of the Soviet Union with a wry nostalgia, as if it had been a paradise for resourceful hooligans, and every so often, at the end of dinner, when everyone was drunk but him—he can really hold his liquor—he sang Stalin's praises, which we chalked up to his taste for provocation. He was incredibly successful with women. He was everyone's favorite barbarian.

Things started to go wrong at the start of the 1990s. He began disappearing to the Balkans for long periods, where he sided with the Serbian troops. One day he appeared in a BBC documentary, discussing poetry with Radovan Karadžić, the leader of the Bosnian Serbs, on a hill overlooking the besieged Sarajevo, and then shooting at the city with a machine gun. He returned to Russia, where in the shambles of post-communism he created a political group with the compelling name the National Bolshevik Party, and which, as far as we knew, was pretty much a skinhead militia. Our amiable friend had become highly unsavory, and I don't remember, in the ten years that followed, talking about him or hearing anyone else mention his name. In 2001 we learned that he'd been arrested, tried, and imprisoned for rather obscure reasons—something to do with arms trafficking and an attempted coup in Kazakhstan. A petition went around calling for his release, but that it was circulated by milieus that put out such tracts as *France Gagged by the International League Against*

Racism and Anti-Semitism, or *Ratko Mladić, Criminal or Hero?* made us all the less eager to sign. At the time I was traveling to Russia often, mostly to Kotelnich, a forlorn city in the provinces where I shot a documentary over a couple of years, but also to Moscow, where one day I bought a book by Limonov, which was translated nowhere except in Serbia, no doubt, called *Anatomy of a Hero.* It had a section with photos where the hero in question— Limonov himself—posed in camouflage fatigues in the company of Karadžić, the Serbian war criminal Arkan, the French right-wing politician Jean-Marie Le Pen, the Russian populist Zhirinovsky, the mercenary Bob Denard, and a couple of other humanists. It seemed like an open-and-shut case, with no chance for appeal. But that didn't stop me from being intrigued by the fate of this man who was so talented, so seductive, so free, and who had wound up *here.* I had the vague impression that this fate said something about the madness of the world, without knowing exactly what.

Then, in October 2006, came the murder of the journalist Anna Politkovskaya. I went to Moscow to write a report. I attentively read her books and articles. Not long before her death, she had covered the trial of thirty-nine National Bolshevik Party militants accused of having occupied and vandalized the offices of the presidential administration, shouting, "Putin must go!" For these crimes they'd been given lengthy prison sentences, and Politkovskaya, without failing to underline the differences she had with Limonov, took up their defense: she believed that the Natsbols, as they're called in Russia, were heroes of the fight for democracy in her country. As my research progressed, I met the tiny group that constituted practically the entire opposition to the government of Vladimir Putin: independent journalists, NGO leaders, mothers of soldiers who'd been killed or wounded in Chechnya. It's a small group, whose members are as respectable as they are atypical, but here I discovered to my astonishment that they all thought of Limonov and his entourage as courageous people of integrity, practically the only ones who could inspire hope in the moral future of their country. Several months later I learned that a political coalition called Drugaya Rossiya (The Other Russia) was forming under the leadership of Garry Kasparov, Mikhail Kasyanov, and Eduard Limonov—that is to say, one of the greatest chess players of all time, a former prime minister under Putin, and an author whom by our criteria you shouldn't even be seen with: quite the troika. Something had obviously changed—perhaps not Limonov himself but the position he occupied in his country. Which is why when Patrick de Saint-Exupéry, whom I'd known as Moscow correspondent for *Le Figaro*, told me he was launching a newsmagazine and asked if I had a subject for the first issue, I responded without a second's hesitation: Limonov. Patrick looked at me with wide eyes. "Limonov's a petty thug."

"I'm not sure. It's worth checking out."

"All right then," Patrick said, not needing any further explanation, "check it out."

It took me a while to track him down and get his number. What struck me, when Limonov answered and I told him my name and why I was calling, was that he remembered me perfectly. We'd crossed paths just five or six times more than twenty years earlier, he was well-known at the time, I was a young, intimidated journalist, no more than a walk-on part in his life; nevertheless he remembered that I had a red motorcycle: "A Honda 125, right?" Right. He said he had no problem with me hanging around for a couple of weeks. "Unless," he added, "they put me back in prison."

2

Two burly young guys with shaved heads, dressed in black and polite, come pick me up to bring me to their leader. We cross Moscow in a black Volga with tinted windows—the typical FSB-mobile, the

driver jokes—and I half expect them to blindfold me; but, no, my
guardian angels just take a quick look around the courtyard, then
the stairway, then finally the landing that gives onto a little dark
apartment, furnished like a squat, where two more skinheads are
killing time smoking cigarettes. Eduard divides his time among
three or four Moscow apartments, they tell me, and moves from
one to the next as quickly as possible, keeping no fixed hours and
never venturing anywhere without bodyguards—that is, party
militants. He comes into the room, in black jeans and a black
sweater. Has he changed? On the one hand he hasn't: still slim,
flat stomach, adolescent's silhouette, the smooth olive skin of a
Mongol. On the other hand he has, because now he sports a gray
mustache and goatee, which together with his glasses and shock
of graying hair remind me suddenly of a passage in his *Diary of a
Loser*, which I'd reread on the plane and copied into my notebook.
I read it out to him, as an icebreaker: "It's great in May, in the
wonderful wet May, to be a head of the All Russian Emergency
Committee, to be in Odessa, and, with a goatee and a leather
jacket, to stand on a balcony facing the sea, to adjust the pince-
nez and breathe in the intoxicating aromas. And then to return to
the interior of the room and, coughing, lighting up a cigarette,
begin the interrogation of a princess N who is deeply implicated in the counterrevolutionary plot and who is famous for her
remarkable beauty—the twenty-two-year-old princess." And another passage, while I'm at it: "I dream of violent insurrection. I
cherish a Razin/Pugachyov-like rebellion in my heart. I'll never be
Nabokov. I'll never run across meadows collecting butterflies on
old, hairy, Anglophone legs. Give me a million and I'll spend it
on weapons and stage an uprising in any country." This was the
scenario he painted for himself at thirty as a penniless immigrant
on the streets of New York, and now, thirty years later, there you
go: he's in the film. "Is that how things stand, Eduard Venyaminovich?"

He laughs. The ice is broken. He strides back and forth in the room where the curtains are drawn and the walls covered with photos showing him with soldiers, some of whom at least must be wanted by the International Criminal Court in The Hague. It's his new role, the professional revolutionary, the urban guerrilla, Trotsky in his armored train. Hideouts, bodyguards, the intoxication of clandestine life and the risks it involves—which are real, because in addition to being thrown in jail he's been severely attacked on several occasions. By whom? Who has it in for him like that? "If you want to see recent threats, read this," he says, and shows me an interview with Andrey Lugovoy in *Komsomolskaya Pravda*. Here I need a bit of attention. Lugovoy is a former officer of the FSB—the body that succeeded the KGB— widely suspected of having organized the poisoning of Alexander Litvinenko, he, too, a former FSB agent, but who fled to Britain to serve Boris Berezovsky, the ex-oligarch and sworn enemy of Putin. Lugovoy, whom Russia refuses to extradite, makes numerous declarations making it clear, first, that he had nothing to do with Litvinenko's murder, and, second, that he knows who was involved: Berezovsky himself, who did not hesitate to have one of his own men killed so people would accuse the Kremlin. This destabilizing operation is only starting, Lugovoy maintains. He has a list of people who are to be killed, which includes the far-left opposition figure (that's how Lugovoy describes him) Eduard Limonov. So watch out for polonium. I get the feeling we're deep in a James Bond film, but who knows? In any case, that's not all, and the rest is less convoluted, more fact-based. There's a militia of pro-Putin youth called Nashi (Ours). Between the Natsbols and the Nashi it's out-and-out war. But each time there's a tussle, the Natsbols are arrested, tried, and imprisoned, while the Nashi get off scot-free. And they're not content just with getting into scraps, they also campaign actively against Limonov. From a bookshelf where they sit alongside situationist or Komintern writings, he pulls out a handful of beautifully printed pamphlets, far higher quality than the newspaper he puts out. I flip through them; later I'll study them in detail. They describe him as a "glam fascist," with photos and quotes to back up the claim. The photos show Adolf Hitler gazing fondly at a little Limonov and are so contrived that they miss their mark. But the quotes are a different story . . . You can always say his words were misrepresented, but I've read *Anatomy of a Hero*. Black on white, it sings the praise of the "three great movements of the 20th century": fascism, communism, and Nazism. Even if it goes on to say that Hitler is admirable for his strategy of seizing power and that he later committed "errors," it's hard not to find that shocking. I say to him, You really wrote all of that? He shrugs; it's rubbish he wrote ten years ago, nothing to get worked up about. Above all, since it's Putin's minions who're calling him a fascist, it's easy to reply: Who're the fascists? Who're the persecutors, who the persecuted? Who abuses power and who goes to prison? It won't be long before I see that here the argument carries weight.

3

What exactly was I expecting? A desperado at his wit's end, meetings with lost souls in suburban back rooms? Nothing doing: he's put all of that behind him, no longer wears military fatigues, is careful not to shoot off at the mouth. Now he only goes to important meetings, such as the press conference he's holding together with Kasparov this morning, at the Central House of Journalists. The former world chess champion has a powerful build and a warm smile. Limonov, at his side in a jacket and tie and clutching a little leather satchel, looks more like an intellectual than an adventurer, and even, I think, a bit like a *chinovnik*, as the bureaucrats in the czarist government were called. The former prime minister Kasyanov, essentially the third member of the troika, isn't here. But Lev Ponomarev is. Like Politkovskaya, this champion of human rights in Russia has defended the National Bolsheviks' cause for the past couple of years. The Russian and foreign journalists, of whom there are quite a few, look on this motley crew of democrats with a somewhat jaded benevolence. They've already covered the story, it's no scoop. Everyone knows full well that they don't have a chance, that they have no political clout or broad support in the country, and that their big hope isn't to win the parliamentary elections in December— let alone the presidential elections in March 2008—but simply to be able to participate, to have their voices heard just a bit. Everyone knows full well that they have no program, that if the swish of a magic wand brought them to power, they wouldn't agree on a thing. I even think that after a week Limonov would be on the street demonstrating against his former running mates—if he hadn't had them shot. So everyone patiently listens to this group list their grievances: meeting halls canceled at the last minute, the publication of Kasparov's book continually being put off, all kinds of wrenches in the works. I think about what my friend Pavel said to me yesterday: this whole business about a democratic opposition in Russia is like wanting to castle when you're playing checkers: it's not part of the rules, it simply makes no sense, and all these opposition figures are fools. Starting to get a bit bored, I flip through my notebook and find another passage from *Diary of a Loser*: "I've sided with evil—with the small newspapers, with the Xeroxed leaflets, with the parties that stand no chance. I love political meetings with just a handful of people and the cacophony of inept musicians. And I hate symphony orchestras. If I ever came to power I'd slit the throats of all the violinists and cellists." I watch Limonov listening to Kasparov. Champing at the bit. Twisting the tips of his mustache with a gesture that looks like a tic, and that starts to get on my nerves. I wonder what Limonov thinks, what he hopes for. Does he believe in it? Does he find it amusing to play at being a more or less respectable politician, he the outlaw, the rabid dog? Is this a tactical ruse? Yesterday I bought and started to read his political autobiography, one of the books he wrote in prison. In it he describes how his party was formed, the first recruits, the hassles, the congresses, the scissions, the persecutions, and as you read on, you can't help thinking that all of that is both heroic and ridiculous—but also that his models, whether communists or fascists, started like that as well. That reasonable people didn't believe in them and then one day things took off, and against all odds these stories about obscure, shabby revolutionaries who never stopped bickering among themselves became history. That's what he must say to himself. And really, who can tell?

In the car coming back from the press conference, we listen to the radio, which is giving a brief rundown on how it went. Drugaya Rossiya, the journalist sums up without a hint of irony, plans on suing the meeting-hall director who canceled their reservation. Limonov shakes his head in annoyance: it was a stupid thing to say; after that it's the only thing the journalists pick up on, and they make the party look like a bunch of losers, guys for whom political activity consists in taking meeting-hall directors to court. In his fifteen years of political struggle, he, Limonov, has learned what to say and what not to say. He's cold and cunning, and proud to be cold and cunning. Not like that dumb schmuck Kasparov, "who always reacts too emotionally." World chess champion, but too emotional. Okay, Eduard, whatever you say.

4

Although the press conference didn't make a strong impression on me, as the days go by, I realize that even if his reputation is tarnished in the West, in his country Limonov is hugely popular. He's even a star. This has no statistical value, but for what it's worth, in two weeks I discussed Limonov with more than thirty people, strangers whose cars I rode in—because anyone and everyone moonlights as a taxi driver for a few extra rubles in Moscow—as well as friends you could safely call Russian yuppies: artists, journalists, and editors, who buy their furniture at IKEA and read the Russian edition of *Elle*. In other words, not fanatics. No one said a word against him, and among the yuppies it was as if I'd come to interview Michel Houellebecq, Lou Reed, and Daniel Cohn-Bendit all at the same time: two weeks with Limonov, what luck! I said, still, just the name alone—National Bolshevik Party—that doesn't bother you? And their flag, a copy of the Nazi flag with a white circle on a black background, only there's a hammer and sickle and not a swastika in the middle? And the shaved heads, the skulls and crossbones on their armbands? They shrugged and considered me something of a prude. That was all just antics, nothing to get worked up about. Anyway, all the humanists keep their hands clean, but in fact they're just chicken. The Natsbols practice what they preach and go to jail for their ideas.

I accompany Limonov to the gala thrown by the radio station Echo of Moscow, the social highlight of the season. He's got his musclemen in tow, but he also brings his new wife, Ekaterina Volkova, a successful young actress: ravishing, delightful, and totally cool. Of all the people who flock to this soiree no one is more photographed or celebrated than the Limonovs, about whom the magazines' "People" sections write gushy—and blatantly Natsbols-friendly—articles. In her interviews, Ekaterina tells with a naive freshness that before meeting Eduard she'd never been interested in politics, but that now she's understood: Russia is a totalitarian state, you've got to fight for freedom and participate in the protest marches, which she seems to take as seriously as her yoga classes. (That said, as totalitarian as this state is, such statements do her as little harm as, let's say, Kirsten Dunst had or felt when she attacked George W. Bush at exactly the same time. It's enough to imagine what would have happened under Stalin, or even under Brezhnev, on the fictitious assumption that such words could have been printed, and I think that there are worse things than Putin-style totalitarianism.)

On another level: fifteen or so prominent Russian writers were recently asked which of their colleagues they valued the most. Ten put Limonov at the top of their list. When Michel Houelle-becq and Frédéric Beigbeder—the two most popular French authors in Russia—were asked the same question, they gave the same answer: Limonov. He was the only one they knew, which confirmed the general opinion. While Limonov was in prison, an upcoming writer, Sergey Shargunov, received a big literary prize from an American foundation, ten thousand dollars, which he publicly turned over to Limonov. Today this Shargunov heads the youth section of the party A Just Russia, a bogus opposition party rubber-stamped by the Kremlin, whose president is Sergey Mironov, chairman of the upper house of the Russian parliament. I offer these few examples, unsorted, to give an idea of the staggering confusion that reigns in this country when it comes to ideological divisions—and incidentally, when it comes to everything else. That doesn't seem to bother the Russians too much, but for Westerners the status of someone such as Limonov is a brainteaser, a minefield—which I tried to shed light on together with Zakhar Prilepin.

5

Zakhar Prilepin is thirty-three and lives with his wife and three kids in Nizhny Novgorod, where he works as a journalist. He's the author of three novels that got him a place on the short list for the Russian Booker Prize, considerable sales, and a reputation that's maturing from promising young writer to confirmed talent: a serious, down-to-earth type, anything but a poseur, who writes acerbic, realistic novels about the lives of real people. His first novel deals with Chechnya, where he served as a soldier; the second with the doubts and wanderings of a young guy from the provinces who believes that by becoming a Natsbol he's giving meaning to the swampy mess of his life. The book is based on his own experiences as well as those of friends his age, because our Prilepin has been a committed Natsbol for the past ten years. He looks every bit the part: stocky, shaved head, black clothes, Doc Martens, and to top it all off he's a nice guy.

•

And this is what Zakhar Prilepin has to say. Because he's an avid reader and self-taught lover of the less frequented regions of Russian literature, he got to know Limonov through his books. He discovered them by accident, and it was the literary encounter of his life: someone who had experienced so many things, with such courage, and who wrote about them with such freedom, such naturalness. Someone who dared everything, a hero, a model. Most of Prilepin's buddies, however, first discovered the party through *Limonka*, Limonov's newspaper. Its name is taken from Limonov's, but it also means "grenade." I've had a look through a couple of old issues. It's influenced by *Mad* magazine and the American underground press. It's terribly trashy and deals less with politics than with rock and roll and style: fuck you, bullshit, up-yours style. Majestic punk. Now, you have to imagine what a provincial Russian city is like. The sinister life the young people lead there, their lack of a future, and—if they're at all sensitive or ambitious—their despair. All it took was for a single issue of *Limonka* to arrive in a city like that and fall into the hands of one of these idle, morose, tattooed youths who played the guitar and drank beer under his precious posters of the Cure or Che Guevara, and it was a done deal. Quickly there were ten or twenty of them, a whole threatening gang of good-for-nothings, with pale complexions and ripped black jeans, who hung out in the squares: the usual suspects, regular visitors to the local cop shop. They had a new watchword and it was *Limonka*. It was their thing, the thing that spoke to them. And there was this guy who spoke to them, too, who was afraid of nothing, who'd led the adventurous life that all twenty-year-olds dream of, and he said to them, I quote, "You're young. You don't like living in this shitty country. You don't want to be an ordinary Popov, or a shithead who only thinks about money, or a chekist. You're a rebel. Your heroes are Che Guevara, Mussolini, Lenin, Mishima, Baader. Well, there you go: you're a Natsbol already."

What you have to understand, Zakhar Prilepin tells me, is that the Natsbols are the Russian counterculture. The only one: everything else is bogus, indoctrination and so on. So of course the party has its share of fascists, and skinheads with German shepherds who get their kicks from pissing off the *prilitchnyi*—the upstanding citizens—by giving the Nazi salute. There are the garden-variety fascists, and also the intellectual fascists, the eternal and melancholic cohort of feverish, wan, awkward young men who read René Guénon and Julius Evola, who develop nebulous theories on Eurasia, the Templars, or the hyperboreans, and who sooner or later end up converting to Islam. But they all blend together, the fascists, the ultra-leftists, the self-taught cartoonists, the bass players looking for people to start a rock band, the amateur-video freaks, the guys who write poetry in private, and those who nurse dark dreams of wasting everyone at school and then blowing themselves up the way they do in America. Plus the Satanists from Irkutsk, the Hells Angels from Kirov, the Sandinistas from Magadan: Natsbols every one. "My buddies," Zakhar Prilepin says softly, and you get the feeling he could have all the success in the world—the Booker Prize, the translations, the book tours to the States—but what's important to him is to remain loyal to his friends, the lost youths of the Russian provinces.

Soon branches of the National Bolshevik Party sprang up in Krasnoyarsk, in Ufa, in Nizhny Novgorod. One day Limonov visited Zakhar's city, accompanied by three or four of his men and a girl who, in these heroic days, was not yet a movie star but rather a leather-clad adolescent with a shaved head, beautiful—Limonov's women are always beautiful. The whole gang showed up to meet them at the station. Those who needed a place to stay were put up here and there, and the gang spent entire nights talking, preparing their next actions—spraying slogans on trains, unraveling banners at official parades, staging agitprop happenings of all kinds. They felt alive. They were against the war in Chechnya, but they defended the rights of Russian minorities in the former Soviet republics; they opposed the oligarchs, cynical leaders, and corruption and called for a return to order, but they also wanted to stir up a maximum of trouble. They set up vague alliances, one day with Vladimir Zhirinovsky, the Russian Jean-Marie Le Pen (Limonov introduced the two politicians, incidentally), another with the Communists. These came to nothing, but the party grew. In Yeltsin's day there was so much chaos that no one paid any attention to them, but things changed when Putin came to power.

6

It's the start of 2001. Limonov and his girlfriend at the time (who's a minor) spend the winter in Krasnoyarsk, in Siberia, where he's started an investigative book on a local oligarch, Anatoly Bykov, a gangster who became an aluminum magnate and one of Russia's richest men. Limonov accepted the offer from a publisher in

Saint Petersburg both because he likes gangsters and because he needs money for his party—little for himself: he's frugal, hates all forms of comfort, and draws aristocratic pride from the poverty that has accompanied him all his life. I started reading the book after getting back from Russia. As I read slowly in Russian, I can't give you a complete account, but the first fifty pages are excellent: Capote without the aestheticism, Mailer without the jerky side, and I think to myself first of all that if I were a French editor, I'd forget about the malaise surrounding the author and publish the book lickety-split, and second, that I would quite like to write a book in the same genre about Limonov. *A Hero of Our Time*; too bad the title's already taken. Anyway, as he goes about his investigation, Limonov feels that he's being watched, followed. He's used to it, but here things are tightening around him. He's in a hurry to finish because before the thaw he wants to join up with a group of four or five Natsbols he left in a log cabin in the middle of the Altai Mountains, charged with spending the winter and seeing how they get along. That's Limonov's idea of a good vacation: a training camp under severe conditions. He leaves his fiancée in Krasnoyarsk and arrives in Barnaul, capital of the Altai region, only to find out that one of his men has thrown himself out of a window, or more likely was thrown out. It's the first death in the party; things are starting to look grim. Limonov makes his way to the mountain retreat where the guys—*rebyata* in Russian, one of the words that comes up again and again in his writings— are languishing, and the next day at dawn the FSB surrounds the camp and takes them prisoner. In the last chapter of his political autobiography, Limonov gives a description of the cap- ture worthy of Alexandre Dumas, ending with a melancholic, drunken conversation with the arresting officer on the long trip back to Moscow. Impressed by his prisoner, the officer practi- cally pleads, "Why aren't you with us? We belong to the same world: we're men, real men, who like commando operations and twisted bodies . . . Why don't you like us?"

Limonov answers disdainfully, "Because you don't deserve to call yourselves chekists. Because you're assholes and your founder, Felix Dzerzhinsky, would turn over in his grave if he saw you. He was a great man, he I respect, but you . . ." The officer lowers his head sheepishly. You'd think he was going to burst into tears.

At the trial, Limonov and his men are accused of arms trafficking and an attempted coup in neighboring Kazakhstan with the intention of creating a separate Russian republic. No weapons were found in the cabin (what surprises me, to tell the truth, is that the FSB didn't plant any there), and as for the coup, Limonov says he had neither weapons, nor men, nor contacts. At the very most he'd toyed with the idea and doesn't deny it: let's say the project was being studied. The prosecution calls for a prison term of fourteen years for Limonov; he's sentenced to four, amid general indifference in Russia and abroad. He serves them in part at the legendary KGB fortress of Lefortovo and in part in a labor camp in Saratov, on the Volga River. Conditions are harsh in both, and Limonov was pushing sixty; nevertheless I believe him when he says without batting an eye that he loved prison. One last quote from *Diary of a Loser*, written thirty years earlier: "I love being an adventurist. It often saves me. Suddenly it rains and I am depressed, and poor, and want to cry. And then I think, 'Don't give up, boy, you've chosen that road yourself, you didn't want a normal life.'" For a man such as him, who's in love with his own destiny and who believes that life is there to try things out, it's a blessing, a golden opportunity to test your strength. And his strength didn't fail him. He's proud of having commanded the respect of the ordinary criminals he was in with. When he was released, they even wrangled with the guards over who would carry his suitcase to the gate. In Lefortovo, the daily promenade on the roof took place at 7:00 a.m., and in the winter at minus fifteen degrees most of the inmates preferred to sleep a little longer. Not Limonov. Often alone, he went out onto the roof and ran, boxed the icy air, did push-ups and sit-ups. In his tiny three-man cell, he found a way to write six or seven books, and he came out with his head held high, in good shape, satisfied with the experience.

7

This prison stint was decisive for his legend, and for the self-awareness of his group. It comes again and again in all my conversations with the Natsbols. He took a risk and paid the consequences, and that in itself was cause for hope. I said to myself, Zakhar Prilepin is a great guy, but he's a writer. I know writers. I have to see the grassroots militants. The gorillas who drove me to their leader almost every day in the black Volga frightened me a bit at first, but I soon found them nice. They didn't talk much, that said, or I just didn't go about it the right way. At the end of the press conference with Kasparov I started talking to a girl, just because I found her pretty, and asked if she was a journalist. She said she was, that is, she worked for the website of the National Bolshevik Party. Cute as a button, graceful, well-dressed: she was a Natsbol. The party had been banned for "extremism" since April 2007, so there were no meetings or headquarters, but through her I met the head of the Moscow branch: a guy with long hair, an open face, friendly, impossible to imagine anyone more sincere. He welcomed me into his somewhat dirty little apartment in the suburbs, where he had albums by Manu Chao and paintings in the style of Jean-Michel Basquiat on the walls, done by his wife. "So your wife shares your political struggle?" I ask. "Oh, yes. In fact, she's in prison. She was one of the thirty-nine in the big 2005 trial." He says it with a big smile, proud as punch—and if he's not in prison, too, it's not his fault, it's just that *"Mne ne povezlo"*— that's not how things worked out. Not yet, it's not too late.

As it happened, there was a trial that day at the Taganskaya District Court, and we went there together. A tiny courtroom with the accused sitting handcuffed in a cage and their friends on the three benches reserved for the public, all of them from the party. Seven are in the dock: six guys with a range of looks, from the bearded Muslim student to the working-class hero in a tracksuit, as well as a somewhat older woman with tousled black hair and a pale complexion, rather beautiful in the style of a leftist history teacher who rolls her own cigarettes. They're accused of hooliganism, that being in this case tussling with pro-Putin youths. They say the others started it and that they aren't being charged with anything; the trial is purely political, and if they have to pay with their convictions, so be it, they'll pay. The judge is neutral, professional, courteous; the guy in a uniform who represents the prosecution mutters an incomprehensible tirade, which he doesn't seem to believe for a minute. The defense points out that the accused aren't hooligans but serious students with good grades, and that they've already done a year of preventive custody, which should be enough. At the end of the trial the guards let the seven Natsbols out of their cage, and they clench their fists in the direction of their friends, saying, *"Da, smert"*—until death. They laugh. Their friends look on with envy: these are heroes. You can say that above all they're boys playing at cops and robbers. But a couple of years in prison in Russia is no joke, and for practically nothing at all—a scrap in which only they were injured—they risk getting two more on top of the one they've already served.

8

One day, we went to the countryside—with the *rebyata*, of course. At first I thought it was for a meeting, some political event, but, no, it was just to inspect a dacha Limonov's wife had bought, a hundred miles outside Moscow. We took advantage of the drive to talk about this and that. Limonov was relaxed, dry humored. I wanted to come back to Serbia, and the film that apparently—I hadn't yet seen it—shows him shooting at Sarajevo with a machine gun. He assured me that he had never shot at human targets, just in the direction of the city, which was far too distant for him to hit anyone. Just for the fun of it, then? My remark annoyed him, enough said. Later, when I was back in Paris, the director of the film, Paweł Pawlikowski, confirmed that it was no doubt too far. He remembers a body-built Limonov who played at being Hemingway, couldn't stop pawing all the weapons, and wasn't taken too seriously by the Serbs. Some of them had read *It's Me, Eddie* and saw him as a joker who got screwed by black guys: not our type. Finally I saw the film: beside Karadžić, Limonov looks like an intimidated little boy, a playground bully who's finally found someone to talk to, and when he gets behind the gun, it's like at the shooting arcade. In the car, I almost asked him if he'd ever killed a man. I think he would have told me the truth, since he's devoid of any type of superego and isn't embarrassed about anything. He's the opposite of a liar, even if these days he does pay some attention to what he says.

Before we arrived, he told me in passing that the property beside the one his wife had bought had been purchased by the Russian American journalist who was killed in Moscow: Paul Klebnikov, you remember? As if I couldn't remember Paul Klebnikov: he was my cousin, and my friend. A correspondent for *Forbes* magazine, he carried out meticulous and courageous investigations into how the largest Russian fortunes were created. He was murdered in 2004, gunned down in front of his office building. My sons adored him, he was their model—the very picture of a great reporter to a little boy: Mel Gibson in *The Year of Living Dangerously*. The inquiry into his murder, like that into Politkovskaya's, has, to this day, failed to turn up anything. Rumors put the blame on a

Chechen warlord to whom Paul had dedicated a book called *Conversation with a Barbarian*. "That's bullshit," Limonov said. "The fact is that this Chechen, Noukhayev, was happy with the book. Very happy. Just like Bykov, the Siberian oligarch I wrote about. He's thrilled with my book about him." Will Limonov be happy with the book I'll write about him, if I write it? I'd talked about him with Paul, not long before Paul was killed. He made a face. For him, Limonov was a brilliant writer doubling as a little fascist thug, and I wondered what Paul would think today if he were here. I wondered what I thought myself. I still do, and I answer that that's a good driving force for a book.

The dacha is much more than a dacha: it's what's called an *usadba*, a veritable manor. Abandoned and vandalized, the old wooden house is immense. There's a pond, and a birch forest. Limonov's wife bought it a couple of years ago for a ridiculous sum, five thousand dollars; now it had to be renovated, and Limonov talks with a local craftsman, the way someone who's done all imaginable jobs himself knows how to talk to a contractor and not get ripped off. And in general, I wish much pleasure to anyone who tries to rip him off. I stroll through the gardens and see his little black silhouette from a distance, gesticulating in a pool of sunshine, his goatee unkempt, and all of a sudden I think, He's sixty-five, he's got an adorable wife who's thirty years younger, a ten-month-old child whose photo he showed to everyone the other night at the gala, including the heavies in charge of security. Maybe he's had enough of war, bivouacs, the knife in his boot, police breaking down his door at dawn. Maybe he finally wants to put his suitcase down. To come and settle here, in the countryside, in this beautiful house, like the landed gentry of the old regime. There would be big bookshelves, deep couches, the shouts of children outside, berry jam, long conversations around the samovar, the gentle passing of time. A novel by Turgenev, a film by Mikhalkov. Happy like Ulysses after a long voyage, he'd

talk about his adventures. To recapitulate: he was a young punk in
Kharkov, an underground poet in Moscow, a magnificent loser in
New York, a trendy writer in Paris, a soldier of fortune in the Balkans, and, again in Moscow, the elderly leader of a party of young
desperadoes. Could his seventh life take place here, in peace? "Do
you see yourself ending your days like one of Turgenev's heroes,
Eduard Venyaminovich?"

I ask him the question on the way back, and it makes him
laugh. No, that's not how he sees things. Really. He's got another idea for his old age. To understand, he tells me, you have to
know Central Asia, where he's been several times with the guys.
That's where he feels the best, that's where he feels at home. You
have to know such cities as Samarqand, Tashkent, Bukhara.
Cities parched by the sun, dusty, slow, violent. In the shadow of
the mosques, over there, under the high crenellated walls, there
are beggars. Whole groups of beggars, gaunt, tanned old men
without teeth, often without eyes. They wear tunics and turbans
that are black with dirt; they place a scrap of velvet before them
and wait for passersby to throw down a few small coins. Most
often they're high on hashish. They're castoffs. They're wrecks.
They're kings.

That, okay, he'd be fine with that.

Published in *XXI*, winter 2008

How I Completely
Botched My Interview
with Catherine Deneuve

1

In fact there is one passage I like: about the ginkgo tree. At one point I asked her about gardening, which I'd been told was one of her big passions, and she started to talk about her favorite trees in Paris, in particular the ginkgo on the Place de l'Alma. I promised to look out for it the next time I was there. She said they'd planted a lot of them in New York, on Fifth Avenue in particular, and that Paris would do well to do the same. They're so beautiful, and so robust, and so beautiful because they're so robust. It's the only tree that withstood Hiroshima. When she says that, you can't help feeling that she identifies with the ginkgo, she withstands everything, she's survived everything. She was just out of adolescence when she became the biggest star in French cinema, and she's been in the spotlight practically ever since. Together we were to look back on her legendary career, which spans almost half a century. Thirty or so film stills chosen by her were to serve as the guiding thread for an eight-page interview. That was the idea, and it seemed reasonable enough; unfortunately it didn't work. I suspected that would be the case when I got home after the interview. I did my best to reassure myself that in two hours of recordings there had to be something worthwhile, but when I received the transcription yesterday and scoured through it, pencil in hand, I had to acknowledge that apart from the ginkgo and two or three other things, there's nothing. And I mean nothing. It's certainly not her fault, I'd like to think it's not entirely mine either, but this verbatim record deserves to be archived as the prototype of the muddled interview, with an interviewer who's completely out to lunch and an interviewee who doesn't feel at all concerned, and I have to ask, How did this happen?

All things considered, I guess I should have seen it coming. A few days earlier I'd read *Close Up and Personal*, a collection of diaries she'd kept throughout her career, most often when shooting abroad. These diaries are remarkable: simple, clear, penetrating. What's also remarkable is that when she shoots *Tristana*, she has the same writing—style and handwriting—as when she shoots *Dancer in the Dark*, thirty years later. Such precocious maturity and such consistency are impressive. Anyway. After the diaries I read a recent interview with her by the filmmaker Pascal Bonitzer. He's a friend of mine, I called him up and asked, How was Deneuve? There was a silence, then an afflicted sigh: "Atrocious. Or at least . . . She was fine, I was atrocious, I'm still pissed off at myself . . ." I reread the interview. Okay, nothing to write home about, but nothing to make you want to commit hara-kiri either. Still, I thought, I'll have to do better than that. I read some more, watched her movies again and again, but didn't prepare any questions. I thought to myself, Things'll happen as they happen, let's put our trust in the flow of the conversation. Because I was thinking in terms of a conversation, and not of an interview. Just why that was the case costs a bit of pride to explain, but I have to explain it, otherwise this whole story would be incomprehensible.

If the people at *Première*, which commissioned this piece, had called me up and just asked me to interview Catherine Deneuve, I would have said, Look, I admire Catherine Deneuve, her

beauty, her talent, her career, but there are other people I admire, I'm no longer a journalist, and even when I was, I didn't like
doing interviews, it creates a relationship that makes me feel uncomfortable, so, no. But they said something else: We're thinking
more of a writer than a journalist, and Catherine Deneuve asked
for you. That's not the same thing. That becomes: Catherine Deneuve would like to meet you, and you answer, yes, absolutely, all
full of yourself. I let my thoughts wander: She's read my books,
seen my films, maybe she'll ask me to write a role for her—or let
me know that she wouldn't be averse to my thinking about it. I
daydream, talk with people I know: Catherine Deneuve wants to
meet me. I'm not a groupie by nature, but still, I'm on the top of
the world this week. I read the great chapter that the author and
politician Frédéric Mitterrand dedicated to her in his memoir
The Bad Life and copy these words in my notebook: "Courteous
even in disdain, distant even in warmth, attentive and inaccessible,
available and secretive, passionate and restrained, bold and cautious, generous and distrustful, aware of the privileges won by
your beauty and reluctant to exploit them, cultured without being
intellectual, loyal to the point of possessiveness, sophisticated and
simple, greedy and self-controlled, free and conventional, bra-
zen and modest, strong and vulnerable, seeking excellence in all
things and despising counterfeits, cheerful and sad, there and not
there . . ."* This list of contrasts will serve me as a guide. I won't
ask laborious questions such as "And how was working with Bu-
ñuel? And Truffaut?" I'm not a journalist looking for anecdotes,
but a writer, like Patrick Modiano, who, word has it, is a good
friend of hers, and he's going to have to move over and make room
for me. This won't be a classic interview but a portrait of the real
Catherine Deneuve, full of nuances and complicity. A conversation, an exchange. An encounter. That's it: an encounter.

---

*From Jesse Browner's translation (Soft Skull Press, 2010).

2

The meeting is set for the Panthéon, that old cinema in the Latin Quarter bought by the film producer Pascal Caucheteux, who produces Arnaud Desplechin's films among others. Desplechin and Caucheteux are almost like a second family to Deneuve, and when the first floor of the cinema was renovated into a lounge-bar, she took charge of decorating it. Rummaging around in secondhand stores and flea markets, she picked out the armchairs, couches, lamps, and bookshelves, which she filled with books that look as if they've been read over and over. The whole place is warm and welcoming, you feel good there. To one of the rare sensible questions I'll ask her—what would you have done if you hadn't become an actress?—she'll reply, "I think I would have married very young, had children very young, and divorced quite quickly, so I would have worked. In an architect's office, maybe, or in decorative art: I've always liked that." But let's take it from the start. She arrives. Blue pants and sweater, glasses, her head of blond hair, and that rapid, so recognizable way of speaking that made the director Jean-Paul Rappeneau say she had the ideal tempo for an actress: the maximum number of syllables in the minimum number of seconds, without missing a beat. I joke a bit, taking obsessive pains to come across as simply and naturally as I can: it's quite something to be face-to-face with Catherine Deneuve—I spent the morning wondering how I should dress, to look good without putting on my Sunday best . . . "So did I," she said. "First I thought I'd wear a skirt, then since these couches are so low, I finally decided on pants . . ." Emboldened by her simple, unaffected air, I tell her about my phone call with Pascal Bonitzer, and thinking it will amuse her and maybe even warm her heart, I say that poor Pascal still has regrets about the interview. She's neither amused nor touched. "He regrets it? He's right. It wasn't good, he didn't work hard enough." O-kay. I hear the warning bells, but they

don't stop me from going into a tailspin of my own. I start saying such things as "One senses that it's important to you to be
meticulous . . ." Dot dot dot.

What was she supposed to answer, the poor thing? "It's true,
meticulousness is very important."

After that, we turn to lucidity, honesty, coherence, her candor
that borders on curtness, all virtues that I ascribe to her in a benign, ethereal tone, as if steeped in an ineffable inner life. Once
we've exhausted the list of her superior moral qualities, we start
looking through the photos she's chosen: "Oh, yes," I say, "I saw
that film a long time ago, but I still have fond memories of it. It
was very beautiful I think."

"I think so, too. Very moving."

Caught up as I am with not going by the book and with having
a simple, natural conversation between two human beings, I don't
ask a single real question, and consequently I don't get a single
real answer. In my defense it must be said that I'm starting to feel
more and more uncomfortable. What am I doing here? She's the
one who asked for me, me and no one else, and she lets me struggle without so much as mentioning it. As the Goncourt brothers
wrote bitterly about a woman they knew: "There was nothing in
her that had read our books." Or seen my films, or anything at
all. Back when I worked as a journalist, I interviewed Sigourney
Weaver, who made a point of asking me if I had any brothers or
sisters. I wasn't naive enough to believe she wanted to know; I
was perfectly aware that she'd no doubt been coached, and that
this was something she had to do in one form or another with all
the journalists she'd talk with that day; nevertheless this effort to
make the interview resemble something like a normal exchange
seemed to me well-intentioned. I wasn't expecting Catherine Deneuve to reverse the roles and start asking me about my life, my
work, or my favorite colors, but still, a wink, a word in passing, to
remind me that she had chosen me would certainly have boosted

my confidence and made me want to write the best article possible about her. At the very least it was in her interest, it would
have cost her little. She must have known that, I suppose, but she
didn't say a thing. Unfortunately, I lacked the presence of mind to
ask her why not. That's what would have been simple and natural
given the situation, but I didn't say anything either, and I still
wonder today what stopped her from taking the first step.

3

In the days that followed I nursed my hurt ego by telling the
story to people I knew. It became a sort of a sketch in which I
was nice but klutzy and she was polite but odious, like the despotic dowager she plays brilliantly in Valérie Lemercier's *Palais
Royal!* Everyone I tell it to ventures an interpretation. Pascal Bonitzer's experience reinforces the view that she intentionally makes
people feel uncomfortable and, what's more, persuades them that
they're the ones who're not up to scratch. Star behavior, crap behavior. However, it's only people who don't know her who think
that way. Without exception, those who do tell a different story.
I've just spoken with the actress Hélène Fillières, who played her
daughter in Tonie Marshall's film *Nearest to Heaven*. She idol-
izes Deneuve and was beside herself with excitement and apprehension at the thought of coming face-to-face with her. And the
woman she met was simple, direct, straightforward, and feisty:
rock 'n' roll, Hélène says, someone who's happy to walk around
the set in curlers because she knows she's the object of universal desire, yet doesn't make a big thing of it. The screenplay had
Hélène kiss her on the mouth, and kissing Catherine Deneuve on
the mouth was both incredibly sexy and incredibly funny, because
with her you can have fun, drink red wine, and talk about men.
While her legend surrounds her, it never weighs too heavily. I lis-

tened to Hélène Fillières, I listened to the actress Nicole Garcia and to my producer Anne-Dominique Toussaint, who's eternally grateful to Deneuve for stepping in on a moment's notice to replace an actress who didn't show up at the last minute: Deneuve rolled up her sleeves, did the job, saved the film, and never said a word about it. These stories don't jibe well with my embarrassing and vaguely humiliating experience, and I tell myself that in wanting to be simple and natural, I put myself in a bad situation from the start: while disdaining the role of simple journalist, I didn't dare adopt another. And totally obsessed with this question, I paralyzed her as well. I quoted to her a sentence I love by Marguerite Duras, about interviewing the opera singer Leontyne Price: "In front of her, I think of her." I find this sentence dazzling for its simplicity and self-evidence. The essence of Zen, and what I would like to attain, if possible, in this life: face-to-face with a person, to think about that person and nothing else. The problem is that when most people find themselves face-to-face with someone such as Catherine Deneuve—and I discovered that I'm no exception—they think first about themselves, and about the impression they'll make on her. As soon as you start thinking like that, you're toast: you're on the asking side, the side of alienation and misery, and even if she wanted to, she couldn't help you. She lets you drown, that's your problem. I think about one moment in the interview. Pascal Caucheteux, film producer and big man around the house, stopped for a moment at our couch and sat down on the armrest. He's quite gruff, with a shapeless jacket and saggy jeans, the type of guy who doesn't even look up from his sports newspaper to say hello. She had lit a cigarette, not the first. Torn between unbounded admiration and mounting hostility, I wondered if smoking in a public place where it was clearly forbidden was a mark of likable rebelliousness or if it simply meant: I'm Catherine Deneuve, and I'd like to see who'll dare ask me to put my cigarette out. Caucheteux jerked mockingly with his chin and said, "Hey!" She pretended not to understand and he said firmly, "The smoke."

"There's almost no one here," she apologized with a laugh, took one last drag, then put out the stub. For just a moment she was the simple, kind woman, not at all annoying or prissy, whom people had told me about and whom I hadn't seen. For just a moment I stopped seeing myself sinking deeper and deeper, looking in vain for the right place, and saw her. And finally I agreed with Frédéric Mitterrand—it had taken me some time—whom I'd called up the day before and who had said in that inimitable voice of his, "You'll see, you won't be disappointed."

Published in *Première*, March 2008

"You Fool, Warren Is Dead!"

I must have been twelve years old when I discovered a collection of Lovecraft's stories entitled *Demons and Marvels* in my parents' bookcase. My uncle had given it to my mother, quite an absurd present because she wasn't at all interested in fantasy literature and must at best have read only a couple of pages. As for me, I was hooked for life.

The narrator of the first story, "The Statement of Randolph Carter," starts by telling about his friendship with a certain Warren, a disturbing character who conducts research into the occult sciences. He's helped Warren with experiments that Warren himself describes as "terrible" and helped him shed light on secrets that are happily unknown to the most intrepid of scholars, until an almost moonless night when the two find themselves in an ancient and sinister New England cemetery. They pry open one slab of a tomb and look down on the first steps of a humid staircase. Warren resolves to go down into the depths. How far will he go? There's no telling, but clearly he hopes to discover something terrible and extraordinary. They agree that while Warren descends, Carter will stay on the surface, and that they'll communicate through portable telephones connected by a reel of wire. The way is long, you'd think the steps led down to the center of the earth. At the start Warren is calm and determined, but as he goes down, he begins to lose his composure. It seems that he sees, hears, feels, and surprises absolutely horrible things that he can't—or doesn't want to—describe. His voice becomes altered, giving vent to an equally indescribable—the indescribable is Lovecraft's trademark—fear. Also terrified, Carter hears a jumble of disconnected words coming from the receiver, as if Warren has gone mad down there or encountered something so abominable that nothing can be said about it and all he can do is scream in horror. Then Warren does start to scream: "Carter! put back the slab and get out of this! Quick! It's too utterly beyond thought!"

"Warren, brace up! I'm coming down!" Carter stutters, but Warren cries in despair:

"Don't! You can't understand! Beat it! For God's sake, put back the slab and *beat it*, Carter!"

Then comes a silence.

"Warren?"

A long silence, no more is heard. Carter is paralyzed with fear. He doesn't dare go down or run away. After a long moment of pure terror, he hears a voice in the receiver, an unforgettable voice that he would give his life to forget, a voice that's both Warren's and not Warren's, the voice of a man and of something that wants to pass itself off as a man, a voice that Carter will hear until the end of his days, and that he will try to flee in vain between the padded walls of an insane asylum. And this is what the voice from the depths of the tomb says:

"You fool, Warren is dead!"

•

I remember precisely the layout of the two last pages of the story. The page on the left was full, with one or two paragraphs; the page on the right stopped halfway down. There was a blank line, then the famous sentence in italics:

"You fool, Warren is dead!"

•

A little later, I had a dream that consisted of a single image: these two open pages, laid out in the same way, and whose last words, on the middle of the second page, were in italics. The story in my dream wasn't Lovecraft's, but I knew that it was a horror story (I'd started to read a lot of them), and that these last words constituted something like the punch line—words that were no doubt ano- dyne but that the context filled with a terrible significance. All the while reading (in my dream), I was afraid to reach the end and thought up one trick after the next, pausing and looking back at the page on the left, so as to put off the moment when I would begin the page on the right, which I knew would lead me like the chutes in Chutes and Ladders to catastrophe, to the words in italics that I could just make out while forcing myself to look the other way.

•

When I woke up, I persuaded myself that the text of these two pages, this unimaginable text that was brimful of such horror that it would certainly kill the person unfortunate enough to read it, simply followed the progression of the reader who was held pris- oner by the dream, tracking and observing his descent into the ordeal of the last paragraph. It said, "The last paragraph, the last words are so dreadful that they petrify like the Gorgon. And for the one who reaches them it's no longer possible to wake up, the dream is over, it's reality and this reality is ghastly. You will get there soon. You're there.

"You're there."

•

The first novel I wrote, *The Jaguar's Friend*, was an extrapolation of this dream. So were those that followed it, though less explicitly. For me, writing has long meant coming closer and closer to the sentence that kills, while at the same time trying to stop my slide toward it. I finally read it, it didn't kill me. It seems to me that it's now become inoffensive. Maybe it's lost the prestige of italics. But when I was asked for this text on fundamental readings, I thought back to that moment when I caught a glimpse of it, at twelve, in this book by Lovecraft. If there's a mantra that determined my vocation, it's the absurd sentence *"You fool, Warren is dead!"*

Published in *Les Inrockuptibles*, June 2009

The Life of Julie

1

Located near Sixth Street in downtown San Francisco, the Tenderloin district is a marketplace for crack and a hotbed of poverty and crime—you even see people smoking cigarettes, to give you an idea. Most of the hotels work with various welfare departments, which pay for the rooms directly to make sure the rent is paid before the residents run out and score their drugs. At the height of the AIDS epidemic in the early 1990s, these hotels also served as annexes to the overcrowded hospitals, housing those for whom nothing more could be done apart from daily injections of morphine. That was the case of the Ambassador Hotel, where the young photographer Darcy Padilla started to come in 1992, together with a doctor she was photographing on her rounds. When that job was done, she came back alone, to photograph some of the patients she'd gotten to know. Still today she speaks emotionally about Dorian, the transsexual who was so proud of his breasts, Diane, who weighed just sixty-five pounds, and Steven, to whom she gave a volume of Salinger's stories and who was so afraid of dying alone that she wanted to promise him she'd be there when the moment came, but she knew you should never make promises you can't be sure to keep. Although she spent several hours a day with him, reading to him and feeding him vanilla ice cream—the only thing he could still swallow—she wasn't with him all the time and he did die alone, certainly in horror and despair, at three in the morning, while Darcy was sleeping peacefully with her boyfriend seven or eight blocks away.

The stories of Dorian, Diane, Steven, and many others were similar: poor and violent families, running away from home at a young age, drugs, prostitution, life on the street, and then the sickness that befell them and turned them into a sack of bones and sores and finally brought them to this black hole in a sordid room in the Ambassador Hotel. These people, who were twenty or thirty at the time, are all dead today, and there's no one to remember them aside from Darcy, who keeps hundreds of photos of each of them at her place, in boxes with their names on them. These black-and-white prints show them laughing, crying, displaying their sores and miseries, and are the only trace that remains of their time on earth. The book that Darcy dreamed of putting

together, which was to be called *Separate Lives, Different Worlds: Living Poor in Urban America*, didn't focus on anyone in particular. She was thinking of a gallery of portraits. And when she met Julie, she didn't imagine she'd spend the next eighteen years chronicling her life, right up to the day she died.

At the Ambassador Hotel Julie and Jack were customers like everyone else, but they stood out because even though they were both seropositive, they weren't sick and had even just had a child together. Julie was nineteen, Jack twenty-one, and Rachel eight days old. With Rachel, Julie spent most of the day in the lobby, where she felt better than in their flea-infested room. She stayed there, next to the big window that looked out onto the street, with the fly of her pants wide open, revealing her stomach, which was still stretched from pregnancy. She was wary and bad-tempered, and when anyone talked to her, she told them where to go. But Darcy asked nicely if she could photograph the baby, whom no one had photographed since her birth, and Julie cooled down. Despite her reluctance to sign anything at all, she signed the form that Darcy held out to her: okay to being photographed, okay to the photos eventually being published. Soon Jack joined them; he took Rachel in his arms and played the tender young father, and above all it was touching to see him go about it so clumsily. They were happy to be photographed as young parents. It was as if they were normal people, as if they had a family. On that day in January 1993, Darcy became their family.

2

Darcy Padilla is an energetic, attractive brunette, and it made her laugh during our first meeting when I said I'd hastily concluded from her self-assured good looks and comfortable manner that she comes from a wealthy background. She turned to her boyfriend,

Andy, and asked, "What would you say? Working class or lower middle class? Let's say lower, lower middle class." Her father was a Mexican American social worker, her mother served meals in a hospital. In the small towns where they grew up in the California interior, Darcy and her brother were always the little Latinos, the Chicanos, and, what's more, the top of their class. Catholic schools, a strict merit system, firm principles. When ten-year-old Darcy ran for student government, her father made fun of her slogan: "Vote for Darcy Padilla." She could do better than that, he said, adding that there are two kinds of politicians: those who make promises they don't keep, and those who refuse to make promises they're not sure they can keep, so she should choose her camp. Advice she remembered when Steven wanted her to promise she'd hold his hand when he died. Her big project—because she was elected, of course—was to put out a class yearbook, for which she took the photos. The day she held a little automatic camera in her hands, she knew what she wanted to do in life, and she did it. I won't go into her—brilliant—studies, her odd jobs, her internships. But at the end of one of them, a three-month apprenticeship at *The New York Times*, she was offered a job. Despite the tempting job security, she refused, because a full-time job wouldn't have allowed her to do what she wanted, the way she wanted. The first photo story she sold featured a homeless person living in cardboard boxes near a bus stop. She then photographed street children in Guatemala, a homeless women's shelter, and AIDS patients in prison. Poverty is her subject: if she was sent to photograph the birthday of a Russian oligarch in the luxury ski resort Courchevel, I think she'd come back with photos of toothless bums wandering through the streets and talking to themselves, or sniffing glue behind the chairlifts. It's in their behalf that she does what she does, but she draws a clear line. She saw misery close up in her childhood, because Mr. Padilla, as he was respectfully called, took all the drug addicts and juvenile delinquents under his arm in the various places his family lived, and she isn't the least bit inclined to put herself in danger. She's not Nan Goldin: none of her close friends has died of AIDS, she's never smoked a joint in her life, she's positive, sporty, pays attention to what she eats, and lives in a nice, well-decorated, tidy apartment. And I think it's because she's so firmly anchored in this ideally straight life that she can take charge of the tattered lives of people such as Julie so well. She's open to them, she never stops asking herself what it's like to be in their place, but she remains in her own. As my friend the judge Étienne Rigal says— and it's the biggest compliment he can pay someone—she knows where she is.

3

Julie was six months old when her mother, who was seventeen, took her under her arm after a violent fight with her husband and left their small town in Alaska for California. She was looking for a better life, but she never found it. An alcoholic, she drifted from man to man, random encounters who were willing to put her and her little girl up for a time. One of them, who lasted long enough for Julie to think of him as her stepdad, raped her when she was still an adolescent, and she ran away in turn. At fourteen, she lived on the street and got hooked on alcohol and amphetamines. When she met Jack, whose story is practically the same, he was prostituting himself. They found out they were seropositive when Julie had a pregnancy test, but neither of them cared as long as they weren't sick. They told themselves that they were in any case going to die young, everyone around them died young, and they were completely incapable of imagining a future for themselves. In the meantime, Rachel gave them a reason to live. They were proud of her, they loved her, they would have liked to be good parents. But they didn't know what it was like to be good parents, no one had shown them how. Darcy, who learned as a young girl to make her bed and clean her room, was appalled at the chaos that reigned in theirs—at the start they didn't dare to invite her—and I was appalled as well when I saw a photo of Rachel sleeping, and beside her a pillow full of cigarette holes, meaning that her father or mother had gone to sleep with a cigarette in his or her mouth not once but more like a hundred times, almost setting fire to the bed where their little girl was sleeping.

Julie, however, made an effort: she wanted to stop taking speed, and it's because Jack didn't want to, or couldn't, that they broke up. Speed turned him into an animal; just his way of walking—which Darcy imitated—scared people on the street. He didn't move far: to another hotel in the neighborhood just a couple of blocks away, but their lives took place in such small radii that he could just as well have gone to live on the East Coast. They lost track of each other; Darcy continued to see Julie and Rachel. Julie introduced Darcy proudly as "my photographer." She liked it when Darcy gave her prints and put together little albums for her, but the photos she preferred were the happy ones, with children in them, and not, as she joked to Darcy, "the ones you like," where Julie looked like a complete wreck. A new couple had moved into the hotel, seropositive drug addicts but not sick, lucky when compared to everyone else around them. They had two children, whom Julie babysat when the parents were too wasted, and she liked it when Darcy came on those days, when three little kids were running on the stairs and fighting on the beds. They all went to McDonald's together; Darcy watched them gobble down the hamburgers she bought them, but she didn't eat anything because junk food goes against her dietary principles. Julie laughed at Darcy for being so stuck-up, and that became one of their favorite private jokes. Once Darcy invited them to eat at a little Vietnamese restaurant just across the street, a place Julie had never even

thought of going. It's still there, I went there with Darcy, and she told me she'd wanted to pay for the meal with her credit card but the owner only took cash. "Okay," she said, "I'll come back and pay you tomorrow." She still remembers how amazed Julie was, first of all because Darcy inspired enough confidence for a merchant to give her credit without knowing her instead of calling the police, and second because she did go back and pay the next day.

When she was starting out as a freelance photographer, Darcy struggled to make ends meet, but she knew that even with her money problems she was incommensurably richer—above all in terms of her future—than all the people she knew in the Tenderloin, and she always acted accordingly. To the extent that she could, she always gave to those who asked, and she never acted as if they were all in the same boat. She told Julie stories about her boyfriends, her photo shoots in countries whose names Julie had never heard. Even if it was impossible for them to be on a completely equal footing, they did develop a relationship in which they saw eye to eye, human being to human being. Julie also talked about her life, with a brutal and sarcastic sense of humor all her own. She was obsessed by the idea that she was like her mother— an alcoholic and a bad parent—and that later Rachel's life would be just as shitty as hers. Darcy listened to her and refrained from saying no, no, and when Julie told her she was pregnant again without knowing which of her one-night-stand partners was the father, Darcy didn't pretend to find it great news. But since Julie had decided to keep the child, Darcy looked after her in her pregnancy. Together with Rachel she was present at the birth, which she photographed. She went with Julie when it was time to register little Tommy. She took the kids to the clinic when they were sick and Julie didn't dare go herself, rightly fearing they'd revoke her custody owing to her intoxication. But Darcy never invited Julie to her place, and Julie, who was intelligent in her way, never asked to go.

4

In 1997 Julie met a certain Paul, with whom she and her two
children moved to Stockton, a working-class city ninety or so
miles from San Francisco. Darcy saw less and less of her. Darcy
wanted to believe that Julie had pretty much put her nightmare
behind her and settled into the life of a suburban housewife, and
that although this life wasn't enviable, it was far preferable to the
utter desolation of the Tenderloin. One night Darcy got a panic-
stricken phone call: Julie was at the hospital after a miscarriage,
and the police had come to tell her that Paul had been arrested
after abusing little Tommy. At first Julie had refused to believe
them. They showed her the report, together with photos: bruises,
cuts, his face covered with vomit. When she got out of the hospital,
Paul was in prison and the two children were in foster care. She
had the right to go see them, but not to have them back for now.
Not for now, okay, but when? That wasn't clear. The counselors
were noncommittal. She knew she was only making things worse
by calling them assholes and shitheads, but she couldn't help it.
Alone in Stockton, she lost her footing, started to be afraid she
was going mad, and for the first time she started to harass Darcy,
calling her up in the middle of the night and threatening to commit suicide. She would have liked Darcy to adopt Rachel and
Tommy. Exasperated, Darcy finally said that if they'd taken the
kids away, it was Julie's fault. "Fuck you," Julie said, and hung up.
If Julie hadn't gotten back in contact, Darcy thinks she wouldn't
have run after her: she'd become too hard to manage. But after a
week of sulking Julie called Darcy up again and shared her latest
concern: she didn't know where Jack was. The last time she'd
seen him was a couple of months ago, and he wasn't doing so well
at all. Darcy called the hospitals, activated her network of doctors
and social workers, and found Jack in a nursing home, in the end
stage of AIDS. The bus from Stockton to San Francisco, where

the home was located, cost twenty dollars, which Julie didn't have, so Darcy paid for her to visit him a couple of times. He had some pictures on his bedside table Darcy had taken of the children and poignantly begged to see Rachel, but Julie couldn't bring herself to tell him that Tommy and Rachel had been taken from her. She avoided talking about it, said Rachel was at school and that she'd come the next time. Jack died without seeing his daughter again—the only gift, he said, that life had given him.

5

In the five years Darcy spent photographing Julie, her big project on urban poverty increasingly focused on her alone, and by 1998, under the title *Birth and Death Certificates*, Darcy applied for a grant from George Soros's Open Society Foundations. She got the grant, two of whose previous laureates were Magnum agency stars Gilles Peress and Bruce Davidson, and jetted off to New York. At the cocktail party given in her honor she noticed a handsome young man with shiny black eyes looking at her intently. His name was Andy; he'd just graduated in economics and was working for an NGO. Puerto Rican from the Bronx, he came from the same sort of background as Darcy and had similar values, only he was more reserved. He had something calm and reflective about him that contrasted with her exuberance. When he told me about their meeting, Andy said, "I'm sure you've noticed: when Darcy's in a room, she's the only one you see, you just can't miss her." This aura intimidated him, but what made him think he had a chance was that she didn't overdo it: there was nothing bohemian about her, none of the posturing he had thought goes with being a photographer. At the start their romance was complicated by the distance, with her in San Francisco and him in New York, but after two years he left his city and his job to join her, not only to

live with her but also to become her partner, agent, accountant, assistant, and soon webmaster. The division of roles between them
is simple: she takes photographs, he does everything else, and apparently it works, because twelve years later they're still together.
They hope to stay together forever—and I hope they do, too.

Almost at the same time, Julie also met someone. It wasn't at
a cocktail party given by the Soros Foundations, but at a rehabilitation center for drug addicts, where they were both enrolled in
a program they never finished. When she first saw him, Darcy
wouldn't have bet a nickel on this Jason. Nevertheless, twelve years
on he was still there as well. While only an adolescent, Jason ran
away from his parents' place in Portland, and since then he'd been
living on the street: drugs, prostitution, seropositivity, the usual
triad, to which in his case was added a less than average IQ
and manic-depressive tendencies, for which he received a disability allowance. Since he wasn't considered responsible enough to
manage this money on his own, he needed a responsible adult

to do it for him, and Julie quickly took on this role. A touching series of photos shows him as happy as a child discovering his Christmas presents while Julie counts out the money with papal solemnity, taking a couple of bills from the wad and handing them to Jason so he can make his life a little less miserable for a couple of hours. He was like the simpleton Lennie in *Of Mice and Men*, and Julie, who in all her life had never dominated anyone, started to dominate him the way Lennie's buddy George dominates him. Like Lennie, Jason wasn't mean, but he could be brutal and even dangerous, Darcy thinks. "Look what he's doing to that cat," she said to me, shocked, showing me a photo in which he grabs the animal by the skin of its neck. It's not something Andy would do, and I'm ready to swear that no cat in the world is treated better than Pablo, the Angora that rules over their pretty apartment on Broderick Street.

6

Julie didn't use any form of contraception. She knew it was possible to have an abortion, but in a purely theoretical way, the way you know it's possible to go to the moon, and between 1993 and 2008 she gave birth to six children. The first two, Rachel and Tommy, as well as Elyssa, the last, are the only ones she had custody of for even a short period of time. The other three were taken away from her at birth by the Child Protective Services, and not without good reason, but this good reason drove her to despair. She knew that her life was a catastrophe, that she'd failed right down the line, and that things were no doubt not going to get any better. The only thing she would have liked to do well, and now felt she could, was to raise a child and give it a small chance of having a better life than hers. That's why she kept enrolling in rehabilitation programs she never finished: in the hopes of acquiring a certificate that proved she had changed and could now be trusted. She hoped Rachel and Tommy would be given back to her, but since she'd gotten together with Jason, they'd been living in San Francisco again, back in the grim Tenderloin, where she always seemed to end up, and Stockton was too far, the bus was too expensive, and she was too down in the dumps to go on visiting them. "I'll go, I'll go," she said, "I'll bring them presents." But she didn't go, and the day of the hearing when their case came up, she didn't show up, so that she was permanently deprived of her parental rights and the two children were given up for adoption. She would never be able to see them again or find out what happened to them, the judge decided. When she heard about the ruling, she was more than eight months pregnant, this time by Jason. She was so afraid her baby would be taken away from her that the day after it was born, she and Jason kidnapped it. They wrapped it in a baby blanket and fled the hospital. Darcy, who had talked with Julie the day before, had a call from the police, who'd started a manhunt. She tried to find them, too, hoping to reach them first and reason with them. Two or three days of extreme confusion followed—sleepless nights, fatigued telephone calls, missed meetings, and negotiation attempts, at the end of which the parent kidnappers were taken into custody. And as they feared, Jordan, the baby girl, was entrusted to Child Protective Services, which immediately put her up for adoption. At the trial Julie and Jason were sentenced to a year in prison. They served six months, during which time Darcy visited them regularly. When they got out, they went back to their life of misery in the Tenderloin. Two more children were born, Ryan in 2001 and Jason Jr. in 2002, both of whom went straight from the delivery room to the adoption center. Julie held them in her arms for at most a couple of seconds. She and Jason were extremely depressed and rarely ventured out of their bed, which was strewn with leftover junk food and all the dismal trappings that the poor acquire. Julie spent her days drinking, Jason smoking grass. The rhythms of their addictions didn't match, their highs and lows were out of sync. Two years passed in this way, during which Darcy didn't see much of them, both because they'd shut themselves away and because Darcy was busy. To increase their earnings Andy got the idea that she should start doing wedding photos, and almost every weekend now she photographed—in color—couples who were wealthy enough to afford her services, which weren't cheap, pledging to love, honor, and cherish each other, surrounded by their smiling friends and family. Thanks to this work Darcy could spend the week photographing homeless people in black and white and submit each stage of her work in progress to prestigious foundations: after Guggenheim, Soros, and after Soros, Getty, each of which bestowed a grant with the congratulations of the jury.

7

While she was putting together the application for one of these grants, Darcy googled Julie's name on the Internet. She was hoping to find articles about Jordan's kidnapping and was surprised to come across a missing person notice: "Julie Baird born 10/10/73. Please contact me I've been looking for you. If you were born in Anchorage Alaska 10/10/73 you're the one." Darcy called, her heart racing: it was Julie's father. After her mother disappeared with her, he'd looked for them desperately, then finally given up. The new resources available on the Internet gave him the idea of posting this message, and what do you know, someone answered: a photographer from San Francisco who knew his daughter. Everything happened quickly after that, so quickly that much to Darcy's regret she wasn't able to be there when Julie and her father met up. Darcy had agreed to do a photo story on Mexican adolescent gangs in Los Angeles, everything was arranged, and Julie didn't want to wait: her father had invited her to Alaska, where she was born and where he was still living, and had offered to buy plane tickets for her and Jason.

She left inextricably excited and distressed, dreaming of a new life with this family she didn't know, terrified at the idea of their deception and maybe their rejection when they saw the wreck that she knew she'd become get off the plane. Darcy had done her best to prepare the terrain by e-mail and telephone, explaining that the thirty-one years that had gone by since Julie had left Alaska as a baby hadn't been easy for her, then Darcy left on her photo shoot. She immersed herself in it, the way she immerses herself in everything she does. Bad news was waiting when she got back three weeks later. No sooner had Julie arrived at her family's place than she fell sick. She was in a hospital in Anchorage. Darcy took the first plane, and when she saw her, she understood right away. Julie was no longer just seropositive: she had AIDS. And what she feared the most wasn't dying, but that her father would find out what she was dying of. She didn't dare tell him and was counting on Darcy to do it. And Darcy, good little soldier that she was, staunchly carried out the task. Julie's father, Bill Baird, is the big guy in the photos, dressed in a lumberjack's shirt and a baseball cap. Darcy liked him right away, he liked her right away. She says he was a nice guy. He cried, understood, blamed himself. He was happy to have found his daughter, sad to have found her in such a state, but she was his daughter, he loved her, drug addict or not, sick or not, he'd take care of her, he'd look after her.

Julie came through this time, but sickness was upon her. She'd lost more than sixty pounds; at thirty-one she looked almost twice that age. Sores in her palate and esophagus that nothing could cure gave her mouth a bumpy appearance and a disgruntled chewing motion, which even someone as unpicky when it comes to feminine grace as Jason admits took some getting used to. Bill

Baird took them to Valdez, where he lived. An hour by plane from
Anchorage when the planes aren't grounded by the weather, six
hours by car, Valdez is practically cut off from everything. Its four
thousand inhabitants live from commercial fishing and canning.
Until he retired, Bill was the cook in the only pizzeria in town;
he'd founded a second family, and his four big children looked on
suspiciously when this scarecrow who was introduced to them as
their half sister arrived. Rumors quickly got around that she and
Jason had AIDS, which didn't make it any easier for them to fit
in. On the other hand, life at Valdez doesn't cost much, the state
pays a premium to people willing to live in Alaska, which, along
with Jason's disability allowance, let them rent a little apartment,
by far the most opulent of all the shabby places they'd lived in.
Bill came to see his daughter every day and took her for long drives
in his car. He showed her the glaciers, the lakes, the eagles, the
wild nature in the midst of which she could have grown up and
perhaps led a simple, calm life if her crazy mother hadn't taken

her away. Bit by bit, she told him about the terrible life she'd led instead, in the big-city jungle. Out of the goodness of his heart, or simply because you can't spend your entire life in absolute despair, Bill pretended it was possible to start over from zero. He spoke of a new start. Then he died of a heart attack. Without him, Julie no longer had any reason to stay in Valdez. Jason liked Alaska, however. He liked the idea of hunting, fishing, and the wide, open spaces, and above all of having a gun. At Bill's funeral they met Bill's brother, a nice guy like Bill whom they called Uncle Mike, who lived with his wife, Aunt Rita, in a sort of cabin in the woods just outside Palmer, Alaska. Near them was an abandoned trailer on an empty lot that had become more or less a garbage dump. There, in the wild, Jason and Julie moved in. No electricity, no running water, but no neighbors either except for the bears and moose, and from time to time they could always take a shower at Mike and Rita's place. Despite its lack of comfort, Darcy approved of this new location, first of all because Palmer is just an

hour's drive from Anchorage, and so from the hospital where Julie would inevitably spend more and more time, and also for egotistic reasons, because Darcy was no fan of the six-hour drive to Valdez, alone at the wheel of a rented car, and sometimes alone on the road for the whole trip.

8

Although she was inconsolable about losing custody of her children, Julie didn't want any more: What was the point of having one if it's just going to watch its mother die at a young age? she thought. But Jason insisted. As he'd been totally dependent on Julie for the past ten years, he'd gotten it into his head that his emotional and sexual life would end when she died, and he wanted, in his words, to have "something of my own" when she was no longer there. Julie berated him: "Something? A child is not something!" Be that as it may, she was soon pregnant again. During her pregnancy one of the new miracles now made banal by the Internet happened. In the fall of 2007, Darcy received a phone call from a certain Karen, who introduced herself as the adoptive mother of one of Julie's children, the one she and Jason had called Jason Jr. before he'd been taken from them in 2002, and who was now called Zach. When Darcy told me the story, I couldn't believe my ears and got her to repeat it. Little Zach knew that he was adopted, Karen told her, but he knew nothing about his biological parents. Nevertheless, he'd had recurring dreams showing them gravely ill and living in the far north, surrounded by bears. They called out to him. Faced with his growing distress, Karen tried to find them, and thanks to an administrative slipup and Darcy's website, she did. Once again Darcy played the role of intermediary. She prepared the ground, spoke of their difficult life with as many euphemisms as possible, but nevertheless told

Karen that they had AIDS. Then Darcy flew to Anchorage, where Julie was preparing to give birth, bearing two letters: one, serious and touching, from Karen, and another from Zach himself, who wrote, "Mom, I love you. I have good parents but I'd like to get to know you one day." Darcy photographed Julie reading these letters, bursting into tears, then smoking frenetically outside to get over her emotion. Elyssa was born several days later by cesarean section. Jason was so afraid Julie would die on the operating table that he didn't want to be present at the birth. Darcy was there, however, as usual. The baby was put in its mother's arms, but this time around, unusually, it wasn't taken away again. It was the first of their four children that Jason and Julie were able to bring home. For the first time, thanks to Uncle Mike and Aunt Rita, they were prepared: they had a crib, a Baby Relax rocker, diapers, and bottles, and while they wouldn't have been called back for a casting as model young parents, it's in this role and in this company that a couple of weeks later they welcomed Zach, the son they'd lost six years earlier. Darcy, who accompanied Karen and Zach, remembers that you could have cut the discomfort with a knife. Everyone was expecting a lot, and nothing happened. Well, nothing: embarrassment, stiff words. The only one who managed to relax the atmosphere at all was Jason, whom Julie had lectured a long time, telling him to behave himself, not swear, and make a good impression. He played video games with Zach, tossed him in the air, and made him laugh a bit. As fathers go, there are better, nevertheless this joking, simple, big-brother figure reassured the little boy, in whose worried dreams his biological parents appeared as violent, dangerous people who could hurt and even kill him. When Karen and Zach left, there was a big hole. Darcy was so stressed-out that she remembers having done something that's not like her at all. When Julie kept chewing her cud and muttering in the same fake voice she'd had during the whole visit that it was all for the best, Darcy blurted out, "Come on, Julie,

stop pretending!," telling her to admit that it had gone horribly and
that she felt like shit. Julie then fell apart, repeating that Karen
was a fantastic person, that she was happy that Zach had a good
mother, but that she wanted to die because she hadn't been able
to be that good mother herself, that she would have preferred
Zach to be unhappy so he'd want to come back to her, and that,
yes, okay, Darcy, she was an absolute piece of shit. Jason went up
to Julie and took her in his arms. Darcy photographed them like
that; it's not the most spectacular of her photographs, but I think
it's one of the ones that moves me the most.

9

The last year, Julie was in and out of the hospital, each time
leaving weaker than when she went in. At home she lay on the
couch the whole time, no longer able to carry Elyssa. Jason, who
was wasted three-quarters of the time, played around with his little
plastic gun but still made sure that she took her thirty-two pills a
day at the prescribed times. They didn't help much: not only was
Julie practically falling apart, but she suffered more and more. She
had huge bouts of bitterness, repeating that it was stupid to have
had Elyssa and that Jason would never be able to take care of her
on his own, but also brief periods of gaiety, especially when Darcy
was there. Julie loved it, for example, when Darcy, who was normally so careful about what she ate, had to have Kentucky Fried
Chicken like everyone else when she came to their place, and what
Julie liked best of all was that it was an old joke between them.
It's something to have known someone for long enough to share
an old joke. It didn't take hours to recite the list of good things
in Julie's life, but there had been Darcy. The same shit without
Darcy would have been worse because there would have been no
witness. One night, after dropping Elyssa off at Uncle Mike and

Aunt Rita's place, Darcy, Julie, and Jason went out to a bar and drank margaritas, and Julie said to Darcy with a wink, "You know what? We should go on vacation, the two of us."

"Where would you like to go?"

"I don't know, Brazil."

"Brazil?" Having adopted over the years Julie's savage sense of humor, Darcy added, "You see yourself on the beach, in a bikini?"

They laughed, and Jason laughed, too, after a moment, but then he didn't stop, the joke made his day. Julie in a bikini: good one!

10

One afternoon in September 2010, Darcy and Andy were at home working when the phone rang. It was Aunt Rita, who told them what the doctor had said when they took Julie to the hospital because she was choking even more than usual: "There's nothing more we can do, take her home and *prepare for the end-of-life procedure.*" After she hung up, Darcy burst into tears. Andy held her in his arms for a long time. He'd never met Julie and would never meet her, no more than he would have met Darcy's patients if she'd been a psychoanalyst. But he'd known about Julie for as long as he'd known Darcy, and his heart was broken, too. They went out to walk for a moment in silence, over to Alta Plaza Park, which overlooks their pretty neighborhood and from where the hills of San Francisco roll down toward the ocean, then went home to book the plane ticket. The whole way Darcy wondered if she'd photograph Julie dying, if Julie and Jason would want her to, and if she herself, Darcy, would have the heart to do it. In the end she did, without the question ever being raised: now that they'd come this far, after eighteen years of this strange cooperation, there was no reason to stop. The file with the last photos is called "julie.end," and I don't see what I could add except that Darcy, who's not religious, prayed that Julie's atrocious agony wouldn't

last too long, but it did, almost three weeks; that Julie had sudden fits of panic and thought the room was full of strangers who were going to hurt her; that Elyssa wanted to play with Julie all the time; and that the last night, Jason, who'd been staying up with her, left her bedside for half an hour to go do something, and she died alone during that half hour, at dawn on September 27, 2010, aged thirty-six.

11

A couple of weeks after the death of its heroine, *The Julie Project*, finally complete, won its author the prestigious W. Eugene Smith Grant. This prize certainly suits her far better than the Helmut Newton Prize, if there is one, and it meant all the more to her in that *Country Doctor*, Smith's famous photo story shot during the late 1940s, was her model and guide when she walked into the Ambassador Hotel for the first time. For Darcy the story ends well. I'm not being at all ironic when I say that, and I sincerely admire the moral health that spares her the frequent pangs of conscience felt by artists whose talent and glory prosper thanks to other people's misery. Darcy doesn't see herself as an artist, with everything that status implies in narcissism, but as a journalist whose job it is to bear witness. And to her, the story isn't over. Julie's death opened a new chapter, whose heroes are her children. Elyssa first, whom she and Andy want to adopt if Jason, as they fear, doesn't manage to bring her up or dies prematurely. But also Zach and the other four. Little Rachel, whom Darcy got to know when she was just eight days old, is now eighteen. She was six when she saw Julie for the last time; she must still have memories of her. With Karen's help, Darcy is now trying to locate Rachel and the others, to let them discover their mother's story if they want.

When Darcy told me that, I wasn't convinced it was such a

good idea. I thought that no one in the world could draw any comfort from knowing that Julie was their mother. Then, the day before I left, I went with Darcy to the Tenderloin, the neighborhood to which she, too, always returns, where she knows everyone and where she's started a new photo story on the patients at a psychiatric clinic that had unfortunately just closed down. She was looking for one patient in particular, whom she'd already photographed once and whose address she didn't have, assuming he had one. So we hung out on the streets, talked to a couple of bums and punks with dogs, and finally ran into him. He was young with a childlike face ravaged by heroin. His whole body shook violently, but he was articulate and even surprisingly well-spoken. He invited us back to his hotel room, which looked to me to be straight out of a nightmare, but Darcy later assured me that Julie's rooms had all been far worse. He talked about his mother, who'd abandoned him when he was four. "I don't know who she is," he said sadly. Then, with the same sense for language that had struck me from the start, he added, "Or was. You see, I don't even know what tense to use when I talk about her. I don't know a thing: where she is, if she's alive or dead. I think she must have been a prostitute and an addict, but I don't care, I'd like so much to know who my mom was, and I'll never know." He said the words softly and started to cry, and I thought that all things considered, Darcy was no doubt right.

Published in *6Mois*, March 2011

The last I heard from Darcy, Jason is serving seventeen years in prison for the sexual abuse of a minor. All six of the children are known to be adopted.

Four Days in Davos

(with Hélène Devynck)

1

You don't expect to see street fights in Davos, even less so during the World Economic Forum. However, around three in the morning, as we were coming out of a bar where a group of young bankers were celebrating their decision to start a hedge fund (that's the kind of thing young bankers do when they're drunk), we ran across two guys in suits slugging each other in the face. Their fight wasn't serious; in fact they were the best of friends and soon made up. We bring it up here because of the unusual reaction of a bystander, a Chinese guy in his thirties, who went up to the two brawlers, tapped one of them on the shoulder to get his attention, and, having got it, bent down and picked up handfuls of snow that he started methodically throwing in his own face. One handful, two handfuls, three handfuls. All the while covering his face with snow, he smiled a benign smile that so alarmed the two that they completely forget their quarrel. This disconcerting ploy, and its no less disconcerting effectiveness, seemed to us to touch at the heart of Zen, and on the way back home we dreamed up ways of applying it in more serious conflicts.

2

The next day we eat in a raclette restaurant, where Felix, whom we'll soon introduce, buttonholed Jean-Claude Trichet for our first interview. The former director of the European Central Bank is a calm, distinguished man who tells us with extreme courtesy that we have five minutes.

First question: "If we'd come here in 2007, we would certainly have interviewed people who anticipated the imminent subprime crisis, about which we knew nothing at all. We didn't even know the expression. So we wonder, what would be the equivalent today? What is it that we don't know, and you—perhaps—do?"

Trichet's astonishingly clear gaze clouds over; it's difficult to say whether he finds the question idiotic, or if he considers it very much to the point. Whatever the case, he gets up, saying it would be better to meet again in Paris for an interview in which we'd set the rules in advance. After which he disappears, replaced almost instantly by the Chinese bystander from the night before, who resolves conflicts by throwing snow in his face. No matter how posh the place, it's customary in Davos to share tables without a fuss, and the Chinese guy has more time for us than Trichet did. With a pleasant twinkle in his eye, as cool as can be, wearing a hooded sweatshirt and big mountain boots, he could be a young Internet billionaire or an advanced martial artist, or both, and when we ask what he does in life, he says he pursues illumination and the expansion of his mind on a quest for permanent happiness. Born in San Francisco, educated at Berkeley, based in Hong Kong, he's a top-notch expert in cognitive sciences, now involved in a vast international project aimed at bringing together a conclave of minds as expanded as his on the island republic of Vanuatu in the South Pacific, with the goal of expounding a new mythology, something that would draw on and go beyond Buddhism and *Star Wars*. And that's why he's come to Davos? "Well"—he widens his Cheshire cat grin—"it can't hurt. And this is the big people's Disneyland, right?"

Before coming, that's certainly not how we saw things. An interview with Klaus Schwab should have made us think again, however. Klaus Schwab is the Zurich economics professor who first organized these meetings of European managers in Davos forty years ago. With the fall of communism, the forum became the unavoidable meetup of the highest-level businesspeople and politicians, over which Klaus Schwab still presides. And if, as Hegel says, reading the newspaper is the modern man's morning prayer, one discovers with surprise that before perusing the stock quotes and the *Financial Times*, Klaus Schwab's morning ritual involves half an hour of meditation. We'll come back to the new age perfume that hovers over this empyrean domain of global deciders, but now it's time to speak of Felix, without whom we would never have come this far.

3

Like Arnold Schwarzenegger, Felix Marquardt is an Austrian American. Handsome, thirty-five, he invented the "thing"—as he himself calls it when he introduces himself—called the Atlantic Dinners. Half think tank, half PR agency, the Atlantic Dinners gather businesspeople and diplomats, but also writers, artists, and rappers, around the world's big players when they pass through Paris, the point being to link up people who at first sight have no reason to know each other, and to see what juicy ideas they come up with. Juicy, or interesting, or funny even, and on this last point we can say it's generally a success: before we went, we had no idea we would laugh as much as we did at a dinner given in honor of Japanese ministers.

Last fall we told Felix that we were interested in the financial crisis and were thinking of together writing something about it from the height of our ignorance—an ignorance that was relative for one of us (Hélène), who as a journalist has often dealt with economic players, and almost absolute for the other (Emmanuel), who counts himself among the three out of four French people who when push comes to shove are unable to say exactly what a bond is. "Okay," said Felix, "then you have to go to Davos."

"But how do you go to Davos? You think we could get accredited as journalists?"

Felix shook his head. "Way too late. The applications have been closed for months now, and they only accept a handful anyway. But I can take you."

Which he did, putting us up in a chalet belonging to some friends of his parents'. In addition to the two of us, there was also an assistant, a photographer, a cameraman, and a sound engineer—all four of whom were to follow us and film everything we did—plus, for good measure, a childhood friend of Felix's who was going through a rough time and whom Felix had persuaded to come along for a breath of fresh air. All in all our group included eight people, who apart from Felix had next to nothing to do with the worlds of business and power. A rather unwieldy number in a place where the top bosses and most powerful ministers can only bring a single escort. For this right, and for the white badge that gives them access to the Congress Center, where the conferences and roundtables take place, they have to fork over seventy-five thousand dollars, while we make do with the humble green badges costing fifty dollars apiece, allowing us to enter the Hotel Belvédère, home to "Off-Davos."

These badges, and the system of castes they articulate, remind Hélène and me of one thing: the Cannes Film Festival, which we know well because between the two of us we've played the most varied roles there, from freelance journalist to jury member. Like Cannes, Davos concentrates a maximum of famous people and other heavyweights in a minimum of space. It's an empire of signs, a theater of privileges and humiliations, where, no matter how important you are, you can be sure that there's always someone more important, that the evening soiree to which you've been invited is not *the* place to be, and that there are always better, more secret rendezvous with even fewer of the happy few. Word has it—at least one would like to believe—that even Bill Gates says that sometimes. The difference from Cannes is that in Davos this implacable hierarchy goes hand in hand with a surprising ease of contact.

That has to do first with the small size of the village: a bigwig banker from New York confided to us candidly that he knew Davos much better than he knew Manhattan, because in Manhattan he only gets around by limousine, whereas in Davos he practices the exotic sport of going by foot. Next, it has to do with the almost complete lack of people, of onlookers, of normal joes: apart from the local population, almost all of whom work for the Forum as chauffeurs, waiters, or security guards, the only people you meet at the Forum are participants at the Forum, so we're ideally among ourselves. Finally, it's because these VIPs, who in normal times are always surrounded by a close guard of ten or so people, are here only allowed one sherpa—rarely a pretty woman, as we'd expected, and in most cases a serious-looking young man, who, when he's accompanying a French dignitary, is generally a graduate of the elitist École Nationale d'Administration and at the start of his career. While at Cannes there can be no question of rubbing shoulders with Sharon Stone if you're not part of her circle, in Davos—even if we didn't drink coffee with Angela Merkel—you can cross paths with Lakshmi Mittal, Ehud Barak, Pascal Lamy, Arianna Huffington, Muhammad Yunus, or Google boss Eric Schmidt as if you were at your local grocery store, and there's nothing to stop you from going up and talking to them if you dare. Going on the logic that if you're there it's because you belong more or less to the same world they do, most of them will be happy to give you five minutes of their time.

Making such contacts is Felix's favorite sport, one he pursues with true social grace, having an easygoing manner, a sparkling sense of humor, a gift for languages, and a profound knowledge of the person's dossier before he goes up to make someone's acquaintance. He's been coming to Davos for ten years and already knows a lot of people, but his one desire is to get to know more, and to put all his friends and acquaintances, old and new, in contact with one another so that they can cut deals, on which in the best of cases he'll receive a commission. ("How much?" we ask. "Ten percent?" "You've got to be kidding! More like a tenth of a percent . . . one-hundredth of a percent. But"—he smiles wolfishly—"the numbers can be big.") One of Felix's major charms is that he's up-front. For him lies are a waste of time, and he makes no bones about having brought us along above all because he likes us, but also because he's counting on our talking about him in our article (he even proposes a title: "The Man Who Whispers in Presidents' Ears"), and because in selling us as a journalist and an author who are writing a book about the crisis ("or better: about globalization," he suggests; better not to use the word *crisis*), he gets us meetings that are a pretext for him to grow his list of contacts.

4

These meetings are a veritable rat race. What's more, the only thing that distinguishes them from chance encounters is that you've made an appointment for a certain place at a certain time, but since neither side stops running into other people on the way, you spend your time telephoning to put the meetings off and in general they never happen, or if they do, it's by chance when you least expect them. For example, we have one inside the Congress Center, and as we can't get in, the person we want to meet kindly proposes to meet us outside. It takes him an hour and a half to cover the two hundred yards that separate us, which we spend walking up and down on the snowy sidewalk and, with Felix's help, getting to know, in this order, a member of President Sarkozy's diplomatic team, who insists on remaining anonymous although he does no more than say hello and complain good-naturedly of summit fatigue; François Henrot, president of Investment Bank Activities at Rothschild Inc., who's heading over to Shimon Peres's Sabbath party; the oligarch Oleg Deripaska's right-hand man, who's known as Little Oleg to distinguish him from his boss; a top manager of the hypermarket retail chain Carrefour, who doesn't yet know that his CEO has just been replaced and that he himself could be on the way out as well; the economist Nouriel Roubini, a shady figure who foresaw the subprime crisis, for which he's acquired the status of international oracle; and finally the crown princess of Norway, who politely refuses to be filmed—because everything's being filmed by Felix's gang. No doubt appearing with this crew gives us a semblance of credibility, which is unfortunately compromised by our bad English. In fact, all of our discussions are limited to polite hellos, asking whom the other person has seen and which party they'll go to this evening. That, too, is much like Cannes, where the people who, while in Paris, had promised to see each other in Cannes, now, not having managed to meet up in Cannes, invariably promise to see each other when they're back in Paris.

As for our more formal meetings, the ones you could call interviews (with an Indian minister, an American banker, the number three at Google . . .), what to say? What do we retain? Not much, but the opposite would be surprising. To pursue the analogy with Cannes, there you can interview the greatest and most original artists for the standard thirty minutes, and they'll all tell you the same thing: the shoot was an incredible experience, the actor or director put his all into it, with such passion, etc. If you're looking for originality, you should do your interview somewhere else. And before giving their answers, it's only fair to say what questions we asked. They were the ones the average, reasonably well-informed Westerner asks when faced with the spectacle of financial capitalism that is obsessed with profit, heedless of its social consequences and the dizzying inequalities it creates, that for the past thirty years has been liberated of any and every form of regulation, privatizing profits and mutualizing losses, disdaining the state as a sort of remnant from Soviet times but counting on it to bail it out when the wind turns, and leading the Western countries headlong from crisis to crisis toward a catastrophe in which the middle classes look set to go down with all hands while the leaders are evacuated on helicopters. Everyone says and thinks such things today; even politicians have cottoned on to the fact that it's what you have to say, if not think, to have any chance of being elected. Everyone, according to the slogan launched by Occupy Wall Street, counts themselves among the 99 percent of underlings and grumbles about the greedy 1 percent, who in reality, like Felix's commissions, make up only 0.1 percent or even 0.01 percent of the population. And while those from the financial world by no means form the majority of those present, Davos is certainly their Versailles, and a new revolution could well be in the making that would quash their privileges. The question, then, is, Are you aware of this? And the answer, clearly, is no.

Let's be clear. With such titles as "Responsible Leadership in Times of Crisis," "Managing Chaos," or "From Transition to Transformation," the talks and roundtables at the official Forum, which we're only too willing to believe take place at a high level, are the equivalent of the films in the Official Competition at Cannes. There seriousness—and even a touch of false piety—is de rigueur. When dealing with the topic of globalization, which it depicts in its most self-assured, victorious forms, the Forum's inaugural report evokes with an exquisite sense of euphemism "a risk of disillusionment." In our conversations, however, it's another story. Disillusionment? Crisis? Inequality? Okay, if you want, but in the final analysis, as the affable CEO of Western Union says to us, let's be clear: if we don't pay top managers what they deserve, they'll go elsewhere. And anyway, just what does it mean to be a capitalist? If you have a hundred dollars saved up and you put it in the bank hoping to soon have a hundred and five, you're a capitalist just like me. And the more money these capitalists like you and me make (that's really what he said, "like you and me," and even if we make a decent living, even if we don't know his exact salary, to say nothing of his stock options, in our view this "like you and me" takes the cake when it comes to the Davos version of turning the world on its head), the more they'll be able to give—to redistribute, that is—to the poor. It doesn't seem to occur to this enthusiastic and, in his way, generous man that it would not be such a bad thing at all if the poor were able to earn enough themselves and didn't need to depend on the goodwill of the rich. Making the maximum amount of money and doing the maximum amount of good—or, for the more sophisticated, doing the maximum of good *by* making the maximum of money—is the mantra of the Forum, where you're not much if you don't have your own charitable foundation. And no doubt it's better than nothing ("What do you want, communism?"). What is not better than nothing, by contrast—and is decidedly worse—is the amazing doublespeak in which this mantra is declined, the words everyone uses to pat themselves on the back: *social commitment, human dimension, global conscience, paradigm shift* . . .

Just as Marxist imagery used to depict capitalists with top hats and potbellies, greedily sucking the workers' blood, today we tend to imagine the superrich and superpowerful who gather at Davos as cynics, like the traders who, in response to Occupy Chicago, posted signs in the windows of their office building proclaiming

WE ARE THE 1 PERCENT. But those small-time cynics were naive, whereas the bigwigs you rub shoulders with in Davos don't seem cynical at all. They seem sincerely convinced of the benefits they bring to the world, sincerely convinced that their financial and philanthropic engineering (to hear them talk, it's the same thing) is the only way to smoothly negotiate the famous paradigm shift otherwise known as the onset of the golden age. Right from the first day we were surprised by the new age aura that hovers over this jamboree of alpha males in gray suits. On the second, it becomes overpowering, and on the third, you can't bear it anymore, you choke in this cloud of discourse and slogans taken right out of personal-development books and positive-thinking manuals. We didn't need to come all this way to understand that optimism is easier to practice for the happy few than for the down-and-out, but its consistent use, its disconnection from all ordinary experience, is exaggerated to such an extent here that even the most moderate observer can't help oscillating between revolutionary indignation, if he's an idealist, and the blackest sarcasm, if he's a misanthrope. In Davos you quickly feel that you know what Kafka meant when he wrote, "We writers deal with the negative," and what inspired such writers as Céline and Cioran. Together with all the enemies of what the novelist Philippe Muray called the Empire of the Good, one wants to laugh aloud at the endless stream of infatuated, overbilled statements inviting those present to "improve the state of the world," "expect the unexpected," "face the talent challenge," or, our favorite, "enter the human age." Yes, that's right: thanks to Davos we can enter the human age! And about time!

5

When we say things like that to Felix, who loves Davos, he laughs and says we're hopelessly middle class. First of all, he says, most of these people we're happy to criticize without lifting a finger are *really* moving their asses, *really* doing useful things for the planet. And second, we're barking up the wrong tree. As far as Westerners are concerned (it's still Felix talking), what's happening today is a crisis, if not a disaster. But for the emerging countries it's a different story altogether: our disasters are their triumphs. Or to put it more crudely: if two Europeans or Americans go broke at the same time as five Chinese or East Indians put poverty behind them, well, then that's not so bad. The only problem is that it doesn't suit us. We were the rich, they were the poor, that's now changing, and if Davos is fascinating, it's because you can see this change taking place, almost like in a laboratory. The big stars are no longer the bosses of France's top forty listed companies, nor the American bankers, nor even the Western leaders. As a rule, they're no longer even white, but Chinese, Indian, Indonesian, African even. Their economies are growing fast, their banks are robust, and this Forum that you view (Felix continues) as the bastion of an oligarchy that's both sated and under fire is in fact the cutting edge of what was formerly known as Third Worldism. You're the ones who're fainthearted and backward-looking; your look of fear when you read your cherished *Dissent* magazine is nothing but a frozen grimace of panic because your countries are becoming the new Third World. Your paltry savings will vanish, and if there is a new revolution, it won't be that of the 99 percent of normal Westerners—among whom you smugly count yourself—against the 1 percent of wealthy Westerners, who are nothing more than a fantasy, but that of the former wretched of the earth against their ex–colonial masters, that is to say you.

It's a strong argument, you have to admit. Although Felix wasn't able to introduce us to a Chinese mover and shaker to back it up—almost none were at Davos this year because the Forum took place right in the middle of the Chinese New Year—he did present us to a distinguished Indian minister and, strangely, to the lobbyist and ex-mistress of the former foreign minister Roland

Dumas, Christine Deviers-Joncour, who apparently fascinates
Felix. By contrast, invited by Christophe de Margerie, the CEO
of the oil company Total—about whom we'll soon have more to
say—we attended a truly edifying dinner on the theme "opportunities for Africa." The half dozen prime ministers and heads
of state identified themselves in their speeches less as Nigeri-
ans, Tanzanians, Guineans, or Kenyans than as Africans. They
stressed that Africa, viewed not country by country but as a
whole, has an average growth of 6 percent per year and can do
still better than that. They didn't shy away from reminding those
present with cutting irony of all the moral lessons that the IMF,
Americans, and Europeans had inflicted on them for their debt.
Subtext: You look pretty silly now. This sort of sharp, incisive
optimism is of a very different tenor than all the globalized positive thinking. For those of us who have lazily become used to
weeping over Africa—seen as a foyer of eternal and irremediable
tragedy, misery, AIDS, and bloody tribal wars—it makes a strange
impression to hear Christophe de Margerie, who after all knows
what he's talking about, announce matter-of-factly that the con-
tinent of the twenty-first century will be none other than Africa.
Two points for Felix, and a stinging rebuke for our critique of the
Forum.

6

The fifth-largest oil company in the world, the company with the
highest market capitalization in the eurozone, present in 130 countries, many of which are not models of democracy, the oil-and-
gas company Total inspires at the very least the most vivid—and
justified—distrust among ecologists and human rights advocates.
But when they meet its CEO, even the fiercest critics generally
come away with sparkles in their eyes. With his bushy mus-

tache, his frank way of speaking, and his cheeky sense of humor, Christophe de Margerie is one of a kind in the stuffy world of France's top managers. Hélène met him as a journalist; he liked her from the start and the feeling was mutual, so one night after he's finished the marathon of meetings that makes up his daily grind, we do the rounds of the after-parties in the company of this top boss. Felix is delighted. Dreaming of selling him his services, Felix flirts with him openly, and Margerie doesn't do anything to stop him, observing Felix with a wry smile the way, in the westerns, John Wayne might look at an impetuous young cowboy who he can see is made of the right stuff. We can tell the Total boss is intrigued, amused, amazed even by the perk of this young man who has too many suits, too much ambition, too many friends, too much charm, too much of everything, and who, arriving impromptu at the most closed events with seven uninvited gonzos in tow, manages willy-nilly to get the whole unpresentable gang inside. Supreme victory, Felix even manages to convince the bouncers that they should let in Margerie, who, clearly delighted with himself, admits that he doesn't have an invitation either. In fact, he's got nothing in his hands and nothing in his pockets. It's the philosophy of the powerful, and when we show our surprise that someone as important as him doesn't even have a cell phone (or, rather, has a crummy little Nokia that he only uses to call his chauffeur), Felix kindly tells us that's how you can recognize the *truly* important people: if they had a cell phone, or worse, if they could read their e-mail on it, it would never stop, so this function is delegated to a subordinate. That said, in the evening Margerie goes around without his subordinate, just as he goes around in three feet of snow in his blazer and tassel loafers without a coat or parka, his walrus mustache blowing in the wind. Sometimes he follows us, more often we follow him, and with one thing leading to another we end up at a Russian after-hours party.

Russia and Davos go back a long way. The Forum took off with the fall of the Berlin Wall, and the stars of the 1990s were the more or less scrupulous artisans of the transition to the market economy in the East. The party's just coming to an end when we arrive. It looks to be standard Russian fare, with iced vodka, beautiful women, and slightly nouveau riche pomp. But things become more surprising when we follow Christophe de Margerie into the cramped back room of this Swiss chalet, where three guys are noshing down pickled herring. They're the conductor Valery Gergiev; the CEO of Sberbank, Russia's largest bank, Herman Gref; and former finance minister Alexei Kudrin. We recognize Gergiev: one of the best living conductors, if not the best. We're familiar with his handsome, slightly banged-up mug—he looks like a cross between a genius and a road bandit—and discover that like Rostropovich before him, he comes to Davos "to see his buddies." He's leaving at dawn to conduct a concert in Milan, but he likes it so much here that he'll be back the next day. Instinctively we want to class the other two as oligarchs. But upon inquiry, we find out they're historic members of the group of Saint Petersburg liberals who've surrounded Putin since he took office. Real power brokers, and at least one of them is reputed to be honest. Revived by the arrival of Margerie, who knows the three well, the conversation is relaxed but soon takes on an allusive, cryptic tone that goes right over our heads. All we can gather is that it's about natural gas, that things will be taken care of but that heads are going to roll, and that the stakes aren't exactly low. Suddenly we say to ourselves that this is the real Davos, the Davos of the masters of the world—not the grand, noble discourses of the Congress Center, nor the hasty, waffled interviews, nor even the ultraprivate parties thrown by Google or *The New York Times*, but this backroom horse-trading between the high and mighty where a word suffices to get your point across. This is what some of the Forum's legendary negotiations must have been like; for example, when George Soros persuaded Berezovsky and the other oligarchs that

Yeltsin had to be reelected if they didn't want the Communists
to come back and confiscate the cake they hadn't finished div-
vying up among themselves. In a flash, with a burst of laughter
drowned in vodka, another scene superposes itself on this one.
What this table loaded with food and bottles, these guys in shirt-
sleeves with mocking faces—so different from the Americans'
smooth expressions—remind us of most is the immortal kitchen
scene in the 1960s classic *Monsieur Gangster*.

7

Radical change of scenery. We're in a little two-star hotel not far
from the lifts. There are no Mercedes or Audis with tinted windows in the parking lot, no chauffeurs waiting in the entrance.
Scribbled in chalk on a blackboard, like the daily menu in a road-
side restaurant, are the words PUBLIC EYE AWARDS, with an ar-
row pointing in the direction of the not exactly plush room where
the event is taking place, attended by thirty or so loyal followers,
including a young woman in a Peruvian beanie carrying her baby
in a sling. When we go inside, however, none other than Joseph
Stiglitz, Nobel Prize laureate and former chief economist at the
World Bank, is explaining what the Public Eye Awards are: prizes
given out, get this, by Greenpeace and several other antiglobalist
organizations, to the companies that do the most harm, cause
the worst ecological damage, and care the least about the public interest. These companies, Stiglitz says, are the rotten fruit
of a sick tree—capitalism driven mad over the past thirty years
by deregulation—and they well represent the dominant state of
mind at the Forum. Eighty-eight thousand Internet users chose
the five short-listed companies. The prize goes to the Barclays
banking group for its food-speculation activities: in the second
quarter of 2010 alone, it put 44 million people below the poverty

line by artificially raising food prices. Stiglitz doesn't say how Barclays reacted to the award, or if it reacted at all. We thought about tracking down one of its top managers and asking why no one from the company showed up to receive this flattering distinction, but not everyone can be Michael Moore: as good as the scene could have been, it never took place.

What is nevertheless amusing about all of this, first of all, is that this nose-thumbing on the margins of the Forum is presided over by an economist who is, let's not forget, a regular and immensely respected guest of the Forum, where he'll speak this year as well. And second, that when you talk about these awards with participants at the Forum—once you've explained to them what they are, that is, because in general they don't know—they all say it's an excellent initiative, because of course there are abuses and they must be corrected: nobody's perfect, neither the companies nor even capitalism. And how should these abuses be corrected? Stiglitz says with government regulations on the one hand, far more government regulations, and on the other, more corporate responsibility, in other words self-regulation. Regarding the first point, everyone pulls a face: everyone knows regulation imposed from outside never works, the states don't know what's good for the economy, they overload it with constraints and taxes. Self-regulation, on the other hand, yes, please! Everyone's in favor of self-regulation, which can't do any harm and has the big advantage of boiling down to virtuous statements of principle such as the one—well, what do you know—by Bob Diamond, the president of Barclays, who never stops solemnly proclaiming that the banks must act like "model citizens"—and who even as we write has just illustrated this policy by lowering the bonuses received by his employees by 30 percent, while remaining demurely silent on what will happen with his own, which is so big that it has all of England up in arms.

One of the strengths of the Forum, we write without irony, is that it is open to what its opponents have to say and offers them a platform for discussion. The problem is that as a consequence it believes it has no opponents, or that its opponents are partners in disguise who have not yet caught on to this reality—but as far as the Forum is concerned, that can be fixed, it would like nothing better. And to that extent the system is truly meritocratic: if you adhere to it, and even better if you're talented, you're welcome. That said, an opponent such as Stiglitz is also one of the clan, at the highest level, and his position is remarkable because he does what he can to reconcile the two sides. But all you have to do is walk the hundred yards from the hotel to where the Occupy Davos movement has set up its igloos and yurts to see what the grassroots opponents are like, and how they're treated. What they look like is no surprise: twenty or so young people, Swiss socialists for the most part, courageously freezing their butts off handing out tracts that aren't revolutionary in the least. Basically they say the same reasonable things that Stiglitz—and what's more our presidential candidates, whether they believe them or not—says: down with finance, our lives are worth more than your profits, etc. For the past few years the police—with whom these opponents have sometimes had violent clashes—have stopped these protesters from staying at the ski resort and confined them to the valley floor. This year the municipality let them use this parking lot, and the mayor, in a gesture of Swiss tolerance, even insisted on assembling the press and laying the first ice block for the igloos. Since the protesters fault the Forum of the masters of the world for its closed, secretive, and hence antidemocratic stance, the Great Manitou Klaus Schwab, the man who meditates every morning, this year proposed to organize a roundtable discussion together with their representatives. The offer caught them off guard, and the resulting negotiations were one of the minor soap operas of the 2012 edition of the Forum, although they caused less of a stir than the visit by Mick Jagger, who had, rumor had it,

come, then gone, stayed just a night, then just two nights, the idea
behind these different accounts being apparently that he was afraid
his showing up in Davos would suggest to his loyal fans that he
had gone over, lock, stock, and barrel—him, Mick Jagger!—to
the side of the rich, the old, and the big of this world. The young
people at Occupy Davos don't have the same image problem, but
they have others, and after long powwows in their yurts they let it
be known that, no, they would not allow themselves to be paraded
around like circus animals in a sanctuary otherwise dedicated to
excluding them. If Klaus Schwab wanted to talk with them, they
said, he could meet them on neutral ground: not necessarily in
one of their igloos—they admitted that wouldn't be fitting—but
in a bar. To which Klaus Schwab answered that was going too far,
maybe another time, but in the middle of the Forum he had other
things to do.

8

Tonight is Felix's last night in Davos. He's got to leave ahead of
time to meet one of his most cherished clients, Georgian president Mikheil Saakashvili, to host a talk with him in a day's time
before an audience of businessmen near Lake Tahoe in California.
To get there Felix has to take a ten-hour flight from Zurich to San
Francisco and then a helicopter, meaning he has to leave before
dawn. He won't go to bed before that, which means we won't
either, and neither will Christophe de Margerie, who'll spend the
night hopping from hotel bar to hotel bar with us, remaking the
world and shooting the breeze. That's the right expression for
it, and it's no doubt one of the reasons why the Total boss is so
popular in Africa and the Arab world. We take our time, don't
go straight to the point, and often there is no point. We talk for
the pleasure of talking, to learn more about the person across

from us, and—something rare in this milieu—without that person necessarily being useful to us. There's no shortage of great communicators on his planet who'll look you in the eye and tell you that what sets them apart in life is that they love people, and already they're looking over your shoulder to see if anyone more important is around to whom they can tell the same thing. It's not our intention to blow Margerie's horn here, but one of the people in our gang was Felix's childhood friend Samuel, who as we said was going through a difficult time, earning his money translating detective novels, whereas in our view he should have been writing them himself. Although he's gruff as can be, he's simply a terrific guy, but don't count on him to let you know. To put it mildly, by Davos standards a guy such as that carries zero weight, even less than the young ideologists in their igloos. They at least challenge the system, and protesters make the best converts, whereas Samuel just couldn't care less and prefers to keep to himself and reread the books of Swiss travel writer Nicolas Bouvier. Nonetheless Margerie spent the better part of this long night shooting the breeze with him, ordering glasses of whiskey at regular intervals, interrupting the conversation from time to time to exchange a few words with the chairman and CEO of the oil giant Saudi Aramco—"Nine million barrels a day! I'm a dwarf beside that guy!" Margerie jokes—then returning to the conversation on, one imagines, life, love, and death with this asocial young guy who only represents himself, and badly at that. Apart from his ability to pay attention to others, no matter how far removed from his own circles they may be, the most astonishing thing about Margerie is his stamina. He's on the job at 8:00 a.m. for back-to-back meetings with men of his caliber, his eyes bright and his voice clear, as tough in business as he is kind in his manners, yet when we say goodnight at 4:00 a.m., happy to hit the sack, he slips in that he won't go to sleep right away. No, once he gets back to his room, he needs at least another hour, hour and a half, to watch television, look at the sky, flip though some files, dream, do nothing, but without going to bed. We wondered if the motor behind his almost frightening activity, curiosity, and availability wasn't a huge pool of melancholy. Aided by our nighttime lack of inhibition, we even asked him. He avoided the question, didn't say yes or no: as open as this man is, that door remains closed.

On this farewell evening, someone drew our attention to the pervasive use of the word *beyond* in Davos. The company of the guy who makes the cocktails is called Beyond Liquids. The slogan of Felix's company, we tease, is Beyond Influence. We even have the business card of someone in an unspecified activity who uses the über-Davosian catchphrase Beyond Global (yes, that's right: Beyond Global). Margerie tells the story of his major rival BP, which decided one fine day that it was no longer so chic for BP to stand for British Petroleum, and that from then on it would stand for Beyond Petroleum. The idea of an oil company that wants to be "beyond petroleum" has Margerie in stitches, because for him his job is finding, extracting, and selling oil: black, dirty, expensive, harmful, but extremely useful oil, and you don't gain a thing by pretending it's orange-blossom water—which is more or less everyone's small sin in Davos, no matter what line the person is in. As for us, without yet knowing what other articles will appear together with ours in this special issue on the financial crisis, we have no doubt that they'll deal with people in Greece, Spain, or Portugal who are not at all beyond unemployment, beyond debt, and beyond the inextricable hassles of life. No doubt all ruling classes, in all ages, have never had the slightest idea—or at best only an abstract, statistical idea—of what the people are really going through. No doubt also all of us, whatever our role in society, would do well to search our souls on this point. Be that as it may, in Davos they really are a little too "beyond."

9

To be alone on the last day in the silent chalet, surrounded by snow, makes a strange impression on us. It's as if a tornado had passed through: Tornado Felix, with his incessant flurry of activity, his frenetic socializing, but also his true sense of friendship, his moments of doubt and solemnity, his way of filling life with rhythm and excitement. Without him we feel a little like orphans, and since we don't have a dozen meetings but just one in the late afternoon, it's almost as if we're on vacation, so we decide to use the day to go on a literary pilgrimage and have tea at Hotel Schatzalp, practically the sole backdrop for Thomas Mann's *Magic Mountain*.

As the gondola takes us up into the heights, the tumult of the Forum—which since it's the last day has already dropped a notch—grows quieter, and when we get to the top, it's like a miracle. We knew that the sanatorium where the novel takes place was turned into a luxury hotel in the 1950s, and we imagined it would be luxuriously nouveau riche. But not at all: it's exactly how we dreamed it would be. Comfortable, more than comfortable, but austere, silent, with no background music or guys yelling into their cell phones. The staff are outstanding, and considerate in an almost ghostlike way, practically gliding over the parquet floors. All you can hear is the wind outside, and the soothing, distant rumble of the grooming machines. You'd think you could even hear the snowflakes falling. Like the young Hans Castorp, Thomas Mann's hero, one can well imagine leaving the hubbub of the world below for a couple of days on the pretext of visiting a tubercular cousin, then putting off the moment of departure from week to week, letting oneself be insidiously won over by the charms of this idle, quilted, languid life that sickness allows you if you have the means, and staying on for a year, two years, three years, among those who dwell on high, gradually losing any reason to go back down. If we were truly rich—a dream that didn't so much as cross our minds among the superrich at the Forum—we'd take up lodgings yearly in this haven of peace and luxury, because this is true luxury, we philosophize, not what the people who fly in and out in their helicopters—and who seem, thank God, to ignore this marvelous place—buy with their stock options between two deals.

In this calm mood—because no matter how you feel about it, you still have to go back down—we arrive at our meeting with Muhammad Yunus, inventor of microcredit, Nobel Peace Prize laureate, and Davos guru. He's a little guy with a big smile who looks a bit like a more handsome version of Yoda in *Star Wars*. Our interview doesn't depart from the official format—strictly timed, with assistants who're as good-natured as they are steel willed—yet, perhaps helped by the spirit of the magic mountain, it seems to us that with Yunus something happens, that we're finally told something. But what? What does Yunus say? In essence that all of the conditions for a major, global, irremediable catastrophe have been met, but that in his view we'll elude it because, not having the choice, we'll become better. We'll throw off the tyranny of our egos and all that goes with it: fear, greed, competition. We'll even—maybe not us but our children—find it exciting and amusing, with the help of the Internet, to invent the instruments of this liberation. In one or two generations our frenetic, desperate, money-obsessed world will have become completely incomprehensible for our children's children: That's how they lived, really? And, Yunus concludes, it's a sign that the first step has been taken when, not knowing which way to turn, the decision makers at Davos finally started listening to a guy such as him, who says just the opposite of what they think and whom they have every reason to consider a harmless visionary. Fine. Nevertheless we have to admit that, charm aside, as we listen to him we're reminded of a yoga master we know, who ends his sessions with a little prayer asking that the world be governed by just men, that rain fall when the crops need it, and that no undue suffering be inflicted on anyone. Such invocations make us smile inwardly; we take them as the price to pay for high-quality teaching. And they're not all hot air: the yoga master has many exceptional—and very real—accomplishments under his belt. The same goes for Yunus. The opposite of a gentle dreamer, he's a man of action who invented a viable economic instrument, the microcredit system. Okay, it's since been somewhat debased and mercantilized, and he's distanced himself—or was distanced—from it to the point of no longer wanting to talk about it. But he never stops coming up with other ideas, and there's no telling if he's not on the cutting edge of some future development. So we can smile and shrug our shoulders all we want, but we have to wonder if we wouldn't have smiled and shrugged our shoulders exactly the same way if we'd been listening to Gandhi. And if, since the world as viewed and managed by the self-proclaimed realists doesn't work, it's not time to give the firmly grounded utopians a chance.

10

We started to wander home slowly along the main street of the resort, which was now almost empty. Night had fallen, the snow crunched under our feet. We were silent, both of us thinking that what we'd just heard was perhaps the truth, the noble truth mimicked by mystico-capitalist inanities on the huge posters that were already being taken down. From the window of a gallery someone called out to us: a nice young guy we'd crossed paths with the night before. "We're having a last cocktail for the road; after that they're closing up. You want to join us?" We went inside; the cocktails were courtesy of a company dedicated to no end of philanthropic endeavors. The buffet was excellent, and our new friend explained to us that after helping Ukrainian oligarch Victor Pinchuk in his charitable activities, he now worked, well, well, for Yunus. "Always thinking about doing positive things makes life positive," he explained to us. "I'm really lucky to be able to do what I do." He wasn't at all ridiculous in saying this, but when a pretty young woman who also works for Yunus arrived—like the two old friends, the two youthful charity-business veterans, that they were—they had a good laugh over the misfortune that had recently befallen them at Zurich Airport, where they'd both managed to lose works by Damien Hirst they'd just bought.

Let's be honest: *real* works by Damien Hirst cost millions, and it would be tempting for the beauty of the story to suggest that it was just such a loss that they were resigning themselves to so good-naturedly. But nothing of the sort: affordable Damien Hirst–derived products, like Salvador Dalí prints in bygone days, now flood the market of art lovers happy to possess something signed by a famous name, even if the signature is done by an assistant. So no huge deal. Nevertheless, Damien Hirst is the artistic transposition of a financier's dream, the leverage effect pushed to its paroxysm: minimum investment (in talent and integrity, we write without wanting to offend anyone), maximum return. An absolute jackpot. It only makes sense that he's the favorite artist of these young people who are so nice, so positive, so sincerely convinced that what is good for their bank account is also good for suffering mankind. As Freud said about the neurosis of one of his patients, "It's so well organized that it's a joy to observe."

Published in *XXI*, spring 2012

Generation Bolotnaïa

1

Toward the middle of the 1990s, Alex wanted to be a psychoanalyst, a profession still in its infancy in Russia. His career took a turn for the unexpected when the fender of his crummy little car nicked that of a Mercedes with tinted windows. The two thugs who got out let him know unceremoniously that the scratch would cost him. As he couldn't pay, they took him along with them. Believing that his last hour had come, Alex tried to engage them in conversation, not so much to talk to them as, more cleverly, to get them to talk. He insists he doesn't know how it happened, but after half an hour one of the two was telling cruel stories from his childhood and bawling his eyes out. The story got back to the boss, a big Uzbek mafioso. Several of the boss's friends had just been killed, and he himself was becoming aware of how precarious life can be; you could say he had a case of the blues, which is how Alex, like in *The Sopranos*, became a psychoanalyst for the Mafia. The story's old, but I'm telling it because, based on his expertise, Alex told me what he believed could be expected from the upcoming presidential elections: nothing. Because politics (it's Alex talking) has no importance in Russia, where real power is in the hands of the Mafias. They act like shareholders who have no problem replacing a CEO with someone a little more presentable, a little more democratic in appearance, the day the CEO stops being popular. So the problem isn't Putin at all, Alex says: of course he'll be reelected, and of course if dissatisfaction grows, he'll be ousted in favor of another straw man, and everything will continue as before. You can travel, say more or less what you want, earn money, steal money, but not participate in governing your country: that's none of your business. For that to change it would take a true revolution, something nobody wants. Which is why Alex, despite having been a hero on the barricades of 1991, doesn't have the least inclination to go demonstrate beside the Akunins, Ulitskayas, Bykovs, Parkhomenkos, and all the other swollen-headed VIPs whom the Western commentators so love and whom the term *champagne liberals* would suit to a T if it weren't already taken. No, on Sunday he prefers to go play tennis.

It was the first day of my visit to Russia, and just after meeting Alex I went to visit Eduard Limonov. We had to celebrate the success of the book I'd written about him; what's more, it's always interesting to hear what he has to say: you can be sure the last thing you'll be treated to is double-talk. What distinguishes Limonov from Alex is that while Limonov still dreams of revolution, Alex doesn't at all. But they do see eye to eye in their disdain for the "bourgeois leaders," as Limonov calls them. He tells me that last fall—when President Medvedev and Prime Minister Putin swapped places, followed by legislative elections that were clearly rigged—there was a popular outcry, but this outcry was hijacked and sapped of content by the group of intellectuals who started to make themselves heard the day it became clear that it was no longer dangerous to do so, and who were soon joined by opportunist politicians, all of whom then left on long winter vacations from December 24 to February 4: the blogger Navalny to Mexico and the others to the beach. In what Limonov says it's hard not to hear the bitterness of the pioneer who was always the first to do something when it took real guts, when you got chucked in jail— and not for a couple of hours but for years—and who now sees his place being taken by people who've run about zero risk. But what he also notes is that two months ago everyone thought he was wide of the mark, while today a lot of people say he was right in maintaining that a real opportunity had opened up, not for a revolution but for effective action, a chance to exert pressure on the authorities and obtain demands—electoral reforms, the liberation of political prisoners—but that the opposition wasn't able take advantage of it. A door opened, then closed, and things went back to how they were before. I'll hear that a lot.

2

Car demonstrations are specifically Russian. For an obvious reason: you freeze less in your car than on foot, but also because average Russians spend a lot of time in their cars, stuck in huge traffic jams and sometimes even wearing diapers to relieve their bladders. One of the signs of the arrogance of the rich and powerful that normal people have the hardest time with is when they clamp flashing blue lights on the roofs of their cars to avoid such mutual submission. For the past two or three years more and more websites have sprung up denouncing violations of the Highway Code by people who have no good reason to have a blue light on their car, as well as the huge black Mercedes sedans that hit elderly people or children and then speed off without any further ado, and whose drivers, or their bosses, get off scot-free. More than any other, this topic unites popular discontent, and ever since a certain Pyotr Shkumatov mockingly stuck a blue plastic bucket to the roof of his car, "little blue bucket" demonstrations have taken off and stirred up the opposition. That's how, my fingers numb with cold, I found myself unrolling duct tape together with a journalist friend to attach one of these buckets to the Audi of Ilya Ponomarev, member of the Russian State Duma from Novosibirsk. I suppose Limonov would make cruel fun of Ponomarev and call him a useful idiot: he's a member of Spravedlivaya Rossiya—A Just Russia—which many consider a bogus opposition party instrumentalized by the Kremlin. But once you start playing that game, no political formation is above suspicion—or rather only one is, namely Gennady Zyuganov's Communist Party. But even if you want nothing better than to throw a wrench into Putin's works, you still have to have a tough stomach to vote for the Communists in Russia. Ponomarev, to resume, is a cheerful, warmhearted young man with a great head on his shoulders, and the six of us crammed into his car had a great time driving on Moscow's inner ring road while honking and lowering our windows despite the cold to exchange encouraging gestures with the occupants of the other cars equipped, like ours, with blue buckets or white ribbons, which have become the symbol of those opposed to Putin, who pretended to believe that the opposition was brandishing condoms. It was like a wedding procession: people of all ages had taken up positions on the sidewalks to applaud the passage of the white-ribboned cars. Some who didn't have ribbons waved balloons or plastic bags, the main thing being that whatever they waved should be white. Ponomarev was telephoning right and left to find out how many people were taking part: three thousand cars according to the organizers, three hundred according to the police. Such a discrepancy is classic, but from inside one of the cars it was impossible to get any idea at all, and even three thousand cars don't make a particularly big procession on a road such as that. Such figures are the stuff of endless one-upmanship: every time the opposition prides itself for having gathered, say, ten thousand people, Putin's party, United Russia, makes a point of gathering one hundred thousand an hour later. Another challenge is getting the permit: you have to say how many people will take part and what route you want to follow. All of that has to be negotiated with the authorities, and those who have a reputation for being good at such negotiations, such as Boris Nemtsov, former deputy prime minister under Yeltsin, are then suspected of having been compromised, or even of betraying the opposition. That's what Limonov accuses him of: instead of running the risk of clashing with the government forces and holding a demonstration near the Kremlin, Nemtsov chose a place that posed no threat to the authorities and is appropriately named Bolotnaïa—the swamp. Throughout my stay, one of my main occupations was following the rumors on the Internet announcing demonstrations and counterdemonstrations practically every day, which not many people at all seemed to know about. The League of Voters (a group formed by the "bourgeois leaders" that Limonov so loves to decry) planned a human chain along the Garden Ring road for the Sunday before the first round of the presidential elections, calculating that thirty-four thousand people would have to take part. A website was opened where you could register and choose your spot; a week before it's due to take place, twelve hundred have signed up. My return flight was booked for just this Sunday; I've decided to postpone it.

3

Moscow's Artplay complex consists of old warehouses transformed into restaurants, art galleries, and architects' offices, and everyone who's anyone in the opposition is squeezed into an exhibition celebrating the creativity of the demonstrators since December: posters, emblazoned T-shirts, carnival disguises, all centering around the theme "Putin must go." Some are quite amusing; still, one hardly knows what to make of the speed with which this new culture of rebellion has become contemporary art, and one is forced to admit that the problem with this Muscovite opposition is its incorrigible trendiness. You'd think you were at a cocktail party where everyone's a journalist, an artist, or a performer: everyone has his or her own website or blog, to say nothing of a Facebook page. The authorities call these young people the "hamsters of the Internet." The young people call themselves "hipsters" (pronounced *gamsters* and *gipsters*, respectively, because an aspirated *h* becomes a *g* in Russian, in the same way they call Hitler *Gitler*). You have to smile when Putin insists that these people are foreign infiltrators and are all paid by the CIA; nevertheless you also have to admit that they represent only an infinitesimal minority of the population, and that they bear no relation to the real Russia. Although no one doubts that this "real Russia" will win the elections—and that the vote won't even need to be rigged—I didn't run across it during this visit. I simply don't know anyone who claims to be part of it, and it's depressing to go to demonstrations alone, especially when it's freezing outside. But these demonstrations do take place, and they're massive, although what you see on the Internet is perplexing. Take the big rally in Luzhniki Stadium, which 130,000 people attended, according to the organizers and the police, who agree for once. Since the permit only specified 100,000, the authorities apologized for having assembled too many people and—in an unhabitual show of respect for the law—even paid the fine of two thousand rubles, or a little less than seventy dollars. Although he's frugal with his appearances, Putin came in person. He harangued the crowd on the topic, precisely, of the real Russia, and the threats posed by those who don't love it. "Do you love Russia?"

The crowd shouts back, "Yes!"

"Are you ready to defend it?"

"Yes!"

All of this is well and good, but when journalists question the people as they leave the stadium, many are wary and steal away; some admit they were paid to come or even pressured into it. The zeal of those who affirm the contrary is suspicious, such as that of the guy with a morose look on his face carrying the sign I'M HERE OF MY OWN FREE WILL. This crowd may be the real Russia, but it looks above all like the Soviet Union. Back then people didn't demonstrate, they marched. Today one Russia still marches, and another demonstrates. The one that marches drags its feet more or less; the one that demonstrates does it because it believes in what it's doing, because it wants to, because it's fun. No matter how many are on each side, as long as that's the case, the second has already won.

4

A film called *Twilight Portrait* just came out in France, and in my view it's the best Russian film in a long time. Since the plotline takes some unexpected twists, I won't give the game away and will just say that it's about a middle-class young woman whose friends, when they drink toasts to her on her birthday, say she's content in every way: she has a nice husband who's not a drunk and earns a good living, an interesting job, an apartment in the center of town. In a nutshell, life is on her side. Until the day she's picked up by a police patrol, raped, and left on the side of the road—and can count herself lucky that she wasn't beaten up, too. She hangs around the place where it happened, recognizes one of the rapists, and instead of taking her revenge . . . I'll stop there, please go see the film, but I can say this: it's universal because it's a love story, but it's also extremely Russian. It puts a new spin on the old antagonism between Westernists and Slavophiles that runs through the entire nineteenth century and all the great Russian novels. On the one hand a rising middle class wants to live, and by that very fact does live, the way they do in Paris or London: young people who use Facebook and type away on their laptops in big-city Starbucks cafés. On the other, there's the Russia of the small towns and villages: backward, alcoholic, brutal, and grubby—but, say the Slavophiles, with soul on its side. The heroine of *Twilight Portrait* embodies the first Russia, the rapist cop the second, and the film undogmatically traces a path between the two. In political terms, the transposition seems to go without saying: the rising middle class owes its growing wealth, comfort, and liberty to Putin, all the while protesting against him; the backward provinces, by contrast, remain faithful to him although they clearly have more reason to complain.

Twilight Portrait was made with little money and a lot of talent by two young women: director Angelina Nikonova, and screenwriter and lead actress Olga Dykhovichnaya. I'd met them briefly in Paris, and when I arrived in Moscow, Olga invited me for dinner at her place. First surprise: her place isn't a little apartment like the ones most of the Russians I know live in, but a magnificent dacha you get to along Rublyovskoe Highway, which accesses the poshest neighborhoods in the west of Moscow and has become the symbol of the flashing-blue-light culture. In these houses, hidden behind high walls and protected by private militias, live the rich and the powerful. Dear Reader, if, like me, you've seen the film and succumbed to Olga's charm, don't be disappointed. There is no ostentation in her, no new-Russian bad taste. As in her person, everything in her house is grace and simplicity. This grace and this simplicity, however, are not those of the middle class the film portrays, but of the elite, and I suddenly realize that this elite has not changed much since Soviet times. There must have been dinner parties just like this one, gathering exquisitely civilized, multilingual guests, interspersed with toasts, stints in the sauna that you access by crossing the snow-covered garden, and rhapsodic songs sung by a beautiful

Georgian woman accompanying herself on the guitar, in dachas just like Olga's, in the days when Nikita Mikhalkov wasn't the dreadful despot he's now become, but a charming and talented young director. When I broach the subject of politics, no one tries to avoid it. On the contrary, everyone loves talking about it. Of course they're all against Putin, but against him the way the cultural elite were against Brezhnev forty years ago. They said bad things about him, and the regime, and the Gulag; nevertheless when you were part of the cultural *nomenklatura* under Brezhnev, you lived like a king; you made the movies you wanted and had no reason to want things to change. So you can laugh—and many do—at ads showing "Russia without Putin" (long lines in front of empty stores, haggard crowds in devastated streets, civil war), but when Putin says, in essence, "The foreign infiltrators wish us nothing better than an Arab spring. But do you want an Arab spring? Do you want Russia to become like Egypt? Or Libya?," everyone apart from a couple of fanatics such as Limonov will answer: No, that's not what we want. We're happy to take part in demonstrations because it's new and exciting to be able to do it. We would love to have cleaner elections because it's a complete embarrassment to have the moral standing of a banana republic. We'd be delighted to have someone a little younger and more open than Putin because it's like with *Rambo*: episodes one and two are okay, but after that you get the feeling it's all rehashed. But we only want all of that if we can avoid tossing out the baby with the bathwater. Putin talks above all of stability, and stability is a must.

5

The Putinists are nowhere to be found. I thought I'd meet some when I left the big city and headed out into the provinces, bastion of the real Russia, but I have to admit that going to see Zakhar

Prilepin in Nizhny Novgorod wasn't the best way of going about it. Not yet forty, Prilepin is respected at home and abroad as one of the best Russian writers of his generation. He's not a product of the Moscow elite, but a guy from the provinces who was a soldier in Chechnya, then an active member of the National Bolshevik Party, Limonov's skinheads. Prilepin still has a shaved head, for that matter. He wears Doc Martens and has expressive blue eyes, and something is extremely touching in how he tries to reconcile his situation as a famous author who's invited abroad and sought out by important people, and his allegiance to the world of the guys he grew up with, and about whom he still writes: not hipsters, but working types who've been left by the wayside. They meet up with Prilepin in groups of three or four, together with a gentle and cultivated guy who likes to read the leftist author Alain Badiou and the right-wing author Julius Evola, and who was for a long time the leader of the local chapter of the National Bolshevik Party, and an old democrat who did time for denouncing the atrocities committed by the Russian army in Chechnya. Prilepin, who was in the Russian army and who went to hell and back with it, remembers that on his return from the front he thought the old democrat was a traitor and even toyed with the idea of killing him. But today, almost fifteen years later, they're the best of friends and agree completely in their analysis of the political situation. It's a strange election, they say, because there's no one you can vote for. There's an enemy everyone knows is going to win, and the people running against him are even less appealing than he is: the eternal nationalist clown Zhirinovsky (whose slogan promises simply, "Zhirinovsky—it will get better"); the old Communist Zyuganov (whose slogan is even simpler: "Vote Zyuganov"); and the billionaire Prokhorov, who's less stale than the others and whose fast-track reform program you'd like to go along with if you could be more sure that in pretending to oppose the Kremlin he's not actually supporting it. Such a situation could be off-putting, especially for people such as Prilepin and his friends, who also don't trust the VIPs who supposedly represent civil society. But they're not put off at all. They have no illusions, they make fun of everyone, but at heart they're optimistic, and it's the nice Badiou fan, the ex-leader of the Nizhny Novgorod National Bolsheviks, who says what is in my view the most sensible thing I've heard this whole trip: "No one in this country wants a revolution," this revolutionary concedes. "And no one can seriously call what's happened a revolution. May '68 in France wasn't a revolution either. It was 'events' that profoundly changed society. Sure, after that you had Pompidou in power, and let's say it was okay to have him. No one wanted Daniel Cohn-Bendit to become president of France. No more than the Russians want someone like Navalny as their leader. But fifteen, twenty years after May '68, the values of May '68 won out. The people who made May '68 happen were in charge. And it will be the same in Russia: the people who made December 2011 happen—those who were at Bolotnaïa—will be in charge here in ten years' time, and they have every interest in there being a soft transition." When he says that, you sense that he isn't personally implicated by what he says. He himself will never be in charge, he's not the type. But his friend Zakhar is. As long as Limonov—who trained him as he trained so many people in this country—is still active, Zakhar won't go into politics. But after that . . . President Prilepin? Minister of culture? We clink glasses and laugh; you want to bet?

6

Twenty-eight degrees outside—almost springtime—and the big demonstration on the last Sunday before the elections is a success. We hold hands the whole way around the Garden Ring. At some places the chain is thick with people; at others it thins out and reinforcements are sent in. People are in a good mood, the circle is completed without too much effort, and while the police say in the evening that eleven thousand participated, we say that by and large the expected thirty-four thousand must have turned out. I went with a group of Lacanian psychoanalysts. The Lacanian psychoanalysts in Moscow aren't old and sententious as they are in France. They wear neither bow ties nor herringbone jackets à la François Mitterrand. They, too, are young, enthusiastic, and trendy, typical of what people are starting to call the Bolotnaïa generation, and they fear Putin's repression far less than the edicts of French Lacanian authority Jacques-Alain Miller. Nevertheless, a shiver went through our little group when young Putinists started demonstrating across from us, holding heart-shaped, mass-produced signs with the words PUTIN LOVES YOU.

"Fascists," my friends murmured, getting a thrill out of the scare, and I felt as if I'd been transported back to the demonstrations of May '68. One contrast speaks volumes: the anti-Putinists tend to be in their thirties, they look prosperous and happy, they know each other, kiss each other on the cheek, and exchange news about their friends, while the pro-Putinists are young, often under twenty, wear ill-fitting, grungy black anoraks, and have surly, unattractive, splotchy faces of the kind you see everywhere among soccer fans, and it made me a little uncomfortable when one of my new friends ironically asked one of them, "You come to Moscow often?" All evidence to the contrary, the other guy shouted back that he was from Moscow, but it was clear that he didn't even know where he was, that he and his buddies had been bused in from their villages in the sticks, and that they'd be bused back that night, without even having the time to party it up in the capital. The question put by my friend, a Muscovite going back three generations, an intellectual who speaks fluent French and English and lives in a beautiful apartment, unwittingly betrayed the most classic class disdain: the yuppie looking down on the worker. It's no secret that revolutions are made by the up-and-coming middle classes in their own interest; nevertheless I thought to myself that they could be a little more discreet.

Published in *Le Nouvel Observateur*, March 2012

The Journalist and the Murderer
by Janet Malcolm

This is a story with three layers. The first is a criminal case: in 1970, in North Carolina, the army physician Jeffrey MacDonald is accused of murdering his wife and their two young daughters. The evidence against him is strong, but so is the case in his defense. Did Jeff MacDonald commit these crimes? He alone knows. He claims he's innocent, so either he's the potential victim of a terrible judicial error, or he's both a murderer and a hypocritical monster.

The moral uncertainty resulting from this doubt makes for a good story, and it's here—in the second layer—that Joe McGinniss enters the picture. He's a fiction writer, author of that hapless thing: bestsellers that don't sell. Hoping to break into criminal nonfiction, which since Truman Capote's *In Cold Blood* has become a literary genre in its own right, he contacts MacDonald's lawyers and signs contracts not only with an editor but also with MacDonald himself, who grants him exclusive rights to his story in exchange for a third of the copyrights. In the years that precede the trial, the two men strike up a friendship, watching football on TV, downing beer after beer, grading women who walk by on a scale of 1 to 5. McGinniss says he's convinced MacDonald

is innocent, and when MacDonald is sentenced to life imprisonment, McGinniss writes aggrieved letters as if he were the one
most hurt by this monstrous injustice. Then his book comes out,
and MacDonald is staggered to discover it portrays him as a psy-
chopathic murderer. The drinking buddy who called anyone who
cast the slightest doubt on MacDonald's innocence an imbecile
or an asshole now says he knows with absolute certainty that
MacDonald killed his wife and children. Outraged, MacDonald
decides to sue McGinniss from the depths of his prison for fraud
and breach of contract.

Enter Janet Malcolm, a journalist for *The New Yorker*, in the
second trial—and third layer—of the story. She has good reason
to be interested in the case: she, too, is facing a multimillion-dollar
libel suit, filed by an American psychoanalyst unhappy with her
portrayal of him in her investigative work *In the Freud Archives*.
She decides to follow this trial, which is absolutely unparalleled
because it's no longer a question of whether MacDonald is guilty
or innocent, or of whether what McGinniss wrote about him
is deceitful or libelous, but only of whether McGinniss had the
right to say it after convincing MacDonald that he believed the
exact opposite. In other words, can a journalist who expresses
false sympathy with someone to win his confidence be found guilty
not only on moral but also on legal grounds? Janet Malcolm wrote
two seminal articles about this riveting case, and then in 1990
this book, which is not an essay but a narrative of rare vivacity:
a model of literary reporting that should be studied in journalism schools as well as creative-writing workshops, and that amply
deserves its classification among the one hundred best works of
nonfiction.

Having said that, however, and having heartily recommended
it, I would like to add that something about this brilliant, stimu-
lating work troubles me. Quite simply, I don't agree with the idea
that its first lines put so well: "Every journalist who is not too

stupid or full of himself to notice what is going on knows that what he does is morally indefensible. He is a kind of confidence man, preying on people's vanity, ignorance, or loneliness, gaining their trust and betraying them without remorse. Like the credulous widow who wakes up one day to find the charming young man and all her savings gone, so the consenting subject of a piece of nonfiction writing learns—when the article or book appears—his hard lesson."

This cynical description of the relationship between an author and his subject is true in the case of McGinniss versus MacDonald. What's more, I'm ready to believe that it's often the case. Nevertheless, and at the risk of transforming this review into plea on my own behalf, I would like to say that's not always how things are. And I'm not talking through my hat: for the past fifteen years I've been writing nonfiction books that describe real events and real people, well-known or not, close friends or distant acquaintances. Some of them I've hurt, yes, but I maintain that I did not dupe any of them. Limiting myself to criminal cases, I no more duped Jean-Claude Romand, the hero of *The Adversary*, than Jean-Xavier de Lestrade duped Michael Peterson, the hero of his extraordinary documentary series *The Staircase*, about which you can't help thinking when you read *The Journalist and the Murderer*. In such undertakings it's a big job—even the biggest and most difficult—to establish a relationship that's honest, not just with the subject of the book but also with the reader.

Janet Malcolm quotes an astonishing scene from McGinniss's book. It describes MacDonald and his whole defense team having fun at a birthday party, throwing darts at an enlarged photograph of the prosecuting attorney. McGinniss describes MacDonald shouting in joy when he hits the target and comments self-righteously, "He seemed oblivious to the possibility that, under the circumstances, it might not have been appropriate for him to be propelling a sharp pointed object toward even the photographic representation of a human being." The problem, as witnesses said at the trial, is that McGinniss himself, that evening, also bellowed with laughter while throwing darts at the photo. Is that bad? Of course not. What is bad is describing the scene without saying just that. It's putting yourself in the role of an impartial, horrified witness. It's not knowing that in telling the story you yourself become a character in the story, as much to blame as all the others.

With a surprising degree of masochism that didn't escape criticism—because after all, it's her own profession she's describing—Janet Malcolm puts all her talent into demonstrating that the relationship between an author of nonfiction and her subject is by nature dishonest, that's just the way things are, and it can't be changed. But I think it can: I think that, yes, there is a border, but that this border doesn't run, as some would like to think, between the journalist—hurried, superficial, unscrupulous—and the writer—noble, profound, beset by moral qualms—but between authors who believe they're above the story they're telling and those who accept the uncomfortable idea that they are also bound up in it. An example of the first school: the pitiful and spineless Joe McGinniss. An example of the second: Janet Malcolm herself, who, all the while declaring such honesty impossible, demonstrates it herself from the beginning to the end of her book.

Published in *Le Monde des livres*, June 2013

Resemblance

1

Exactly two years ago, in June 2012, I was here in Florence, both as writer in residence at the Santa Maddalena Foundation and as finalist for the Gregor von Rezzori Prize. That was the first time I'd been a writer in residence anywhere, and I was a bit scared. I'd been told it can be a dream or a nightmare, depending on how you get along with Beatrice. It turned out to be more of a dream, and I venture to say that I got along well—very well even—with Beatrice Monti della Corte, the founder and moving spirit behind this "retreat for writers and botanists," and of the event that brings us together today. It's true, she can be intimidating. Her irony and her complete lack of sentimentality can be hard to take, as can her close friendships with the famous and talented of this world: if she tells you about a nice young guy who started a rock group with some friends, it's Mick Jagger. What I love are the stories of how she traveled to Ethiopia with Curzio Malaparte when she was ten; how sometime later she shacked up at Henry Fonda's place together with Rex Harrison, James Stewart, and Laurence Olivier; and how my favorite author, Henri Michaux, timidly flirted with her when she was a young—and, she admits, "pretty foxy"—gallerist. In fact she was a knockout, and still is. I loved it when she told me about her friends, her houses, her loves, and above all about the love of her life, the person around whom and for whom she made Santa Maddalena: Gricha.

Like everyone here, I started calling the celebrated Austro-Hungarian writer Gregor von Rezzori, who would have turned one hundred this year, by his nickname, Gricha, as if he hadn't been dead for the last fourteen years and we'd just taken the dogs for a long walk in the countryside. I'd read and admired *The Snows of Yesteryear* and *Memoirs of an Anti-Semite*, and since my first visit I've read his other books. I admire his supple, roving style, his madcap freedom, his way of not giving a damn about anything. I love him the way I used to love Nabokov, only he's less pedantic, less full of himself than Nabokov. When you open the door to one of his books, you don't feel as if you have to watch your step. Gricha is friendly, welcoming. Even when he pokes fun at you, you feel he likes you. God knows he's present in his books, as he's present in every room in Santa Maddalena—in particular the little office on the first floor of the tower where I so liked to work, and which he discusses in depth at the start of his marvelous *Anecdotage*. His presence is everywhere, you'd think he'd just gone shopping in the village, but above all he's present in Beatrice's conversation. I think that's what I liked the most here. The way she loved him, the way he loved her, and the good vibrations with which this love still fills the build-ing, the garden, right down to the conclaves of glowworms that gather once night has fallen around the pyramid dedicated to his memory. You could tell this story from Beatrice's point of view, but as I'm a man and a writer, I tend to associate myself with Gricha, and I think that Gricha completely lucked out. He led the life of a high-class vagabond, and then at over fifty he met Beatrice and spent the next thirty years with her. He lived with her at Santa Maddalena and wrote the great books that he'd had neither the leisure nor perhaps even the inclination to write before that. I think Gricha was a happy man. It's not often that you can say that of a writer.

That's the first topic that I'd toyed with for this lecture: Is it possible to be both a great writer and a happy man? Are there examples? Who? I started to hunt around, then branched off into another subject that also has much to do with my trip to Florence two years ago.

2

As I said, I was a finalist for the Rezzori Prize. I didn't win, Enrique Vila-Matas did. A timid, starry-eyed man, he seemed saddened by the news, as if from then on his less fortunate comrades would turn their backs on him. We tried to console him by saying that he deserved it, and that not just the prizewinner but also all the finalists receive a check. This generosity deserves to be mentioned because I believe it's unprecedented. Before the prize was awarded there was a lecture like the one I'm giving today, by the Canadian novelist Michael Ondaatje. Back then it was held in the Medici Riccardi Palace. As all art lovers know, the Medici Riccardi Palace houses a chapel whose four walls are decorated with a fresco by Benozzo Gozzoli, representing the procession of the Magi to Bethlehem to worship the baby Jesus. The chapel isn't big, and you can only visit it in small groups at specific times. That's better than nothing. Still, with at least twenty people per group, by far the best option is to visit it outside opening hours, like a museum on the day it's closed—which I was able to do thanks to Max Rabino.

Max Rabino is a dear friend of Beatrice's. A dilettante, a lover of art, and a wellspring of knowledge, like some characters in Chekhov's plays he seems to belong to the house. I had a friendly crush on Max. What I liked about him was his blend of ancient wisdom

and childish innocence: a real Taoist, this Max. To continue: With
him I had the privilege of visiting the Chapel of the Magi, and
during this visit he remarked, If you look at the procession of the
Magi, you see dozens of people, maybe even a hundred (I didn't
count them). Among them, the figures in the foreground are per-
sonalities at the Medici court: Cosimo, Lorenzo, Lorenzo's three
sisters, the *condottiero* Sigismondo Malatesta, as art historians tell
us. The others were apparently picked at random in the street,
around 1460. Whether it's the noblemen and noblewomen in the
foreground or the masses behind them, they were without doubt
all painted from nature. Even if you don't know who the models
were, you're sure they looked just like that. Once you reach the
holy infant, however, the faces change to those of angels, saints,
and a host of heavenly figures. All of a sudden they become more
regular, more idealized. What they gain in spirituality they lose in
expression, in originality, in vitality: you can be sure they were no
longer painted using real models.

3

I like landscape paintings, still lifes, and nonfigurative works, but
above all else I love portraits. When I visit a museum, the portraits first grab my attention, and I think that if I'd been a painter,
I would undoubtedly have been a portraitist. In my domain I
consider myself a portraitist. I'm sure that's why Max's comment
affected me the way it did. Since then I've tried the experiment
a number of times, and I recommend that you try it, too. Look
at a portrait, any portrait. You'll see that instinctively, intuitively,
without even realizing it, you'll distinguish between those that
are painted using a model, and those that represent fictious characters based solely on the imagination. You don't need a guide to
know that Ingres's Monsieur Bertin and Bellini's Doge Loredan

really existed. With Michelangelo's characters and Raphael's virgins, however, it's another thing altogether. I'm not saying that one is better than the other; I'm just saying that they're different, and that this difference jumps out at you. And what I wondered next is if this difference that is so evident in painting can also be seen in literature.

The question interests me all the more in that for the past twenty years or so I have no longer written novels—that is, if you take novels to be works of fiction dealing with fictional characters. I now write what for lack of a better term you could call works of nonfiction. And I'm the first to insist, perhaps even over-insist, that what I'm telling is true, that the characters I'm trying to represent all have their models in reality and aren't creatures of my imagination.

People rightly say that this appeal to the "real" calls forth a whole slew of objections. I can repeat all I want that Limonov exists, for example, but that doesn't stop the Limonov in my book from being partly the real Limonov and partly a character I made up. Even I don't quite know where the one stops and the other starts, and I'm forced to admit that there is no clear-cut boundary between the two. This ambiguity is peculiar to literature and doesn't exist in the cinema. Film critics will tell you that things are complicated, that the boundary between documentary and fiction is becoming increasingly fuzzy. But that doesn't stop there from being one, and it's clear: in a fiction film the characters are played by actors, and in a documentary you see the real people. In my view it's as simple as that, and I defy you to name a film that escapes this binary classification.

Allow me to digress. Ten years ago or so I shot a documentary called *Retour à Kotelnitch* in the small Russian town of Kotelnich, which no one knows except the people who are unlucky enough to live there and those who've seen the film. I spent several months there, filmed the inhabitants, and struck up relationships that were often complex. They couldn't figure out why I was filming them or what I wanted to do with the images, and it wasn't easy to explain because I didn't know myself. I was waiting for something to happen, and something did happen, something terrible: a young woman whom I liked and who had worked for us as an interpreter was brutally murdered, killed together with her eighteen-month-old baby by a madman with an ax. The film crossed a line. Instead of drifting in search of a subject, it started telling something, something that was both tragic and fiction-like, and some of the inhabitants of the town whom we had filmed without knowing what story we would tell became, by the force of events, tragic, fiction-like figures as well. The most tragic and fiction-like figure of all was the husband of the murdered woman and father of the murdered child, who was also the local officer of the FSB—the organization that used to be called the KGB. He was mysterious, both charismatic and disturbing, wary to the point of paranoia when he was sober and, as soon as he'd had a drink—which happened often—able to tell us his deepest secrets as if we were the best of friends. That said, the story I want to tell takes place not in Kotelnich but in Venice, where the film was presented at the Venice Film Festival in 2003. The producer had brought the poet and scriptwriter Tonino Guerra to the screening, and I was both touched and daunted to show my film to a man who had written the screenplays of so many masterpieces by Fellini, Antonioni, Francesco Rosi, the Taviani brothers, Theo Angelopoulos, and Andrei Tarkovsky. After the screening we all went out for a drink at a café on the Lido. With his white mustache, cap, and corduroy vest, Tonino Guerra looked every bit like an Italian patriarch dispensing justice under an oak tree. We waited for his verdict, which he finally handed down. He didn't like the film. He found it both confusing and sinister—I was devastated, as you can imagine—but he found one good thing about it: the actors were extraordinary, especially the FSB guy. I said timidly, "In fact he's not an actor, he's really from the FSB. There are no actors in the film, just real people from Kotelnich."

"Really?" Tonino Guerra said with a suspicious look.

"Really."

He didn't seem convinced. The more I repeated to him what seemed to me to go without saying, the more he suspected that I was kidding him, and I finally decided that it was the best compliment anyone could—or would—ever pay my film.

4

Max's comment both disturbed and enlightened me for another reason, having to do with the book I was working on during my stay in Santa Maddalena. Only three months ago I wouldn't have said a thing about it because it wasn't finished, and I know from experience that you shouldn't talk about your books as long as they're still in the works: every secret you divulge, especially when it's tinged with optimism, is sure to cost you a week of discouragement. But now the book's done, it's set to come out in France this fall and in Italy next spring. So not only *can* I talk about it, I want to.

That's not easy to do briefly because it's a big book, to which I dedicated seven years of my life. In a nutshell, it's an account of the first days of Christianity. It takes place between A.D. 50 and 100, when no one so much as suspected that they were living "in the year of our Lord." It's set in Greece, Jerusalem, and Rome, and the main figures are the men we call Saint Paul, Saint Peter, Saint John, and so on, but who at that time were simply called Paul, Peter, John, et al. They weren't saints with halos but men, complex and fallible like the rest of us. Like us, they bickered among themselves, they were jealous, and each was convinced he knew more about their faith than the others. The only thing they had in common was an extremely strange belief, and the strangest thing of all is that this belief, which should normally have disappeared with them, endured, that in less than three centuries it devoured the Roman Empire from within, and that today still a quarter of humanity continues to adhere to it.

As you all know, this belief is about the life, teaching, death, and—if you believe the believers—the resurrection of a Galilean preacher called Jesus of Nazareth. You can think what you want about him and what was done to his message, but you can't deny that he's a major historical figure. I don't think it's going too far out on a limb to say that of everyone in history, he's the one who's been represented the most. And all of these representations, whether in paintings, literature, or film, are based on four short accounts that, put back-to-back, fit in a pocketbook and that were written by four very different authors, let's say, fifty to eighty years after Jesus' death. I wanted to know who one of these authors was. For reasons that I won't go into here and that you'll understand, I hope, if you read my book, I chose Luke. My book, consequently, became a biography of Luke the Evangelist. As we know almost nothing about him, it's largely imagined. I tried to picture who this Luke was, what he thought, what he believed, and to reconstruct the physical and mental context in which his life took place. Since what we call the Gospel According to Luke is a portrait of Jesus, I found myself making a portrait of the portraitist.

So unavoidably I came up against the question of resemblance. Does the portrait Luke painted of Jesus resemble the real Jesus? The question isn't absurd because the real Jesus isn't imaginary. He existed. Whether he was resurrected or was the son of God is another thing, a matter of faith. But that he lived in the place we now call Israel, that he breathed the same air as we do, that he ate and drank and pissed and shat like any other human being, no one aside from a few screwball atheists will contest. Take any famous scene from his life: his appearance before the

Roman governor Pilate, for example. You're obliged to imagine
it; nevertheless it's not imaginary. It's not even subject to doubt,
such as the raising of Lazarus or the adoration of the Magi. Roman historians refer to it. It took place. It came about in a space
and a time that we can't determine with absolute precision but
that, like all points in space and time, was absolutely precise. It
happened at a certain place, at a certain time, at a certain tem-
perature. These two men, Jesus and Pilate, weren't mythological
figures, gods or heroes, living in a fantasy world where everything
is possible because nothing is real. They were a colonial officer
and a local visionary: men like you and me, who had specific
faces, wore specific clothes, and talked with specific voices. Their
meeting didn't take place like things we imagine, in one of an
infinitely variable number of ways, but the way all things happen
on earth, that is, in one specific way that excludes all others. We
know next to nothing about this specific way, this unique way,
that had the privilege of passing from the virtual to the real. Yet
it happened. Tons of fiction and legend have been grafted onto it,
but it does not belong to the realm of fiction or legend: it belongs
to reality. So while it may be illusory to try to make a realistic
representation of it, it's perfectly legitimate.

      As Kafka said, "I'm very ignorant. The truth exists nonethe-
less."

5

With the exception of John, perhaps, none of the four Evangelists
witnessed the events they describe. None of them even tries to
give the impression that he did. Luke wrote fifty years after Jesus'
death, and he states clearly that his is a second- or even thirdhand
account. That doesn't stop you from reading his Gospel the way
you read any historian, or from asking about each detail: Is it

true? Did Jesus say what Luke has him say? Did this anecdote happen? Is this trait authentic?

The more I read the Gospels—the Book of Luke and the three others—the more I came to appreciate the difference I mentioned above, between portraits that were done using a model and portraits done from the imagination. Between characters, speech, and anecdotes that could have been distorted but that nevertheless resemble something real, and others that fall under the category of myth or pious imagination. Another example: Jesus' arrest on the Mount of Olives. There, too, the scene is so real you could cut it with a knife. In the middle of the night, a commando hastily arrests a guerrilla leader. Dim lanterns, truncheons, semi-darkness: it's like something out of a painting by Tintoretto or Caravaggio. One of the leader's men tries to resist. He takes out his sword, swings, and cuts off a soldier's ear. This soldier, John the Evangelist tells us, was named Malchus. Luke adds that Jesus touched the wound and healed it. For me this short scene contains a striking juxtaposition of two registers. I believe the cut ear, and I believe that the guy whose ear was cut was named Malchus—otherwise why write it? But I don't believe that the ear was then miraculously repaired, not just because I'm skeptical about miracles, but above all because the detail clearly belongs to the category of those that are meant to edify, and not of those that are told simply because they happened.

What I wonder, deep down, is whether an internal criterion allows you to say whether a portrait resembles its model, and if an anecdote is authentic. I think there is, but I'm forced to admit that it's hugely subjective: it's what you call ringing true. You feel it, but you can't demonstrate it. However, another, more objective criterion is what the exegetes call the embarrassment criterion: when something must have been embarrassing for the author to write, when he would certainly have preferred to omit it, but retained it out of scrupulousness, you can say chances are good that it's true.

When Mark tells us, for example, that Jesus' brothers and sisters thought he was mad and wanted to have him put away, you believe it. When Mark shows the disciples bickering like cats and dogs instead of outdoing each other in piety and nobility of spirit, you believe it. And when the four Evangelists, for once unanimous, tell us that Peter, the most senior and faithful of Jesus' disciples, the rock on which Jesus wanted to build his church, denied his master three times in the night that followed his arrest, you believe it, too, because it's not at all flattering for Peter. It's exactly the same thing with painting. If a court painter gives the king a noble, energetic face, you think that it might resemble him or might not: there's no way of telling. But if he paints him with a squint and a wart on his chin, you can be sure of one thing: the king had a squint and a wart on his chin. The bottom line is that what we believe bears a resemblance is, if not ugly, then at least imperfect.

6

I didn't attempt Jesus' portrait: I wouldn't have risked it. More modestly, I tried to make a portrait of one of his four official portraitists. I tried to paint a plausible portrait, if not a perfect likeness, of Luke. Not an easy undertaking, as we're dealing with a man not only about whom we know nothing but who lived nineteen centuries ago. Many times I asked myself how to write a historical novel that doesn't ring hollow. I reread the masterpieces of the genre, one of the most famous being *Memoirs of Hadrian* by Marguerite Yourcenar. Even if it's a bit long, I'd like to quote the passage in which Yourcenar explains how she proceeded:

> The rules of the game: learn everything, read everything, inquire into everything, while at the same time adapting to one's ends the *Spiritual Exercises* of Ignatius of Loyola, or

the method of Hindu ascetics, who for years, and to the
point of exhaustion, try to visualize ever more exactly the
images which they create beneath their closed eyelids.
Through hundreds of card notes pursue each incident to
the very moment that it occurred; endeavor to restore the
mobility and suppleness of life to those visages known only
to us in stone. When two texts, or two assertions, or perhaps two ideas, are in contradiction, be ready to reconcile
them rather than cancel one by the other; regard them as
two different facets, or two successive stages, of the same
reality, a reality convincingly human just because it is complex. Strive to read a text of the second century with the
eyes, soul, and feelings of the second century; let it steep
in that mother solution which the facts of its own time
provide; set aside, if possible, all beliefs and sentiments
which have accumulated in successive strata between those
persons and us. And nevertheless take advantage (though
prudently, and solely by way of preparatory study) of all possibilities for comparison and cross-checking, and of new
perspectives slowly developed by the many centuries and
events separating us from a given text, a fact, a man; make
use of such aids more or less as guide-marks along the road
of return toward one particular point in time. Keep one's
own shadow out of the picture; leave the mirror clean of the
mist of one's own breath; take only what is most essential
and durable in us, in the emotions aroused by the senses
or in the operations of the mind, as our point of contact
with those men who, like us, nibbled olives and drank
wine, or gummed their fingers with honey, who fought
bitter winds and blinding rain, or in summer sought the
plane tree's shade; who took their pleasures, thought their
own thoughts, grew old, and died.*

---

*From Grace Frick's translation (Farrar, Straus and Giroux, 1963).

I find this passage beautiful. I approve of its proud, humble method. The poetic list of invariants—"those men who, like us, nibbled olives and drank wine, or gummed their fingers with honey, who fought bitter winds and blinding rain, or in summer sought the plane tree's shade; who took their pleasures, thought their own thoughts, grew old, and died"—leaves me pensive because it touches on a huge question: What is eternal, unchanging, in what Yourcenar calls "the emotions aroused by the senses or in the operations of the mind"? And what, as a consequence, is not part of history? The sky, the rain, thirst, the desire that pushes men and women to mate: fine, but in our perception of things, in the opinions we form of them, history—that is, the changing nature of things—quickly creeps in and never stops occupying places we thought were beyond reach. But what I can't go along with in what Yourcenar says has to do with keeping your shadow out of the picture and leaving the mirror clean of your breath. That is, the presence of today's author. I believe profoundly that that's something you can't avoid. I think that shadows—and the tricks by which you try to remove them—will always be visible, and in that case it's much better to accept them and work them into the narrative. It's like shooting a documentary. Either you pretend that you're seeing people "for real"—as they are when you're not there to film them—or you admit that by filming them you change the givens, and that what you're filming is a new situation. I'm not bothered by what's known in technical jargon as the direct gaze: when people look straight into the camera. On the contrary, I work it in and even draw attention to it. I show what this gaze is interacting with, the things that are supposed to remain off-screen in classical documentaries: the team during the shoot, me directing the team, our quarrels, our doubts, our complex relationships with the people we're filming. I'm not saying this approach is better. Of the two schools, all you can say in favor of mine is that it's more in tune with modern sensibilities, with their penchant for

suspicion, making-ofs, and looking behind the scenes, than Marguerite Yourcenar's proud and somewhat naive claim to step aside
and show things as they are in their true essence.

7

What's amusing is that unlike more modern painters such as Ingres or Delacroix, who were careful to depict Tacitus' Romans
or biblical Jews realistically, the old masters naively applied the
modernist credo and Brechtian-style detachment. If they'd been
asked, many of them would no doubt have admitted that Galilee
in Jesus' day probably didn't look much like Flanders or Tuscany
in theirs, but the question never occurred to most of them. The
desire for historical realism wasn't part of their intellectual frame-
work, and I think that basically they were right. They were truly
realists, to the extent that what they represented was truly real.
It was them, it was the world they lived in. The Blessed Virgin's
home was the home of the painter or his funder. Her clothes,
which were painted with such care and love of detail, were those
worn by the old masters' wives or lovers. And they didn't hesitate
to put themselves in their paintings. One work I love, painted by
the great Flemish master Rogier van der Weyden, shows my hero
Saint Luke painting a portrait of the Virgin Mary—because one
tradition that has absolutely no basis in history, but that nevertheless enchants me, is that Saint Luke was a painter: he's even
the patron saint of painters. In the painting by Rogier van der Weyden, this portrait of Saint Luke is among those that leave you in no
doubt. It was modeled on someone real: Rogier van der Weyden
himself. His Saint Luke is a self-portrait. I was thrilled when I
discovered that, because in my book I did exactly the same thing:
I painted myself as Saint Luke. Just as Flaubert says of Madame
Bovary, I could say, "Luke is me," and honestly I think that was

the most reasonable choice. No doubt my Luke bears no likeness to the real Luke; no one knows what the real Luke was like. But at least it resembles me, and that's a start. Whom your work resembles doesn't matter that much, I believe; what counts is that there's a resemblance.

Speech delivered in Florence in June 2014

In Search of the Dice Man

1

Toward the end of the 1960s, Luke Rhinehart worked as a psychoanalyst in New York and was bored stiff. He lived in a pretty apartment, with a nice view looking onto his neighbors' windows, and his neighbors had a nice view of his. He practiced yoga, read books on Zen, dreamed vaguely of joining a commune but didn't dare. Instead he wore bell-bottomed pants and sported a beard that made him look a little less like a depressed shrink and a little more like an unemployed actor. As a therapist, he was resolutely nondirective. If an obese patient who still hadn't lost his virginity was plagued by sadistic impulses and said on Luke's couch that he'd like to rape and kill a little girl, Luke's professional ethics obliged him to repeat with a calm voice, "You'd like to rape and kill a little girl? . . ." With a noncommittal question mark followed by three long dots. No judgment. But what he wanted to say was "Well, go ahead, then! If what really turns you on is raping and killing a little girl, then stop boring me with this fantasy. *Do it!*" He checked himself before coming out with such monstrosities, but they obsessed him more and more. Like everyone else, he stopped himself from going through with his own fantasies, although they were pretty harmless—not enough to get him sent to prison, unlike his sadistic patient's, if he were to let himself go. What Luke would have liked, for example, was to sleep with Arlene, the sexy wife of his colleague Jake Ecstein, who lived across the landing. Luke suspected she wouldn't say no either, but as a faithful and responsible husband he let the idea simmer away in the back of his mind.

•

So life plods on, calm and dreary, until one night after a dinner party when he's had a little too much to drink. Luke sees a die lying on the carpet, a banal playing die, and gets the idea of throwing it and acting on its instructions.

"If it lands on a number from 2 to 6, I'll do what I would have done anyway: bring the dirty glasses back to the kitchen, brush my teeth, take a double aspirin to avoid having too bad a hangover in the morning, go to bed beside my sleeping wife, and maybe masturbate discreetly thinking of Arlene. But if I roll a 1, I'll do what I *really* want to do: I know Arlene's at home alone tonight, so I'll go across the hall, knock on her door, and sleep with her."

The die lands on 1.

Luke hesitates, feeling vaguely that he's standing on a threshold: if he crosses it, his life could change. But it's not his decision, it's the die's, so he obeys. Arlene opens the door in a negligee; she's surprised but not put out. When Luke comes back home two extremely pleasant hours later, he realizes that he has changed. This change may not be enormous, but it's more than anything one might expect of psychotherapy—as he's paid to know. He did something the normal Luke wouldn't do. A bigger, less inhibited, more audacious Luke is breaking through the surface of the prudent, conformist Luke, and perhaps still other Lukes whose existence he doesn't even suspect are waiting behind the door for the die to open it.

•

In all circumstances, from now on, Luke consults the die. Since it has six sides, he gives it six options. The first is to do what he's always done. The five others depart more or less distinctly from this routine. Let's say Luke and his wife had planned to go to the movies. Antonioni's new film *Blow-Up* has just come out, and it's exactly what a couple of New York intellectuals such as them should go see. But they could also go see a film that's *even more* intellectual, a Hungarian or Czech film that's even more artsy, or they could see a blockbuster of the sort they generally disdain, or even a porn flick in a skid row movie house in the Bowery, where people like them have never set foot and never would. Once it's been subjected to the die, even the most anodyne choice, that of a film, a restaurant, what to eat at a restaurant, opens, if you watch out for it, a vast array of possibilities for putting your routine behind you. At the start, Luke takes it easy. He chooses prudent options, not too far from his habits. Small side steps that spice up his life without disrupting it, such as changing places in bed, or positions during sex. But soon his choices become more audacious. He starts thinking of everything he's never done as a challenge to be faced. Going somewhere he'd never go, getting to know people he would otherwise never meet. Undertaking to seduce a woman whose name he found in the phone book. Borrowing ten dollars from a complete stranger. Giving ten dollars to a complete stranger. Venturing into a gay bar, flirting with men, turning on the charm, and—why not, he the affirmed hetero?—sleeping with a man. Acting pushy, impatient, and despotic with his patients. To the patient who believes he's a piece of shit, blurting out, "And what if you really *are* a piece of shit?" To the writer with a block: "Instead of slogging away at your bullshit novel, why not go to the Congo and get involved with a revolutionary group? Why not go all out: sex, hunger, danger?" And to the guy who's inhibited by his passivity: "Why don't you do my receptionist? She's ugly, okay, but she wants nothing better. Go ahead and kiss her when you leave. At worst she'll slap you, what do you stand to lose?" He pushes his patients to leave their families and jobs, to change their political and sexual orientations. The results are disastrous and his reputation suffers, but Luke doesn't care. What he likes, now, is doing the exact opposite of what he'd normally do: putting salt in his coffee, jogging in a tuxedo, going to work in shorts, pissing in the flowerpots, walking backward, sleeping under his bed . . . His wife finds him strange, but he says it's a psychological experiment, and she lets herself be lulled into believing it. Until the day he gets the idea of initiating his children.

•

Here he has no doubt that such an undertaking is dangerous, very dangerous even. But it's a rule of thumb that every option you start by imagining winds up being submitted to the die and, one day or another, can end up being rolled. So one weekend when their mother isn't there, Luke gets his little boy and girl to play this apparently innocent game: you write six things you'd like to do on a piece of paper, and the die chooses one of them. It all goes well at the start—it always does: they eat ice cream, go to the zoo, and then his son becomes bolder and says that one thing he'd like to do is go beat up a boy who bugs him at school. "Okay, write it down," Luke says, and that's what the die rolls. The boy thinks his father won't make him go through with it, but his dad says, "Go ahead." The boy goes to his friend's place, hits him several times, and comes back to the house with his eyes shining and asks, "Where are the dice, Dad?"

That makes Luke stop and think: If his son so naturally adopts this way of being, it's because he's not yet completely warped by the absurd postulate put forward by his parents and society that it's good for children to develop a coherent character. What if they were brought up differently? Giving pride of place to contradiction, multiplicity, and relentless change? Tell lies, dear children, disobey, be inconsistent, lose the bad habit of brushing your teeth before you go to bed. We're told children need order and discipline; what if they need just the opposite? Luke seriously thinks of freeing his son of the dismal tyranny of the ego and making him the first man entirely subject to chance: a child in the spirit of Lao-Tsu.

Then the children's mother returns and discovers what's been going on. Not finding it funny in the least, she leaves Luke and takes the children with her.

•

So our hero is now without a family. That makes him sad because he loves his family, but the die is as insistent as Jesus Christ, who also demands that his followers abandon everything.

Then it's his profession that Luke abandons, after an evening with the cream of New York psychoanalysts. The road map given to him by the die (though it must be said he'd smoked a lot of drugs while listing the options) is to change personality every ten minutes, the six roles he must alternately adopt being those of a well-mannered psychiatrist (him before the die), a mental retard, a sex maniac, a Jesus freak, a radical leftist, and a right-wing extremist spouting virulently anti-Semitic remarks. The evening was a scandal, after which Luke is interned and has to appear before a disciplinary council. He uses this unexpected tribune to announce to the world what he calls a revolutionary therapy. His colleagues are horrified: his revolutionary therapy is the programmed destruction of the identity. That's right, Luke concedes, but isn't that the best thing that can happen? What we call the identity is nothing but a straitjacket of boredom, frustration, and despair. All therapies aim at pulling this straitjacket tighter, whereas true freedom means bursting out of it, no longer being held prisoner by yourself and being able to be another self, dozens of selves . . .

"What do you really want?"

"Everything, I guess. To be everybody and to do everything."

•

After this profession of faith, the visionary is chased from his professional community—just as another visionary, Timothy Leary, the apostle of LSD, was chased from his. With no family, work, or personal ties, Luke is free, and given over to the vertigo that comes with freedom. He has discovered—and experimented on himself—a technique that at first spices up his life, but whose logic of escalation calls his existence into question at every moment. At the start it was like marijuana, enjoyable and amusing, now it's like acid, enormous and exulting, laying waste to everything in its path. To give free rein to the suppressed tendencies in his personality, he moves from transgression to transgression. His discovery becomes a form of asceticism, no longer at all hedonistic or amusing. The last safeguard to explode is the pleasure principle. Because he who starts down the path of the die at first does things that he'd never have dared to do but that, more or less secretly, he'd always dreamed of doing. Then the day comes when the die pushes him to do things that not only he'd never dared to do but he didn't *want* to do, because they ran counter to his tastes, his desires, his whole personality. But that's just it: the personality—the miserable, petty personality—is the enemy to be done away with, the conditioning that you have to free yourself from. To cease being held prisoner by yourself you have to agree to follow desires that you weren't aware of, and even that you didn't have.

Take sex: you start by changing your sexual routines to the satisfaction of both partners, then you change partners, then you leave your wife (or in Luke's case, she leaves you), then you sleep with all the attractive women who cross your path, and then, to broaden your horizons and to be a little less a slave to your petty preferences, you move on to women you don't find attractive—old women, fat women, women you'd never have even looked at in the past—and from there to men, then to boys, then to rape, and then to sadistic murder à la *American Psycho*, why not?

•

Sooner or later, no serious practitioner of the die can avoid writing murder on his list of options. It's the supreme taboo; it would be fainthearted not to violate it. When the die orders him to do it, Luke imagines two subcategories: killing a person he knows, and killing someone he doesn't. He'd like it to be the second option, but he rolls the first, and he's forced to draw up a list of six potential victims, in which he courageously includes his two children. Luckily for him he's spared that particular ordeal, like Abraham the murder of his son Isaac: the die simply demands that he kill one of his former patients.

If you believe his autobiography, he went through with it. Certain commentators doubt it, and almost fifty years later the facts seem impossible to verify. By contrast what does seem certain is that having totally ruined his career, his family life, and his reputation, Luke was ready to become a prophet, and that's what he did. In these remote years when the most paradoxical therapies flourished from one side of America to the other, a guru with a die had every chance of attracting followers. That's how the celebrated and scandalous Center for Experiments in Totally Random Environments—where you enroll of your own free will but undertake not to leave until the experiment is over—saw the light in a peaceful New England village. The novices start off with emotional roulette: you choose six strong emotions, which you express as dramatically as you can for ten minutes. The more advanced students move on to role plays of varying durations:

you list six personality types—let's say philanthropic and cynical, hardworking and lazy, normopathic and psychotic; these potentialities exist in each of us—and for ten minutes, an hour, a day, a week, a month, or a year (also according to the verdict of the die), adopt the one that comes up. For someone who's not a psychotic, living for a year as if you were one is quite trying. At the end of the course, the most daring attempt total submission, also for a variable duration, depending on the will of someone else who not only throws the die but also selects the options. In this way Luke became the slave of a completely neurotic woman who was imaginative enough to have him live a month of sadomasochistic delirium, during which time he believes he learned more about himself and life than he did in the forty years before that.

Some of the followers of dice therapy went crazy. Others died or wound up in prison. Some, it seems, reached a state of awareness and joy similar to the nirvana of the Buddhists. In the year or two of its existence, Luke's center became as scandalous as Timothy Leary's communities: a school of chaos posing as serious a threat to civilization as communism or the satanism of Charles Manson, as the conservative newspapers had it. The end of the adventure is shrouded in obscurity. It's said that Luke was arrested by the FBI, that he spent twenty years in a psychiatric hospital. Or that he died. Or that he never existed at all.

2

Everything I've just told comes from a book, *The Dice Man*, published in the United States in 1971 and translated into French the following year. I was sixteen when I discovered it, along with the nutty, paranoid works of Philip K. Dick, and it made almost as big an impression on me. I was a terribly timid adolescent with long hair, an afghan vest, and little round glasses, and for a while I walked around with a die in my pocket, counting on it to give me the self-confidence I lacked with girls. That worked more or less well—actually less rather than more—but notwithstanding that, *The Dice Man* was the kind of book that not only pleases readers but also gives them a set of rules for life: a manual of subversion of the kind they could dream of following. It wasn't clear whether it was fiction or autobiographical, but its author, Luke Rhinehart, had the same name as his hero, and like him he was a psychiatrist. According to the back cover he lived in Majorca. And at the time I'm describing, Majorca and Formentera—where Barbet Schroeder filmed *More*, his movie on drugs featuring the marvelous Mimsy Farmer and the heady music of Pink Floyd—were the ideal refuge for a prophet at the end of his tether, who's just managed to escape from his shipwrecked community of maniacs. The years passed, *The Dice Man* remained a buzzword, the object of a minor but persistent cult, and each time I met someone who'd read it (almost always a pothead, and often a follower of the *I Ching*), the same questions came up: What was true in the book? Who was Luke Rhinehart? What had become of him?

Later on I started to write books of my own, many of which dealt with the temptation held out by multiple lives. All of us are prisoners of our personality, terribly confined by our own small way of thinking and acting. We'd like to know what it's like to be someone else, at least I would, and to a large extent I became a writer to imagine just that. It's what inspired me to tell the story of Jean-Claude Romand, who spent eighteen years pretending he was someone other than himself, and that of Eduard Limonov, who lived ten lives at least. A couple of months ago I discussed this subject with a friend, who countered the temptation of multiplicity with the Stoic tradition, for which accomplishment is the fruit of coherence, faithfulness to oneself: patiently sculpting a personality that's as stable as can be. As you can never take all the paths in life, wisdom is following one's own, he said, and the narrower this path is, the fewer forks it has, the further it will take you. I agreed: with age I've also come to see things that way. But then I thought of Luke Rhinehart, the apostle of dispersion, the prophet of the kaleidoscopic life, the man who said that you have to take all paths at once, no matter if they lead nowhere: a phantom of the bold and dangerous 1960s, when people believed they could experience everything, try everything. And once again I started to wonder what had become of this phantom, and if he was still alive.

In the past, people were pretty much dependent on their own imagination regarding such questions. But today there's the Internet, and in an hour on the Internet I learned more about Luke Rhinehart than I had in thirty years of idle conjecture.

His real name is George Cockcroft; though no longer young, he's alive. He's written other books, but none was as successful as *The Dice Man*, which more than forty years after it came out is just as much of a cult classic as ever. Dozens of sites are dedicated to it, and just as many legends circulate about it. Ten times it was almost adapted for the cinema. The biggest stars in Hollywood, Jack Nicholson, Nicolas Cage, fought to play the role of Luke, but mysteriously the project never came about. Communities of followers of the die still exist all over the world. As for the mythical author, he lives as a recluse on a remote farm in Upstate New York. No one has seen him for three decades. A single photo of him makes the rounds: it shows under a Stetson a sarcastic, gaunt face that bears a striking resemblance to another magnificent phantom: Dennis Hopper in *The American Friend* by Wim Wenders. It strikes me that there's a story here, and I pitch it to Patrick de Saint-Exupéry, editor in chief of *XXI*, as if Luke Rhinehart were Carlos Castaneda, William Burroughs, and Thomas Pynchon rolled into one: an icon of the most radical subversion transformed into an invisible man.

Sold, of course.

3

One detail should have warned me: my invisible man has his own website, through which I was able to contact him. He answered my message in less than an hour, with surprising good grace for a recluse. I wanted to come from France to interview him? What a good idea! When I filled him in on the reason for my visit, he told me nicely that he hoped he wasn't going to disappoint me: on my search for Luke Rhinehart I was going to meet George Cock-croft, and George Cockcroft, in his own words, was an old fart. I took this warning as false modesty.

For the past couple of weeks I've been in contact with some followers of the die on the Internet, and on my way through New York I invite one to dinner. Ron is thirty, introduces himself as a conceptual artist and urban pirate, and heads a community of dice people who meet every month for what, under all the new age jargon, seems to be good old group sex, where the die above all decides who'll be on top, who on bottom, and who'll be doing what in which hole. No such thing is planned for the days when I'll be there, I learn a little to my regret, but the urban pirate appears impressed by my boldness: Knocking on Luke Rhinehart's door! Pulling on the tiger's whiskers! That's really venturing into the dark side of the Force. I answer that to judge by the author's messages, he seems like a nice old guy. Ron looks at me pensively, with a touch of pity:

"A nice old guy . . . Sure, why not? Maybe the die ordered him to play that role for you. But don't forget that a die has six sides. He's showing you one, you don't know what's behind the other five, or when he'll decide to reveal them . . ."

•

It's a two-hour train trip from Pennsylvania Station to Hudson in Upstate New York, through an enchanting countryside. The man waiting for me when I arrive is wearing the same Stetson as he is in his only photograph, he has the same jagged features, the same faded blue eyes, and the same slightly sardonic smile. He's tall and has a bit of a slouch; you could even find him sinister, but when I hold out my hand, he gives me a big hug, kisses me on both cheeks as if I were his son, and introduces me to his wife, Ann, who is just as warm and welcoming as he is. We all pile into their old station wagon and drive through the sleepy town. White wooden houses, verandas, lawns: it's not the suburban America of series such as *Desperate Housewives*, but a far older, more remote, more rural America. Don't be fooled, Ann tells me: it's charming in spring, but four months out of twelve it's covered in snow, the roads are often blocked, and to live here year-round you need inner strength. As we drive past the orchards and through the woods, I realize that the winter version of this decor is that of one of my favorite novels: *Ethan Frome* by Edith Wharton—one of the saddest novels in the world, which makes *Wuthering Heights* seem like *The Sound of Music*. When I say that, my hosts are enchanted: it's one of their favorite novels as well, George has often taught it to his students.

To his students? He's not a psychiatrist, or a psychoanalyst?

"Psychiatrist? Psychoanalyst?" George repeats, as surprised as if I'd said cosmonaut. No, he was never a psychiatrist, he's been a college English teacher all his life.

Really? But on the cover of his book . . .

George shrugs as if to say, *Editors, journalists, you know, there's almost nothing they won't write . . .*

From Hudson we drive for about an hour; he handles the wheel with an abruptness that contrasts with his good humor and makes his wife laugh—with the affectionate, teasing laugh that underscores the little quirks of those we hold dear. It's moving to see how the two love each other: not a look or gesture passes between them that's not tender, caring, brightened by a life of complicity: they're Baucis and Philemon reincarnated, and when Ann tells me in passing that they've been married for fifty years, I'm not surprised. But that image doesn't square at all with the Luke Rhinehart whom I'd imagined on the basis of his book.

•

They live in an old farmhouse that's been renovated to withstand the harsh winters, with a yard that slopes down to a duck pond. It would cost a fortune today, but they were lucky to have bought it forty years ago when it was within their means, and they haven't left it since. They have three grown boys, two of whom live nearby. One's a carpenter and the other's a housepainter; the third still lives at home. He's schizophrenic, Ann tells me matter-of-factly; he's doing fine at the moment, he's not having any crises, but I shouldn't worry if I hear him speaking a bit loudly in his room, which is right beside the guest room where I'll be staying for the weekend. (I invited myself for the weekend, but I get the feeling that if I wanted to settle in for a week or a month, it wouldn't be a problem.)

Ann serves us tea, and George and I take our mugs out onto the terrace for the interview. He's swapped his Stetson for a baseball cap, and since I ask him to tell me about his life, he starts from the beginning.

4

He was born in 1932 in Albany, just a few miles from where he now lives and in all likelihood where he'll die. Semirural middle-class, hard hit by the Depression, in spite of which he looks back on a more or less happy childhood and youth. Good in math, a bit of an egghead, and not adventurous in the least, he reached age twenty without having felt the slightest creative urge. But when he went to college (to study civil engineering like his father), he got bored and forked off into psychology. At the start of the 1950s, psychology as it's taught in college isn't Freud or Jung, Erich Fromm or Wilhelm Reich, it's tedious experiments on rats, and George decided it was better to read novels—something that had never so much as occurred to him until then. While working night shifts as an intern in a hospital on Long Island, he devours Mark Twain, Herman Melville, and the great Russian writers of the nineteenth century. He starts working on a novel that takes place in a psychiatric hospital (well, well). The hero is a young man who's been interned because he thinks he's Jesus, and among the hospital staff is a doctor named Luke Rhinehart, who practices dice therapy (well, well, *well*). The character's first name was chosen in honor of Luke the Evangelist, which delights me all the more because I've just written a long book about that same Luke— which delights George, too, when I tell him. As for the die, it's a quirk the young George picked up in college with a group of friends. They used it on Saturdays to decide what they were going to do that night—there wasn't a lot of choice, anyway, between eating a hamburger and going to the drive-in . . . Sometimes, they dared each other to do stuff: hop around the block on one foot, go ring a neighbor's doorbell, nothing too mischievous, and when I ask hopefully whether he pushed these experiences further as an adult, he shrugs his shoulders and smiles apologetically because he can tell that I'd like something a little spicier.

"No," he admits, "all I asked the die was, for example, if I'd had enough of working: Do I stay at my desk for another hour? Or two hours? Or do I go for a walk right away?"

"What are you talking about?" says Ann, who's come onto the terrace to offer us some blueberry crumble, which she's just taken from the oven. "Don't you remember at least *one* important decision that the die made you take?"

He laughs, so does she, they're as touching as ever, and he tells me that he'd noticed an attractive nurse at the hospital, but was shy and didn't dare talk to her. The die made him do it: he drove her home, took her to church, but the church was closed, so he invited her to play tennis. Of course, the attractive nurse was Ann.

•

Ten years later they have three little boys, and George, who's become an English teacher, applies for a job at the American school in Majorca. This expatriation is the big adventure of their lives. Majorca in 1965 was enchanting, but they experienced none of what fascinated me in *More*. George doesn't take drugs, he's faithful to his wife, he hangs around with other teachers like himself. Still, he doesn't completely escape the zeitgeist because he's started to read books on psychoanalysis, antipsychiatry, oriental mysticism, Zen—all of 1960s counterculture, whose grand idea, to cut to the chase, is that we're conditioned, and that we must free ourselves from this conditioning. Influenced by this reading, he suddenly becomes aware of the revolutionary potential of something that he'd thought of as no more than a simple game, and that he'd more or less given up since his adolescence. Although since his marriage he'd also given up on the idea of writing books, he now gets fired up about what will become *The Dice Man*. He spends four years writing it, supported faithfully by his wife, and that, too, surprises me. Because while they're both open and tolerant, they're basically very much on the up-and-up, very family, and no matter what you say about it, the book is monstrously transgressive—even today it remains shocking.

I ask Ann, "Didn't it bother you to read it? To discover that your husband, the father of your children, had all these horrible things in his head?"

A touched smile. "No, it didn't bother me. I trust George. I thought it was a good thing; I was proud of him."

In her candor, she was right: right to be proud of him, right to trust him. Much to their surprise, an editor paid good money for the book, and the rights were sold to Paramount. Then *The Dice Man* started to live its erratic, unpredictable life: success in Europe but not in the States—in line with the malediction that seems to be the lot of the great bizarre writers from Edgar Allan Poe to Philip K. Dick—regular new editions, and finally a cult status given a new kick ten years ago by the Internet. There were disappointments: for one obscure reason or another the film was never made; Paramount sat on the rights although dozens of independent filmmakers would have loved to do it; none of his other books had the same success; and he remains forever the author of an unclassifiable classic. But that's already a lot, and life hasn't been too cruel to him, or to them. The rights from *The Dice Man* allowed them to buy this beautiful house in the land of their fathers and to age with dignity, he writing, she painting, both of them caring for their big sick son, their only worry being that they could die before he does.

•

That day was Mother's Day, and the two other boys came over to celebrate it with their parents. They're good American kids: Bud drinkers, trout fishers, who wear checkered shirts and have their feet firmly on the ground. Their schizophrenic brother came out of his room for a short while, and despite being a little slow he didn't cut a bad figure. All three told Ann she was "a terrific mom," and I'm sure it's true. After dinner, we finished the evening at the house of one of their sons, also in the middle of the countryside. He has an outdoor Jacuzzi, in which George and I continued to drink while looking up at the stars, with the result that I don't quite remember how I made it back to my room.

I woke with a start around three in the morning. My throat was dry; all you could see from the window was the dark, oppressive mass of trees that surround the house; while a couple of yards away a monotone, throaty voice was intoning sentences I couldn't understand. A ray of light shone under the door that separated the schizophrenic son's room and mine. I was distraught and took a moment to calm down. As so often, literature assuaged my fear. I thought of all the stories that deal with visits to a reclusive old writer in a wooden house in the hills—the classic of classics being *The Ghost Writer* by Philip Roth, in which the young Nathan Zuckerman discovers that the enigmatic secretary is none other than Anne Frank, who has survived. I said to myself: It's strange how much you can project onto a photograph. The one of Luke Rhinehart made me imagine a whole novel: a dangerous, sulfurous life filled with excesses, transgressions, ruptures. Numerous women, femmes fatales, some of whom are on drugs and at least one or two of whom committed suicide. Bordellos in Mexico, communities of madmen in the Nevada desert, delirious, mind-expanding experiences. And this face, the same face with strong bones and eyes of steel, is in fact that of an adorable old man who is approaching the end of a sweet, comfortable life together with his adorable wife, a man whose only departure from the norm was to have written this alarming book, and who in his old age must softly, gently explain to people who come to see him that you mustn't confuse it with him, and that he's simply a novelist.

•

Really? But what did I know about the reality? I remembered the warning of Ron, the urban pirate. What you see, the adorable old man, is just one side of the die. It's the side that the die ordered him to show you, but at least five others are in reserve, and maybe tonight he's due to change them. Perhaps the Stephen King option will surface tonight. The lovely farm with white shingles, the tender old companion with her blueberry crumble, Mother's Day, the idle chitchat in the Jacuzzi, all of that will revert into the shadows. The tall, slouched silhouette—the silhouette of an ogre when you think about it—is already heading to the barn to fetch the scythe . . .

5

At breakfast I could see that George was worried he'd disappointed me. At that moment he wasn't wrong: I had no idea what I could write. So he took me kayaking on a lake, and as our kayaks skimmed slowly over the calm water, he told me the stories of some of his disciples. Because what he was content merely to imagine, others did for real. Take the extravagant tycoon Richard Branson—the guy who created the Virgin Group and got huge media coverage with his attempt to circumnavigate the globe in a balloon, or by dressing as a stewardess and serving passengers on one of his airliners after losing a bet. He told anyone who wanted to hear it that all of his choices in business and in life had been taken thanks to the die, influenced by Luke Rhinehart. He quotes Rhinehart the way others quote Lao-Tsu, Nietzsche, or Thoreau: an emancipator, a liberator. The readers of *Loaded*, a trendy London magazine, agree: in a referendum they voted *The Dice Man* the most influential novel of the twentieth century. That gave the editor in chief an idea for a story, which he gave to his most gonzo journalist. The assignment: Follow Luke Rhinehart's example for three months. Let all of your decisions be taken by the die, and tell what happens. The funding was, if not unlimited, then at least sufficiently large for him to satisfy *almost* any whim: take a plane to the remotest destination, shack up in a fisherman's hut, rent out the top floor of a palace, hire a killer, pay a huge bail . . . The journalist, a certain Ben Marshall, took the assignment seriously enough, it seems, to trash his love life and his professional life, and to disappear without a trace for several months.

"A funny guy, that Ben," George tells me. "You can see him in *Diceworld*, a documentary made by an English TV channel in 1999."

I'd never heard of this documentary and ask if he has a DVD we can watch. All of a sudden he looks embarrassed. He says it's not great, and he's not sure he even has it. But I insist so much that in no time we're sitting on the living room couch in front of the big TV, zapper in hand, and the film starts. It's true, it's not great. The editing is choppy, the clip effects wear on you, but it does show Ben Marshall, who volunteered to gamble his life on the die. He's young, fidgety, with a shaved head and a fixed stare, who explains convincingly how he stopped before he went mad, because the die can drive you mad; it's the most exciting thing in the world, but it'll drive you mad, you have to know that. He's like someone who's returned from somewhere far away, a little bit of paradise and a lot of hell. And lo and behold, whom do we see next? His inspirer, our friend George, or rather our friend Luke, as he was fifteen years ago: the Stetson, the gaunt face, the steely eyes, handsome, but not at all like the doting grandfather I know. In a low, insinuating, hypnotic voice, he says into the camera, "You lead a dull life, a life of slavery, a life that doesn't satisfy you, but there's a way to get out of it. This way is the die. Let yourself go, submit yourself to it, and you'll see, your life will change, you'll become someone you can't even imagine. Submitting to the die will make you free. You'll no longer be someone, you'll be everyone. You'll no longer be you, you'll finally be you."

Saying this, he looks like a televangelist, a mad preacher in a novel by Flannery O'Connor, the head of a sect filmed just before his followers commit mass suicide. He's frightening. I turn to look at the person beside me on the couch, the nice pensioner in slippers holding his mug of herbal tea. He gives me an embarrassed, apologetic smile, you'd believe him on the spot, and says that the Luke in this film isn't him: it's a role the director asked

him to play. He, George, wasn't so keen on it, but the director insisted, and since he doesn't like to hurt people . . .

Ann, who can hear us from the kitchen, laughs gaily. "You're
watching the film where you play the spook?"

He laughs, too, beside me on the couch. Nevertheless when I
see him on the screen, I find him awfully convincing.

6

I met other followers of the die over the Internet: one in Salt Lake
City, one in Munich, one in Madrid. All men: I don't have an explanation for it, but the die's a guy's thing, like westerns or science fiction. The guy in Munich said, "To write an article on the
dice life that's worth its salt, you have to become a dice man."
Strangely, that frightened me. So much that I didn't even dare to
let the die decide as minor a question as which city I'd visit: once
I'd eliminated Salt Lake City, I chose Madrid over Munich for the
wimpy reason that I like it more. Oscar Cuadrado, who came to
meet me at the airport, is young, a bit pudgy, and nice. On the
way to his place in his 4×4, he made what was by now a familiar
joke: "I may look nice, but you never know what the die's got in
store for tonight: maybe I'm a serial killer and you'll find yourself
chained to my basement wall."

He lives in a stylish house in the suburbs, together with his
wife and his little girl, and without further ado we sat at a lawn
table and consulted the die: Do we have a drink right away, or do
we wait until we've done the interview? Three sides for a drink,
three against: we could just as well have tossed a coin. The answer: right away. Now, do we drink beer, table wine, or the
bottle that Oscar's saving for his daughter's eighteenth birthday?
Two sides for the beer, three for the table wine, and just one for
the special bottle, because although he'd open it willingly—you

don't refuse the die—still . . . Finally, it's over a glass of table wine—not bad at all—that he explains to me how he uses the die.

Oscar's no fan of philosophical or perverse flights of fancy. Like everyone, he's heard of people who've ruined their lives by setting extreme conditions such as leaving their families from one day to the next, going halfway around the world and never coming back, having sex with animals, or stabbing someone at random in a crowded train station in India. Stories like that circulate on all the sites dedicated to the die—including the one he's been managing for the past ten years—but they don't interest him. Lacan said that psychoanalysis isn't for idiots or crooks; Oscar believes the die isn't for nutcases or people with a death wish. He recommends a hedonist use, one that makes life more fun and surprising.

For that to be the case, he has three rules. The first is to *always* obey, to *always* apply the decision of the die. But obeying the die is ultimately obeying yourself, since you set your options. Hence the second rule, concerning the decisive moment when you list the six possibilities. Coming up with six ways of reacting to each of life's challenges takes imagination, and to do it you have to examine yourself and try to find out what you want. It's a spiritual exercise, aimed both at getting to know yourself, and getting a better grasp of the infinite possibilities offered by the real. The options you select have to be pleasant, but at least one—the third rule—has to be a little difficult, it has to make you overcome resistance and break with habit. It's got to make you do something you wouldn't normally do. You've got to surprise yourself and even be hard on yourself—but gently, with tact, knowing yourself and not going too far. When you throw the die, your desire has to be tinged with fear. Ever since he discovered the Spanish translation of *The Dice Man* when he was seventeen, this sort of small challenge has been second nature to Oscar. Like his father, he's a tax lawyer, but since it's not fun to be a tax lawyer, thanks to the die he's also become a wine importer, a webmaster, a Go teacher, a fan of Iceland, and the publisher of the Mauritian poet Malcolm de Chazal. Uh, how's that? Well, first he thought it'd be good to get to know a foreign country, a distant one if possible. Six continents, six options. The die fell on Europe, then, narrowing the choices, on Iceland. Fine. Now, how should he visit it: on foot, by car, hitchhiking, by boat, by bike, or on a skateboard? He was afraid he might chicken out if the die fell on skateboard, but it landed on bike and he went through with it. The only problem: he'd never ridden a bike. So he learned, toured Iceland by bike, and even went back with the young woman who would become his wife. On this trip the die got him to make the proposal, which was accepted. For their honeymoon, the young couple traveled to Mauritius—a present from his parents-in-law, not the die. But once there, Oscar made up for it. He looked around for something to read, an author with something to do with Mauritius, either someone who came from there or had written about it. The list included Bernardin de Saint-Pierre, J.M.G. Le Clézio, Charles Baudelaire, Joseph Conrad, and the poet Malcolm de Chazal. Bingo: Oscar fell completely in love with de Chazal, a creole surrealist whom such people as André Breton, Jean Paulhan, and Jean Dubuffet had all been crazy about. Seeing that Malcolm de Chazal hadn't been translated into Spanish, when Oscar got back from his honeymoon, he founded a publishing company to change that. He knew nothing about publishing, no more than he'd known about bike riding. But when he pulls the books from his bookshelf, I can understand why he's proud: they're magnificent. He sums up, "It's through Luke that I discovered Malcolm, and now it's thanks to him that I've met you. Funny, isn't it?"

With the help of a bottle that's considerably less average than the first, we're now good buddies, Oscar and I, and I'm ready to admit to him how uneasy I felt when his Bavarian counterpart said that to write about the dice life, you have to be a dice man. I'm

not a dice man. Because I like my life the way it is? Out of a philosophical conviction? Or simply because I don't have the balls?
Whatever the reason, for the past two months that I've been
working on this story, I haven't once dared to take the plunge.

"Try it," says Oscar, taking a die from his pocket and placing
it between us on the table. I panic, as if in five minutes, without knowing what happened to me, I'll be obliged to massacre
my family with a machete or—the light version—climb Mount
Everest in flip-flops. Nothing doing: Oscar says I can simply let
the die decide where we eat. I'd planned on inviting him to a good
restaurant downtown. "Fine, write it down: that's the first option."
The next is that he'll invite me. The third, we'll go to the most
expensive restaurant in Madrid and toss the die again when the
bill comes. The fourth, we'll stay home. I grow more daring: the
fifth, we'll stay home and I'll prepare dinner. Oscar smiles, seeing
that I'm taking to the game. I rack my brains, trying to come up
with a last, more radical option. I say, "The sixth is that we'll take
the car and go to eat, say, in Seville."

Oscar nods. *"Bueno.* Now throw the die."

All of a sudden I'm afraid it'll land on 6. Because if it does,
I know that we'll *really* get up, get in the car, and drive to Seville, which is more than three hundred miles away; it's almost
10:00 p.m., and we've already drunk two bottles of strong red
wine. I throw the die, and—phew!—it lands on 5.

Now, I won't try to sell you the hours that followed as a major
transgression or a complete breakdown of the senses; nevertheless, tottering back and forth in the kitchen of a complete stranger
with a glass in your hand, opening cupboards, and mixing just
about everything you can find into a casserole with a wooden
spoon is quite amusing. My beef miroton was ten times too spicy,
and when I emerged from the kitchen carrying the steaming
dish, the whole family was waiting at the table. I was congratu-
lated for my cooking talent, and we agreed that such role plays can

be a good way of breaking the ice in somewhat tense situations. It would be interesting to use them to resolve international conflicts, we said. In Ukraine, for example. Once again that evening I noted how relaxed dice men's wives tend to be about their husband's foible. Susana Cuadrado doesn't seem any more worried than Ann Cockcroft that an addiction to chance will lead her family from one peril to the next. No doubt they're both right to be so trusting. But I continue to think I'm right to be wary.

7

Dear Friend,

It is our pleasure to inform you that Luke Rhinehart is dead. He very much wanted us to tell you this as soon as possible so that you wouldn't be annoyed that he wasn't replying to your e-mails. In recent years he had gotten great satisfaction out of his interaction with friends on the web, and he told us he had tried to avoid dying so he could continue these dialogues. Unfortunately, Chance had other ideas.

Luke didn't fear death, although he confessed to being a bit nervous. Death to him was just another one of life's unknowns, like traveling to a new land, starting a new book, trusting a new friend. Luke liked to laugh at death, but then again he liked to laugh at everything. He felt confident that death wasn't all it was cracked up to be. He promised to report back as soon as he could and let us know what he had found. He was confident we would all get a good chuckle out of it. However, at this point we still haven't heard word.

Some of you have asked about Luke's last days. They were no different from days from any week over the last several decades. For a man who believed in chance and change, Luke was discouragingly consistent. In fact, many of us who knew him were disappointed in his willingness to roll along on his familiar patterns. People who came to see him on the basis of his books were sometimes discouraged to discover how attached he was to his habits. Even when he threw the die, it was always to do more or less the same things.

"It's not rolling along in the same old patterns that is bad in itself," he said, "but rather if you're enjoying the rolling. If you're comfortable in the selves you're rolling along with, then roll on. Most people aren't. They don't like who they are. It's with them in mind that I wrote all those things about the die. But I'm fine as I am."

Luke's wife, Ann, was with him to the end.

"I'm dying," he said to her at one point early in the last week.

"Big deal," she said, straightening his pillow.

"It's just that I find it interesting. I've never died before."

"Well, a lot of people have."

"Right. And that's a quite comforting thought. All those people waiting to greet me on the other side."

"Or ignore you."

Luke stared at the ceiling. "That would be boring," he finally said.

"Typical Luke—always worried about being bored."

"Are you going to miss me when I'm gone?"

"Oh, come off it. You've been underfoot for more than fifty years. Instead of tripping over you as I have been I'll probably trip because you're not where I always assume you are."

"That's comforting, too."

"Of course I'll miss you."

●

When I received this e-mail, I was surprised, then sad, then moved. I'd only spent two days with George and his wife, but I liked them. So, since I had their number, I called Ann to express my condolences. When she picked up the phone, she was as cordial as ever and happy to hear from me, but she sounded a bit hurried and said she'd pass me on to George. I wondered if she'd lost her mind, or if I had, and I stuttered something about the e-mail I'd just received, and she answered like someone who was used to this sort of little misunderstanding: "Oh, the e-mail! Of course . . . But don't worry: it's not George who died, it's Luke."

When he got on the line, George confirmed, "Yeah, I was getting a little tired of Luke. I'm getting older, you know. I still love life: seeing what the weather's like when I look out the window in the morning, doing the gardening, making love, going kayaking, but I'm less interested in my career, and my career was basically Luke. I wrote that letter for Ann to send it to my correspondents when I died. I kept it in a file for two years, and one day I decided to send it . . ."

Ah, okay, I get it.

I asked him two more questions. The first: Before sending this e-mail, which is after all quite unusual, did he throw the die? Was it the die, finally, that decided Luke's death?

George seemed sincerely surprised: "Oh, no, that didn't even occur to me. The die can be useful when you don't know what you want. But when you know, what use is it?"

Second question: Apart from me, how did his correspondents take the news?

He gave his mischievous little laugh, like an old prankster. "Well, a few thought it was in bad taste. Aside from them, some thought: 'That's George!' And others: 'That's Luke!'"

"And you, what do you think?"

Published in *XXI*, fall 2015

Letter to a Woman of Calais

1

As surprising as it might sound, Hôtel Meurice in Calais is the parent of the famous five-star Le Meurice in Paris, and not the other way around. This former coach inn is even the ancestor of luxury hotels in Europe. Granted, today its luxury is somewhat stale; nevertheless, for the price of an Ibis hotel it long seduced English tourists. The problem, as any salesperson in Calais will tell you, is that the English tourists have all scrammed because of the migrants, and more generally because of the chaos that reigns in the city. Monsieur Cossard, the owner, would like to sell the business; unfortunately you can't sell anything in Calais. He'd also like to attract the CRS, or riot police, as customers. No less than eighteen hundred are stationed around the Tunnel and the port, a windfall for the managers of the low-cost Ibis and Formule 1 hotels. But the people who make the billeting decisions at the Ministry of the Interior must have deemed the Hôtel Meurice's bourgeois decrepitude, faded Jouy wallpaper, wobbly sofas, and outmoded trim ill-suited to the harsh tasks facing the riot police. A new group of customers appeared several months ago, however, composed half of journalists and half of filmmakers and artists from all over Europe, who've come to report on

the migrants' misfortune. At times you'd think you were in the
legendary Holiday Inn in Sarajevo, where practically all of the war
correspondents stayed at the height of the siege. At the end of
breakfast, they all pull warm down jackets over their multipocket
vests, grab their cameras, and get into cars rented at the Avis
agency on the Place d'Armes to head off to the Jungle, as if they
were heading to the front.

2

But I don't go to the Jungle—or not yet. I stay in the city. And
this morning before leaving the hotel I was given a letter at the
reception starting with the lines:

> No, not you!
>   This afternoon it was Laurent Cantet, last week Michael
> Haneke, and Charlie Winston's been here as well. So, no,
> Monsieur Carrère, not you! That's what we say here: we've
> had enough of these "People"—excuse the word—who
> come to Calais to earn their bread and who treat those
> of us trapped inside like laboratory rats! What have you
> come here for? To spend two weeks between *The King-
> dom* and your next opus, sleep at the Hôtel Meurice, write
> a few pages for *XXI*, and hand down your judgment on our
> city? You see that I write "our city" like a true Calaisian.
> Monsieur Carrère, do you know that in the three years I've
> spent in this hole I've been asked about the situation no less
> than once a week by people who've come in from outside
> and who wanted, like you, to write, film, and talk into the
> mike about what they've seen, perhaps believing that they
> can do it better than the rest, or wanting to assuage their
> imperious desire to throw in their own two bits? Calais

has become a zoo, and I'm one of the keepers. I know the ropes, so I wonder: Which trap will you fall into? Where will you settle in? At the Channel (I saw you there)? Or the Betterave (I saw you there, too)? Or Café Minck (where, of course, you were taken to shake hands)? I don't know, I can't quite put my finger on it, but what I'm sure of is that whatever you try, it'll be a failure.

The letter goes on like that for eight pages, more sad than cruel, well written, and signed with a name that sounds like a pseudonym: Marguerite Bonnefille. After reading it, I can't help getting lost in thought as I head over to Café Minck. On foot, which is uncommon in a department that's so poor that its tax revenues come principally from vehicle registration. I walk up Rue Royale, the main artery of Calais-Nord, which was simply *Calais* until the nineteenth century and is more or less an island. Rue Royale is known as the "street of thirst" because of all the bars that line the road. It's home to numerous brawls on Saturday nights. The bars are closed in the morning, as are some of the stores. The stores, however, aren't about to reopen, first of all because there are fewer and fewer people in Calais to buy anything at all, and second because Calais residents now do all their shopping, have their fun, and go to the movies—at least those who have the money— at Cité Europe, the huge mall situated near the entrance to the Tunnel in the neighboring town of Coquelles.

Cité Europe, the Tunnel: everything seems to conspire to make Calais *intra muros* completely superfluous. It remains a port, however, which you reach after crossing the Place d'Armes. This square, like the entire city, was rebuilt after the war by an architect who'd made a name for himself mostly on the French Riviera and in Casablanca, and who gave the city a Mediter-ranean touch that poorly matches the climate. The immense, windy plaza is decorated with two statues representing General de Gaulle and his wife, Yvonne—a native of Calais. Just a few days after I left, these statues would be tagged FUCK FRANCE. The tag is credited to the mysterious No Borders activists, who have neither nationality, structure, nor hierarchy, and who are very present in the Jungle. Although they're idealistic and dedicated, everyone here concurs that they're more or less like evil trolls, always on the lookout for any way they can wreak havoc.

In passenger transport, the Port of Calais is the biggest in France and the second-biggest in Europe, after Dover. For a long time it was the biggest employer in the city, along with the lace factories. The last word in that regard has not yet been spoken: an ambitious project baptized Calais 2015 (which is still not far along at the start of 2016) is set to double both the port's size and its capacity. But competition from the Tunnel, the depressing liquidation of the ferry company SeaFrance, and the daily incidents with the migrants have thrown up some major obstacles.

These subjects come up repeatedly among the regulars at Café Minck, where, as Marguerite Bonnefille rightly assumed, I was taken as soon as I arrived. My guides were a journalist who writes for *La Voix du Nord*, Bruno Mallet, and his wife, Marie-France Humbert, who works at *Nord Littoral*—which is pretty much like working for the Capulets and the Montagues, respectively, because even though they belong to the same group, these two dailies compete ferociously with each other. That said, everyone makes up over a glass of muscadet at Café Minck, one of the most convivial places in Calais, and, I think, in the world. By and large the customers are getting on in years: most of them retired sailors, fishermen, Chamber of Commerce employees, or labor unionists, who would make the day of any casting agent tasked with recruiting actors for a nostalgic film celebrating the working-class heroes of way back when.

The most remarkable thing, however, isn't this extraordinary concentration of ancient, ruddy, guileless faces, or that any number of those present must vote for the far-right National Front, but the custom, established by the owners, Laurent and Mimi, that all who come in the door—accompanied by the obligatory gust of sea wind—go from table to table to shake hands with the other customers, whether they know them or not, before placing their order. Despite my reserved nature, I, too, got in the habit of shaking twenty or thirty paws when I came in. And I was happy to do so until I learned in Marguerite Bonnefille's letter that I was acting pretty much like the tourist in Paris who gets around by Bateaux Mouches and spends his evenings at the Moulin Rouge.

3

Yes, that's right! I have a glass of muscadet at Café Minck in the morning, and in the evening I knock back a few beers at the Betterave, a trendy bar in Calais-Nord and a satellite of the Channel, which I'll talk about in a moment. Propping up the bar at both, I confirmed the truth of the cliché that people in northern France are as warm and hospitable as their climate is gloomy. It's like with the Russians: it's said they're drunks, sentimental, extreme—and it's true. Since I got her letter, however, I've suspected each face I see to be that of my mysterious correspondent: lying low, on the lookout, smirking ironically as I reel off my little couplet about what I've come to do. "Regarding your take on Calais," she writes, "the angle you've chosen is original, I grant you. Talking about Calais *without* its migrants: talking about the rest—if I understand correctly—that's somewhat new. You don't stick to the beaten path, bravo!"

You're unjust, Marguerite Bonnefille. I never said that I want to talk about Calais without its migrants—why not talk about Warsaw in 1942 without its Ghetto? I just want to focus people's attention on the city and its inhabitants. Everyone I talk to approves of this take: "It's true," they say, "we've had enough of people only talking to us about the migrants. And we've had enough of talking about nothing else." After which, they start talking about just that. Some aren't afraid to take sides, but many say that the worst thing is not being able avoid taking sides, being forced at every turn to say you're either "pro-migrant" or "anti-migrant." It's like with the Dreyfus Affair, which rocked France in the early twentieth century. A cartoon done at the time shows a large family dinner. In the first image, the head of the family says, "Please, let's not talk about *it*." In the second, the table's a wreck, the guests are at one another's throats, and the caption reads, "They talked about it."

4

Pro-migrant and *anti-migrant* are strange terms. Strictly speaking, no one's "pro-migrant," in that no one in this town of seventy thousand wants a shantytown of seven thousand poverty-stricken migrants on its outskirts, sleeping in tents, exposed to the elements, in the mud, in the cold, and who inspire, depending on your character, foreboding, compassion, or a guilty conscience. While I have met some people who're "anti-migrant" in the extreme sense of bawling "Drown them all!" or "Send them back home!"— which in many cases would amount to the same thing—they're not all that common.

A lot of people say things were fine when it was just "the Kosovars." Originally the term was used to describe those who arrived at the end of the Yugoslav Wars in the 1990s, but now the elderly above all use it to mean any foreigner in an irregular situation. Back then when there were only a couple of hundred of them, everyone made the best of things. But now that "the Siberians" are here as well, it's too much. Twice I heard people talking about "the Siberians." It took me some time to understand that by that they meant the Syrians, and with them the Kurds, the Afghans, the Eritreans, the Sudanese, all of whom, now in their thousands, have come from the war-torn regions of the Middle East or East Africa, which television depicts every day in blood and ashes, so you can understand that the poor people wanted to flee, but did they have to flee to our gardens, of all places? Fine, they've got to be taken in, but must it be here? Why Calais, which is already having such a hard time as it is?

No one is thrilled by the cumbersome presence of the migrants; the migrants themselves are in despair at being here. Only the anti-migrants hold them directly responsible—with a good dose of racism, it's true—while for the pro-migrants the problem lies with the state, with Europe, and above all with England, where they all want to go, which doesn't want anything to do with them, and which played the nasty trick of shifting its border to our side and getting us to guard it. This swindle goes under the name of the Le Touquet agreement, and even the people who call the Syrians "Siberians" know more or less what that is.

5

You get firsthand experience with the results of the Le Touquet agreement when you exit Highway 16 onto the beltway leading to the port and the ferry terminal in the east of the city. It's like in a war film or a postapocalyptic video game. Dozens of CRS patrol wagons are parked along the shoulder, looking out over the biggest shantytown in Europe. When night falls, young guys dressed in black anoraks and beanies emerge from this encampment and launch an assault on the beltway, using no end of tactics—chucking branches, rolling carts, and so on—to divert the attention of the CRS and slow down the traffic in the hopes of clambering on board a truck. Accidents abound, sometimes they're fatal, and even those who manage to climb aboard a vehicle stand practically no chance of going undiscovered when they get to the port, what with all the checks, dogs, infrared cameras, heat sensors, and heartbeat detectors.

It's a nightmare for everyone: the migrants, the CRS, the truckers, and the drivers, who're afraid either of being attacked by a migrant or of running over one—another, more basic version of the opposition between anti and pro. The road leads between two ramparts of white fencing, four meters high, topped with razor wire (the model called concertina). These fences cost the British government 15 million euros—it's their contribution; France supplies the personnel—and stretch as far as the west of the city, where they surround the Tunnel, which is the other way of getting to England.

There, what used to be a green, rolling landscape has been transformed into a gigantic moat. Last fall the Eurotunnel Group had 250 acres of trees felled to facilitate video surveillance and stop the migrants from advancing under cover: now a rabbit couldn't hide there. For good measure, some months later it flooded the entire zone. As Bruno Mallet said to me in Café Minck, if they could bring in crocodiles, they would. What's more, the sky, the sumptuous, ever-changing sky of the Opal Coast, is perpetually crisscrossed by helicopters. The blue lights gyrate, the sirens blare, men chase men. I don't want to heap too much criticism on the Eurotunnel, which has to protect its traffic, and it's hard for me to say who bears the brunt of responsibility for this situation—the French state, which doesn't do what it should; England, which takes what it wants from Europe and leaves us to sort out the rest; or ex-president Bush, who set the Orient on fire when he invaded Iraq. I'm not forgetting that my subject is the Calaisians and not the migrants—and if I did, Marguerite Bonnefille would no doubt remind me—nevertheless, I had to paint this backdrop to show how it's not easy here to think of anything else.

6

But that doesn't stop people from trying: from thinking about their work, their children, their friends, and from trying to lead a normal life. I wonder what it would mean for me if instead of spending two weeks here as a journalist, I'd come to live in Calais for several months or even years. "Two weeks, Monsieur Carrère, two weeks! Do you really think you can get to know Calais in two weeks? If you want my opinion, you should live here for a while and write a book." I hear the advice, perhaps it'll sink in. In the meantime, I wonder how I'd make a niche for myself if I lived in Calais for a while, where I'd hang out, whom I'd hang out with. The answer is easy, my correspondent had little chance of being wrong: at least at first I'd hang out at the Channel.

Created by the Calaisian theater director Francis Peduzzi and situated along the beltway in the city's former slaughterhouse, this huge space is a prestigious national theater, with the concomitant subsidies. Rightly presenting itself as "living space," it has roomy redbrick buildings, industrial parquet floors, a bookstore, a bistro, comfy couches and armchairs, and was all customized—a little Gustave Eiffel, a little Jules Verne—by the Nantes artist François Delarozière, who's accompanied the project for the past twenty years and whose every visit is awaited by the entire community like the return of the Messiah.

Because the Channel, where it's easy to believe you're in New York or Berlin, is a community. Everyone knows everyone, everyone kisses everyone else on the cheek when arriving: the team, the regulars, but also the students from the nearby high school who come to do their homework here. It's the arty, well-heated

lung of a downtrodden, divided city. It's also, as one can well imagine, the most solid bastion of the pro-migrant camp in Calais. The
migrants' help associations meet here informally on Wednesdays
(along with the organic-food producers); the Appel des 800—a
group of filmmakers, writers, artists, and intellectuals who
were the first to sign a manifesto bringing attention to the refu-
gees' plight—has natural allies there; plenty of cool young people
are always ready to serve as guides for the Parisian artists who
want to visit the Djeungueule, as they call it. Because at the
Channel you don't say *la Jungle*, as you'd say in French, but "la
Djeungueule"—making it sound English. As I quickly found out,
saying *la Jungle* is uncool, not to say square.

7

At the Channel there's an excellent bookstore belonging to the
publisher Actes-Sud, run by Marie-Claire Pleros. Marie-Claire
is pretty, with a grave demeanor and gentle manners, and a beautiful voice. Everyone loves her. She helped me a lot when I first
arrived, introduced me to people, some of whom opened their
homes to me and whose names I want to mention here: Dominik
and Marie-Claire Richard-Multeau, Jean-Louis and Annie Bou-
gas, Pierre-Yves and Mimi Chatelin. By Calais standards, with its
13 percent unemployment, they're among the privileged, and
they know it, even if their privileges aren't boundless: a chartered
accountant, a teacher, the manager of a holiday village, a newly
retired phys ed teacher who, after completing the single-handed
Route du Rhum yacht race several times, is now preparing to sail
around the world—four years, five years, he predicts, and his
wife laughs tenderly: One or two will do, don't you think? . . .
These regulars at the Channel vote unfailingly on the left, read
such magazines as *XXI*, which commissioned this story, and

bring up remarkably open and friendly children who go to good universities in Lille or Paris, and who know full well that even if they wanted to, they couldn't live where they were born because there's no work now and probably won't be any in the future. They live in the Saint-Pierre neighborhood, that is the former town of Saint-Pierre-lès-Calais, which emerged in the nineteenth century with the lace industry and is now part of the city.

That's where the factories and workers' houses were built because the upper classes of Calais—which wasn't yet called Calais-Nord—didn't want to be disturbed by the incessant rumbling of the Leavers machines and Jacquard looms, which worked around the clock. People my hosts' age—my age, that is, late fifties—remember this nerve-jangling sound with their entire bodies, which doesn't stop them from getting all nostalgic when they talk about it. Then it stopped. The lace industry, which employed some twenty thousand people before the war and five thousand just twenty years ago, today employs no more than four hundred. Of the hundred or so factories, only four remain. The buildings of the others are no more than enormous, blackened, empty brick carcasses, whose courtyards are invaded by rust and weeds, ideal for squats. It's there that the migrants took shelter, until city hall evicted them last year and crammed them into the Jungle, where they would be less annoying to the people of Calais, or so the idea went. So that they wouldn't be tempted to return, all the doors and windows were boarded up.

In the streets of this formerly bustling and industrious neighborhood, two out of every three houses are up for sale. Those that aren't empty have been subdivided by their owners—who have themselves moved to the more peaceful neighboring villages of Marck and Coulogne—into minuscule apartments, which they rent out to welfare recipients through the city's human services agency. No light shines through the cracks of the closed blinds. The deserted, ashen streets are bathed in an atmosphere that's part curfew and part siege. So it's all the more warm and comforting when friends open their door to you. These houses, where I would certainly have my napkin ring if I lived in Calais, are like cabins on board the *Titanic*: full of books and records, with sparkling kitchens and framed quotes in the bathroom by various apostles of antiglobalization and degrowth, such as Pierre Rabhi, whose theory of the hummingbird was expounded to me over a plate of Maroilles and boulette d'Avesnes, the classic, deliciously stinky cheeses of the Nord department.

There's a forest fire, all the animals flee, but the hummingbird flies to the river, fills its tiny beak with water, and heads back as fast as it can to pour the contents on the blaze. It flies back and forth like that all day, and when a hippopotamus remarks that pouring these few of drops of water on such an inferno is a joke, the hummingbird replies, "Maybe, but I'm doing my bit." For my friends in Calais, as long as the migrants were still squatting in the center of town, their bit consisted of bringing them food, blankets, and clothing, and talking to them. And, now that they've been evacuated to the Djeungueule, in doing more or less the same thing but less often. My friends feel guilty, what's more, and worry about how courageous they would have been during the Occupation. They'd like to do more—as would I: in my neighborhood in Paris there are all the Afghans and Kurds I'd need if I wanted to be a more energetic hummingbird.

8

You know what's the most difficult thing in this city, Monsieur Carrère? It's the inertia of things. It quickly brings you back down to earth, dashes you to the ground, even, when you see what's wrong. Everything's solidified: the yuppies in their bubbles, the dimwits in their high-rises, the politicians in their politicking, the barbed-wire professionals along the beltway and the near Tunnel. I think I'm getting depressed here, Monsieur Carrère. At night the wind gusts up to sixty miles an hour, and we come home to our warm houses while . . . Oh, right: we said we wouldn't talk about that.

You know, Marguerite, I do what I can. I meet people, a lot of people. Not just the yuppies in their bubbles, as you say—even if I find it reassuring that there *are* yuppies in their bubbles in Calais. You invited yourself into my report, so fine, you can help me. Let me quote you again:

> When we found out what your angle was, my friend and I smiled. We said that way you'd be able to talk about the unemployed, the alcoholics, and the incestuous offspring who populate the city. About the firemen who vote National Front and the couples who wind up in court for initiating their adolescents into incestuous sex, when they aren't sucking off their German shepherds. About the fights that break out on the first of every month because everyone's received their welfare checks and can't wait to line up at the ATMs, go shopping in a cab, then get plastered and butt heads in the bars of Calais-Nord.

There, Marguerite, you're talking about the Urban Priority Zone of Beau-Marais and the neighborhood of Fort Nieulay: frightening places, whose violence someone such as my friend Marie-Claire finds far more frightening than the petty crime of the migrants. They're what's known as "priority" neighborhoods, except that now, as Kader Haddouche says with a tired smile, the entire city has become priority. Kader Haddouche is thirty-nine, his parents are illiterate Algerians—his father's a retired asbestos worker, his

mother a cleaning lady—relatively uncommon origins in a city
where, unlike in the coal mining areas, there was practically no
immigration. There was no need for additional laborers: the lace
industry already had all the workers it needed.

Paradoxically, that was Kader's chance: the lace industry only
took "long-standing Calaisians," as he says. Coming from an Arab
background, he had no chance, so he had to go to university, an
idea that never crossed the minds of his childhood friends, who
counted on getting jobs in the lace industry. That's how Kader became a biology teacher at the vocational school, while his "long-
standing Calaisian" friends all figure more or less predominantly
in the tableau vivant that you obligingly painted for me, dear
Marguerite: unemployment, alcoholism, despair, racism. Polling
stations 20 and 21 of the Calais Metropolitan Area, where more
than 50 percent voted for the National Front in the last munici-
pal elections, are in the Beau-Marais district, where they puke
on migrants although they never see any because like everyone
else the migrants have no reason to go there.

Kader took me for a walk around Beau-Marais, where he
grew up, where he still lives, and where he feels at home—
which he doesn't in Fort Nieulay, where he's not on his own turf
and keeps on his guard. Under a cold, drizzling rain, we wandered between peeling towers and playground slides that make
you want to cry, talked with teenage dropouts who freeze their
butts off smoking shit in a devastated, windswept hall ("Got any
better ideas? There's nothing to do"), visited the Social Center,
whose director says, "Here we foster coexistence, well-being, and
a sense of togetherness." Once she's said that, she gives us an
apologetic smile: she knows it's doublespeak—even if, as Kader
tells me, it's here that he read his first *Tintin* comics, and it's here
that his mother still comes each week for gym classes; that's not
nothing—and in addition to being not nothing, that's all there
is. The last businesses in the neighborhood, the home appliance

store But and the discount store La Foir'Fouille, have left. The only thing that's opened up in recent years is the employment agency Pôle Emploi. That way there's no need to go downtown, and apart from looking for a fight on Saturday nights, no one does. These details struck me as telling, Marguerite, but I admit that all things considered they're slim pickings, and I didn't see a single person sucking off a German shepherd.

9

I dragged my feet and circled the Jungle, but put off the moment of going there. In your letter you call it "this thing that eats away at all of us, all the time." You do get the feeling that it eats away at people here, that it obsesses and divides them, and that this division isn't just between generosity and egotism, openness and withdrawal, the educated and the dregs of society who've found people to hate who're even more miserable than they are, but also, concretely, between people who have gone to the Jungle—some of whom have even gone there more than once—and people who've never set foot there. I'm not taking a dig at the second, I might even be one of them if I lived in Calais. And I have more respect for Marie-Claire, who has refrained from going there until now for fear of being overwhelmed by emotion and her powerlessness, than I do for so many hardened tourists of adversity.

We finally went there together, accompanied by a young woman, Clémentine, who works at the Channel and knows the camp well and often takes visitors there. I won't tell the story of our visit. I tried, but I get caught up. Right away it takes up too much space, you can't limit it to a couple of paragraphs. I'd simply like to say a word here about those Calaisians who, like the brave Clémentine, go to the camp in their Pataugas sneakers with packs on their backs to help, care, and inform.

They say what volunteers of all nationalities say. At first it got on my nerves, like a sort of missionary romanticism; nevertheless I think it's true: The Jungle is a nightmare of misery and filth, terrible things happen there, accounts are settled and women are raped, its inhabitants are not all peaceful engineers, enthusiastic students, and virtuous people who've been persecuted for their political beliefs—far from it. However, there's also something tremendously exhilarating about it: the energy, the thirst for life that pushed these men and women to undertake long, perilous, heroic journeys, of which Calais, no matter how much it looks like a dead end, is just one stage.

Which is exactly what the fresco done by graffiti artist Banksy on a concrete wall at the entrance to the Jungle expresses. The city authorities wanted to have it painted over before they realized it was a work of art and, what's more, one by the most famous—and most expensive—street artist in the world. Now it's part of the city's heritage, like Rodin's statue *The Burghers of Calais*. It shows Steve Jobs carrying a bundle and stick and a vintage computer and evokes the fact that the Apple founder was the son of a migrant to the United States from Homs, in Syria. But his situation was different from that of today's migrants, and the parallel is all the more flawed in that Steve Jobs was only of Syrian origin, that he was born in San Francisco and was adopted. Nevertheless while some migrants will die trying to get to England and others will hang around the margins of Europe leading a life of humiliation and poverty, a Syrian or an Afghan who has braved a thousand dangers to arrive in Calais and who is, God knows, going through hell in the Jungle, can still view the camp despite everything as a moment in his life, a transitional ordeal, a stepping-stone to making his dreams come true. While the situation of the little white guy who lives on unemployment benefits in Beau-Marais is less precarious, to an extent it's also more logjammed, more irremediable, and I wonder if, more or less consciously, that doesn't go some way in explaining the resentment he feels.

10

Him: . . . We bend over backward, welcome them with open arms, make sure they're warm. Okay, there's a war raging where they come from, and people say they're poor, but when you're poor, you don't have seven-hundred-dollar smartphones, designer clothing, or basketball shoes that cost ten times more than mine. They're just pretending to be poor, but don't you be fooled, they're richer than we are. They don't pay taxes, they're given food and a place to sleep, the associations give them everything they want, and they take the money and go to the hardware store to buy screwdrivers, hammers, electric saws, everything they need to cut the fences and break whatever they can. And who pays? We do, with our tax money.

Her: And now on top of everything they're given driving lessons so that they can pass the road test, while my son doesn't have the money.

Me: Really? They're given driving lessons?

Her: Yes. I saw it on the Internet, and I saw two of them coming out of Gambetta Driving School. I can tell you, they were grinning to high heaven. We go shopping for the week at Auchan, and when we compare our carts to theirs, theirs are filled to overflowing with bags of fresh bread, huge packs of soft drinks and chips, and all the best brands. Those overflowing shopping carts are horrible, just horrible. They have stores in their Jungle. Is that legal? A French store pays taxes, it needs a license, you think they pay for one? The French are left high and dry, it's up to us to make ends meet, and they're given everything on a silver platter.

Him: They drop things from bridges and cross the highway as they please. If a French person did that, he'd go to prison, but they can do what they like. Now I think, if one of them crosses the highway in front of me, I won't slow down, I'll speed up.

Her: They walk around in groups of thirty or forty. They squint at you, looking for things they can steal. My sons are twenty-one and seventeen, but when they go out, I'm afraid they'll be attacked. You go to town, you're all alone, and there are tons of them. People get mugged all the time.

Me: Have you been mugged?

They look at each other: No.

Me: Have your sons?

Her: No.

Me: Do you know someone who's been mugged? Someone I could meet?

Her: No, but there are some. There's a woman who lived on the Chemin des Dunes, which borders the camp. It was her place, and now that the migrants have made her life impossible, she's the one who's had to go.

Him: She made a video, it's on the Angry Calaisians' website. They wanted to get organized and protect themselves, but they had to stop because it got too dangerous. They're fathers and mothers, and no one's protecting them. The police told them that they couldn't protect them, that they're not allowed to protect French people.

Her: You know what's written at the entrance to their camp? "One cop, one bullet."

11

I've got reams and reams of text like that, Marguerite, and you must know it all by heart. It's the constant litany of those you talk about in your letter, "who say their last names first and their first names last: Delcloy, Kevin, or Carpoulet, Monique." Those are the grassroots Calaisians, and it's difficult to hear them talk without a tinge of haughtiness, because more than being unpleasant, their remarks betray both their financial and their educational poverty. It's also hard to know how much of what they say is true, and just how unsafe Calais has become. The police and city hall didn't answer my requests for a meeting—which weren't exactly pressing, it's true. Like the perceived cold, the perceived unsafety varies depending on whom you're talking to. But even people such as my friends with Pierre Rabhi quotes in their bathrooms, who tend to play the violence down for ideological reasons, acknowledge that a climate of threat lingers over the city.

The pro-migrants dread it, the anti-migrants hope for it, but everyone awaits the catastrophe that will upset the existing order: either the murder of a migrant by a Calaisian—which, I'm given to understand, has no doubt already happened—or of a Calaisian by a migrant—that, no, not yet: we'd know. Unless . . . The Angry Calaisians are convinced it has, and that while the local papers splash outraged stories across their front pages whenever a migrant sprains his little finger, going on orders from on high, they carefully hide acts of violence committed on French people. The Angry Calaisians think the government sides with the migrants against the locals, and that *Nord Littoral* has been infiltrated by the No Borders people (that's not the impression I got when reading it every morning). And the Angry Calaisians have shouldered the task of fighting disinformation by doing the work that the journalists should be doing: talking about what's really going on in Calais, what people don't know, and what, if people knew it, would spark a civil war.

Going on what's perhaps an excessive taste for nuances and the complexity of the world, I would have liked to paint the portrait of some Angry Calaisians who are not complete rednecks, but those I met fell very much into that category. Did they attack first, before retreating into vigilante journalism and tirelessly filming with their cell phones as the riot police or trucks on the beltway got pelted with stones? Were the nighttime rounds they went on before being stopped by the police racist attacks pure and simple—as testified by a video uploaded by their sworn enemies in the No Borders movement? Or, as they affirm, were they infiltrated by chaotic, racist, and violent elements, whereas they themselves are none of the above?

I have no idea. All I can say is that although I didn't return to the Jungle, I did go back to its perimeter, accompanied by two Angry Calaisians: a burly young guy who works as a security guard and a frail, silver-haired woman, both, dear Marguerite, the type of people who introduce themselves first with their last name, then with their first. Except that they don't introduce themselves because they prefer not to tell me their names. They have good reason to be wary of journalists, and I'm afraid that this article, if they read it, isn't about to change that. The goal of our excursion was to "come to the aid of a resident."

I've already said that I found the Angry Calaisians neither open nor particularly endearing. I must also admit that the resident in question has every reason to complain, and that living as she does on the Route de Gravelines, which borders the Jungle to the south, must be sheer hell. It's a hell to which everything contributes: on the one hand the incessant hordes of haggard, fierce young migrants on the potholed, muddy road—no doubt in advanced sexual frustration like those who went on the rampage in Cologne this past New Year's Eve—who take shortcuts through private gardens to get to the highway, and who steal wood, give residents the finger, flash their cocks, and catch pets for food (or so people say); and on the other hand the presence, certainly reassuring but no doubt a burden in the long run, of the CRS patrol wagons, which never stop pulling up in front of the house and then screeching off again; and finally because this house, which she worked her fingers to the bone to purchase and hasn't even finished paying off, is no longer even worth the nails that hold it together. It's certain, if ever someone was in need of people coming to her aid, she was, and I didn't exactly see myself preaching to her about France, the land of refuge, or quoting Matthew 25:35: "I was a stranger and you welcomed me." But I did ask her if everyone in the neighborhood shared her views. Speaking for her, the silver-haired Angry Calaisian pointed to a little house down the street and said, lowering her voice as if we could be overheard, "She's against us."

12

Of course, I go and ring the doorbell of the little house. No answer at first, but seeing that a car is out front, I insist. I don't doubt that from her window the resident we've come to aid is looking at me. The door finally opens, revealing a young woman holding a baby in her arms. North African, early thirties, with a pleasant air. I reel off my intro, explaining that I've come with an Angry Calaisian who told me that she was on the other side. She nods with a smile and invites me in. She tells me her name and allows me to publish it: Ghizlane Mahtab. She's not at all suspicious and likes to talk:

She and her husband have lived here for a year. He's a delivery driver; she's an unemployed lab technician, and while waiting for something better to come up, she works at McDonald's (the Angry Calaisian's daughter works at Burger King). The couple have four children aged between two and eight. People call their home "Wi-Fi house" because before the fences went up, thirty or so migrants were always out front. The neighbors were certain she gave them her password, but she didn't; it's just that the reception was good, and she didn't mind it when they were there. She's never had any problems. It's true that her neighbor has had some; maybe she exaggerates a little, but she's certainly had problems. All that Ghizlane can say is that she hasn't. No one's ever peered in her windows, stolen socks from the line, or swiped a loaf of bread from the trunk of her car while she was taking in the groceries. The thing is, she likes people, she smiles at them, she's interested in them. The kids from the Jungle come and play with her children, her little girl calls them "the neighbors," the biggest calls them "those poor guys." Even if he's more reserved than Ghizlane, her husband thinks as she does. He gave his shoes— his wedding shoes, even—to a guy who was walking barefoot, and it doesn't bug him when she takes the kids to go have tea in the Jungle. The neighbors aren't happy, they call the police and get them to move the migrants who're gathered in front of her place, and some people in her family no longer kiss her because they think she could have scabies, or worse. Others think she has a lover in the Jungle, but she doesn't care. She knows that people get robbed and raped, that drugs are sold, and that shitty things happen, and she's really pissed off at the two hundred assholes who blacken the reputation of six thousand good people—but isn't it the same thing in Calais? Aren't there assholes everywhere? As for these Angry Calaisians who put on balaclavas and throw rocks at the migrants, who come and do their rounds night and day, they can't have anything better to do. The two who spend so much time at the house I've just come from, don't they have kids, don't they have housework to do?

I listen to Ghizlane as she serves Chicken McNuggets to her little girl, and I'm encouraged by her words. I tell her, and she smiles as if to say it's normal, the least she can do, we're all human, right? Two months ago, journalists from *Paris Match* interviewed and photographed her; she doesn't know if it's come out, she should find out. She's excellent in the role of the positive, open, spontaneous heroine, as good as the woman you see on TV all the time who's installed dozens of power strips at her place and lets the migrants come charge their cell phones.

We say goodbye and I head back over to the resident's place. She's still being aided by the Angry Calaisians. I tell them I've just visited the neighbor who's "against them"—which they know perfectly well—and that she says she hasn't had any problems. At that point the Angry Calaisian twists her mouth into a smile and scores a point: "Well, if she doesn't have any problems, why doesn't she ever open her blinds?" It's funny, I'd noticed but hadn't given it any thought: it's noon, the weather's nice, it's dry and sunny, yet her metal blinds were down. Our conversation had taken place under the dining room light, and no matter how much Ghizlane beams, her house is closed up tight like that of the last humans in a zombie film. A bit put out, I say, "That's true." The Angry Calaisian is triumphant and repeats at least three times, "Well then, why does she live with her blinds down? Huh? Why does she live in the dark?"

13

I'm nearing the end, Marguerite. You were right: two weeks is a joke. I've seen nothing of Calais—or very little. And of what I saw, there's so much I couldn't find room for . . . I'd have liked to talk about the lace industry, its grandeur and decadence, the dozens of highly specialized trades it involves: drawer, designer, pointer, card puncher, wheeler, bobbin presser, warper, embroiderer, seamstress, darner, and cartwright, with all of these meticulous skills converging around that of the loom operator, the veritable hinge pin of the textile industry and respected tamer of the twenty-ton, twelve-yard-long machines that produce what will become, first and foremost, delicate underwear and bras.

I'd have liked to portray Anne Le Deist, whom you must know; she's a regular at the Betterave: a designer who used to work for Noyon Dentelle, one of the last factories still in operation, and who now works as a freelancer for Chinese clients; or Bruno de Priester, the last person in Calais to punch cards by hand, whom I saw officiating at his machine like an organist; or factory boss Olivier Noyon, a handsome, jovial son of an entrepreneur from the Nord region who carved out a career for himself in the audio-visual business in Paris at the Cité des Sciences, and then in music, before going through a midlife crisis and coming back to head the company so it would stay in the family. His wife, a film editor, was probably not at all thrilled at having to relocate to Calais. At the start he didn't have a clue about lace, so he learned and came to love it. And it seemed to me that he—"Monsieur Olivier," as everyone calls him at the factory—is much loved in return, even though since he arrived his job has basically been to rise to the Asian challenge, delocalize to Sri Lanka, and push through three major layoff plans in fifteen years.

And Abbé Delenclos! I'm sure you know him as well, Marguerite: the priest at Fort Nieulay who's been there for fifty-three years and who's straight out of a work by Georges Bernanos or Maurice Pialat. A fatigued colossus who loves to laugh and is the only person I know capable of saying, "All things considered, Fort Nieulay's quite a pretty place." A long time ago he used to have parishioners; now he has almost none. His church is empty, but he finds it normal for the old to go and not be replaced by the young. "We don't eat, sleep, and breathe religion in these parts, and we're not here to fill quotas either, just to remind people that Christ exists." Although he has precious few worshippers, he still has neighbors who come to ask his advice, and whom he helps not do too many grossly stupid things. As long as men like that exist, even if it's just one in each city, you can't despair entirely. Still, he's eighty-four . . .

Okay, Marguerite, I have to wrap things up. I have a maximum of nine thousand words and no longer have the space for the ship broker Antoine Ravisse, although he well deserves it, a man who hasn't gone to bed a day in his life without going to the port and looking out at the sea. Or for his new partner Valérie Devos, who's a lawyer and as hyped as he is calm, and who, while he looks out over the English Channel, talks in a machine-gun staccato about the terrible reprisals between the Albanian human traffickers she's been appointed to defend. I have to thank you, Marguerite Bonnefille, for challenging and guiding me, while at the same time hiding from me your name, your face, your profession. However, you gave me a big hint: Do you remember this bit from your letter? "I just went out in my car to cover the tensions in the city. Are you familiar with these tensions, at night? I trembled as I approached, afraid that someone would throw a rock at my windshield or start banging my car with a stick. But shh! You've chosen another angle."

14

Someone who goes out in the night to "cover tensions" is called a journalist. You cover crime stories, Marguerite, you must work in the same offices as my friend Bruno or his wife, Marie-France. Since you're one of us, you'll know how important the end of a story is. Ghizlane Mahtab's drawn blinds kept gnawing at me. I called her up to ask about them. She took it nicely, as if I were questioning not her confidence in humanity, but her ability as a housewife: "The blinds were closed? Then I hadn't done the cleaning. But come over now and you'll see: all the blinds are open."

It struck me that starting from this one detail you could tell two entirely different stories. On the one hand, the version with a ray of hope, a corner of blue sky, according to which when you're open to others and smile at them, you'll receive openness and smiles in return. On the other, the version that would please the self-proclaimed realists and the cynics who pride themselves on their lucidity: not only is the Jungle a hell, but the ray of hope is a lie. This young mother tells journalists her rainbows-and-lollipops story, although in fact she's barricaded herself in. "In the dark," as the Angry Calaisian said, and even if they're not particularly likable, at least the Angry Calaisians tell the truth. I wondered which version I'd choose if I were writing a fictional account. But I'm not writing a fictional account, so I went back to the Route de Gravelines on the day I left. I know this has no statistical value and that what's true one moment can be false the next, but still, Marguerite, I was happy to see that on January 22, 2016, at eleven o'clock in the morning, Ghizlane Mahtab's blinds were open.

The report you've just read was published in the magazine XXI in the spring of 2016. During the months that followed, not much changed. Each night migrants blocked the port beltway with tree trunks or concrete blocks to force the trucks to stop, slicing their tarpaulins and hiding inside in the hope of reaching England. The Jungle perimeter thronged with the usual mix of Afghan or Eritrean teenagers, police officers, Angry Calaisians, representatives of humanitarian associations, and more or less big-name celebrities—the most recent being Pamela Anderson. Calais was nicknamed "the blue city" and "Las Vegas" because of all the flashing lights. So business more or less as usual. Then, at the end of October 2016, what had been pending for months happened: the Jungle was dismantled.

I didn't go, but I heard all about it through my correspondent Marguerite Bonnefille. After my story was published, we struck up a friendly correspondence and she told me her real name: Marie Goudeseune. As I had suspected, she works for a local paper, La Voix du Nord, and it's through her that I have most of my information. The dismantlement lasted four days and was well organized—well organized from the point of view of the authorities, less well from that of the Jungle inhabitants. The police crammed most of them into buses bearing optimistic and poetic slogans such as TO THE END OF MY DREAMS. *They were taken either to the neighboring camp in Grande-Synthe, or to the shelter for minors in Saint-Omer, or to villages in the four corners of France. Once the Jungle had been more or less emptied, guys dressed in orange suits arrived, the bulldozers went to work, and the shelters were burned in front of an avid army of journalists and a dismayed last group of inhabitants.*

"Everything's fine when you talk about migrants in general," writes Marie. "It's a pure management question. But it's not the same when you talk about Saleh, 16, who bursts into tears in front of the burning Kid's Café because he doesn't know where or with whom he'll sleep tonight, because he's desperately alone." The Jungle literally went up in flames; today you'd think it was the ruins of a village ravaged by war or a natural catastrophe. After that, almost no migrants were seen in Calais or the surrounding area. The police routed out the last squatters and ad hoc campers, applying "zero tolerance." The weary Calaisians breathed a sigh of relief.

Two months later, however, several dozen migrants came back, and La Voix du Nord, *where Marie works, asked worriedly, "Are they back?" (For the moment this return is marginal: between 150 and 200 people, whereas the Jungle was home to at least 8,000.) A second question arises: When Britain leaves the European Union, how will that affect the way in which the British border is guarded—a role the French now grudgingly assume? And a third: What will become of the immense wasteland where the Jungle used to be? There's talk of an equestrian center, and also of a nature reserve administered by the Coastal Protection Agency. The people at the agency have only one thing in mind, Marie tells me: to use it as a resting area for bank swallows. Ironically, bank swallows are migrant birds, and here they'll be given a far warmer welcome than their human predecessors: let them fend for themselves.*

Orbiting Jupiter: My Week with Emmanuel Macron

The man does not perspire. I discovered that on September 12, 2017, on the island of Saint Martin, a French territory in the Caribbean that had been devastated a few days earlier by Hurricane Irma. Uprooted trees, roofs ripped from houses, streets blocked by mountains of debris: for three hours Emmanuel Macron, president of France, has been walking through what remains of the village of Grand Case in the sweltering, clammy heat amid the strong odor of burst sewage pipes—or in other words, of shit. Everyone accompanying him, including the author of these lines, is dripping with sweat, literally soaked, with large circles under their arms. Not him. Although he hasn't had a second to change or freshen up, his white shirt with elegantly rolled-up sleeves is impeccable. So it will remain until late in the night, when the rest of us are exhausted, haggard, and reeking, and he's still as fresh as a daisy, always ready to shake new hands.

Every interaction with Macron follows the same protocol. He turns his penetrating blue eyes on you and doesn't look away. As for your hand, he shakes it in two stages: first a normal grip, and then, as if to show that this is no ordinary, routine handshake, he increases the pressure while intensifying his gaze. He did the same thing to Donald Trump and it almost turned into an arm wrestle. Then, with his other hand, he clasps your arm or shoulder, and when the time comes to move on, he relaxes his grip while lingering almost regretfully, as if pained to cut short an encounter that meant so much to him. This technique works wonders with his admirers, but it's even more spectacular with his enemies. Contradiction stimulates him, aggression galvanizes him. To those who complain that the state took its time bringing relief, he explains calmly and patiently that the state does not control extreme weather conditions and that everything that could be anticipated was anticipated. At the same time—and we'll come back to this *at the same time*—he never stops repeating, just as calmly, just as patiently, "I came to Saint Martin to hear your anger."

It's a good thing, too, because up comes an angry woman named Lila, who bars his way and accuses him of not giving a damn about the victims' suffering, and of coming "just to perform" before the TV cameras in his ironed shirt and plain tie that doesn't look like much but must have cost a fortune. She's so vehement that the group of islanders who've gathered around them start booing and jeering and saying that's no way to talk to the president. Anyone else would have taken advantage of the situation and said, "You see, the people are behind me." Not Macron. For him, Lila is a challenge. He takes her hand and his face divides in two—something I've often seen it do: the right half, brow creased, is determined, grave, almost severe, giving you the feeling that whatever he does, he's doing it in the eyes of history. The left half, meanwhile, is cordial, optimistic, almost mischievous, giving you the feeling that now that he's here, things will be all right.

For five, ten minutes, he soaks up Lila's wrath. He has a schedule to stick to, and his team's in a hurry, worried about running overtime—and they will run overtime, they always do.

Nevertheless, it's as if he has all the time in the world, and he does: he's the boss. One wonders if he'll win over Lila, who, now feeling self-assured, growls cockily, "I'm a bit of a pain in the ass." To which he responds with his most charming smile, "I admit, that didn't escape my attention." Good one: she smiles back, she's going to back down, she backs down. Then at the last moment, as they shake hands before parting, she has second thoughts and says, "Let go of my hand, damn it! Let go of my frigging hand!"

For me this "Let go of my hand!" was like a desperate attempt to cling to her anger—and her integrity. To escape the president's hypnosis, his persuasiveness worthy of the Pied Piper of Hamelin, his almost frightening seductiveness. Watching him, I was reminded of the opening credits of the TV series *The Young Pope*, in which Jude Law, dressed in an immaculate cassock, advances across the screen as if on a cloud, in slow motion, weightless, and turns and winks at the camera. Macron winks often. He did it to me. No matter what you think of him, whether you see his rise as a political miracle or a mirage destined to fade away, everyone agrees: he could seduce a chair. The professional commentators who started to drop him after just a few months of his presidency can keep calling him a powdered marquess, a megalomaniac with royal pretensions, a rich man's president, or a communicator without a cause, but he couldn't care less. The people, by contrast, with whom he is directly, physically in contact are his bread and butter. Anyone who's had his or her hand shaken by Macron is lost to the opposition: he or she is destined to vote Macron and to convert to Macronism. But you can't shake hands with everyone in the country. And anyway, just what is Macronism?

•

Let's take another look at his file: Just three years ago this young man was totally unknown to the general public. By contrast, he was well-known to a small Parisian milieu in which politics, finance, and the media are almost incestuously intertwined. Everyone in this milieu—which he looks down on today, as if he'd never belonged to it—is proud of being his friend, having his mobile phone number, and getting upbeat text messages from him in the middle of the night. At thirty, he's an investment banker at Rothschild & Co.—in this line of work, you can't do any better. At thirty-four, he joins the cabinet of then president François Hollande as deputy secretary-general. And, let it be said in passing, for one-tenth of what he was making as a banker: it's not money he's after. I remember seeing a documentary on the new Socialist president at the time: everyone, starting with Hollande, seemed stiff, like stuffed animals dressed up in the dark suits of power. Everyone, that is, but one sharp-witted, vibrant guy with sideburns, the only one in this gallery of mummies who seemed alive. That was the day I learned the name Emmanuel Macron.

Just two years later, this young man is minister for the economy, industry, and digital affairs. Hollande adores him: he's the ideal son who's so good at charming his elders that a big name in the Socialist Party calls him the "old folks' man." The old folks in question, his mentors, tell him that if he wants to make a career in politics, he has to choose a constituency, run for office, and become a member of parliament: that's how it's always been done in the Fifth Republic. Macron thanks them for the advice, but doesn't run; he's not interested in doing what's always been done.

The presidential election approaches. By all accounts it will play out between the Socialist left, burdened by Hollande's morose five years in office; the right, caught up in fratricidal quarrels; and the eternal populist wild card that has borne the name Le Pen for the past forty years—business as usual. Then, in April 2016, exactly one year before the election, the young and dashing minister of the economy announces to a sparsely filled room in his hometown of Amiens that he is creating his own party, En Marche!—with an exclamation mark. It will take some time before the commentators figure out that the initials EM also stand for the name of this young man about whose ambitions and convictions little is known. One month later he hands in his resignation to a confused Hollande and leaves the government. Even if his intelligence and charisma are generally recognized, no one would put a penny on his winning the presidential election. Or almost no one, that is. To the first people who attend his meetings and join his party, Macron repeats like an incantation that they will remember it all later, like those who joined de Gaulle in London in 1940: they were there, right at the start of the adventure.

And what an adventure! This is a guy who only runs for a single office in his entire life, that of president of the republic, and wins. A guy who understands that the parties that have structured French public life since the end of the Second World War are clinically dead, and that it is time to offer the French something new. What we're seeing, he maintains, is a clash between old and new, navel-gazing and openness, routine and audacity, conservatism and progress—and it goes without saying that he, Macron, embodies progress, openness, audacity, the new. He says he's neither on the right nor the left—although saying that usually means you're on the right. So wouldn't it be more accurate to say he is on the right and on the left at the same time?

•

And here we are again, back at the famous *at the same time*. This banal, everyday expression has now become practically unusable in France, except as a running joke. For a normal French person today, saying "at the same time" is already making a joke about Macron, who has raised this speech mannerism to the level of a philosophical position. As soon as he thinks something, he says to himself that you can also think the opposite, that other people think the opposite, and that you have to see things from their point of view, too. When adopted as a general principle, this "at the same time" quickly gets us to the old centrist utopia: overcoming rifts, choosing the most open and the most competent people from each camp, governing in the center, bringing people together. Many have dreamed about what in the last century was still called "the third way," between economic liberalism and social democracy. But in recent years, no one has been able to revive it, until Macron appeared with his stainless self-assurance and phenomenal good fortune.

It's said that when inquiring about an officer he didn't know, Napoléon asked only one question: "Is he lucky?" In his staggering rise to power, the young man, who has nothing against being compared with Bonaparte, benefited from an unprecedented planetary alignment. President Hollande decides not to run again—partly because this spiritual son, about whom he'll say, "He betrayed me methodically," is also in the running. The Socialist Party chooses as its candidate Benoît Hamon, who's likable but a lightweight. The conservative candidate, François Fillon, ruins any hopes his camp may have had with a string of scandals and lies. That leaves Marine Le Pen, who will self-immolate during the one-on-one debate with Macron by showing just how sectarian and unfit to govern she is. The way is clear. At thirty-nine, Macron becomes the youngest president in French history, and an international star. The country's entire political class is dumbfounded. Stunned, former president Nicolas Sarkozy is said to have commented with disconcerting humility, "It's me, but better."

During the campaign, Macron changed. At Orléans, on a day of fervent tribute to Joan of Arc, he all but explicitly compared himself with the Maid of Orléans: heralding from a distant village, alone, unknown to all, she hears voices that command her to save France—and what's more, she does. Macron, meanwhile, this former student of the École Nationale d'Administration (for decades, the finishing school for the nation's political elite),

banker, high official, and young minister—the absolute prototype
of the insider who knows the rules of the game like the back
of his hand—reinvents himself as an inspired outsider, a mystic capable of ending a meeting by whirling around in front of
eight thousand people, his arms folded in front of him, his eyes
half-closed, chanting "I love you!" until his voice goes hoarse.
François Hollande, just after being elected, said he would be
a "normal" president. France, ungrateful, wasted no time in
finding that "normal" wasn't a quality they wanted in a leader.
Macron, who saw his predecessor get bogged down and sys-
tematically takes the opposite stance, announces that he'll be a
"Jupiterian" president.

Such ambitions give one pause for thought. The same goes
for Macron's decision to do away with the traditional televised
Bastille Day interview, on the grounds that the questions put by
the journalists risked not doing justice to the new head of state's
"complex thoughts." The words *complex thoughts* were the butt of
a good many jokes, but they weren't uttered by accident. Placed
in quotation marks, they were approved by his communication experts, and one imagines that *complex thoughts* is the new name
for thoughts *at the same time*, thoughts that view reality from on
high and take account of its many facets. In the same way, in Macron's entourage there's no longer any talk of "reforming" the country, but straight up of "transforming" it. That, incidentally, was
one of the first things he said to me: "If I don't radically transform
France, it'll be worse than if I did nothing at all."

But still, aside from glorifying Macron's personality, what
is Macronism about? Almost six months after his election, the
question feels more and more pressing. The new president gained
power thanks to his charm, and by offering the country a breath
of optimism it badly needed. Like Britain, France was once a world
power. It dreams of regaining that status, and Macron promises
that with him, it can; that if France follows him, it will become as

seductive and competitive as he, Emmanuel Macron, this young president and envy of the world.

For several months we did feel good about ourselves, but now it seems that this Prince Charming effect is dissipating. The number of French people who approve of Macron has plunged from 66 percent to 32 percent since the elections—a historic drop. Why? Because a statesman who wants to make things happen will inevitably become unpopular? That's what he says, and it's true. Because he promised to act fast and he is acting fast, and because to do that he's willing to force through his policies? Because his labor law reform, fast-tracked by executive decree, better suits bosses than workers? Because by scrapping the wealth tax he's favoring the rich? Because, although his campaign focused on overcoming divisions, he's increasingly moving rightward in a way that shocks voters on the left? A bit of all of that, and above all, a hint of arrogance and class contempt. When he criticizes "slackers" and those who "kick up bloody chaos," it's the poor and unemployed who feel targeted. When he talks about train stations where "the successful cross paths with those who are nothing," no one hears what he surely meant to say: that inequality saddens him and that he's trying to reduce it. No, everyone hears that the unsuccessful are nothing in his eyes.

•

I spent a week with Macron and his entourage to write this article, and as it was a week of traveling—to Athens and then to Saint Martin—my conversations with Jupiter took place, logically enough, in the sky. All power elicits courtlike phenomena, which you can observe at leisure in the presidential plane. But this court is hypercool because the president's inner circle is made up of young people who, at thirty, have jobs you can normally only get at fifty, if at all, and who, while never ceasing to be total control freaks, have all adopted the boss's direct, easygoing style. Yet, as easygoing and direct as he is, the boss never forgets the historic dimension of his role, and it's in this made-to-measure suit that he goes on his first official visit to Greece.

What's at stake, and in my view what makes the trip such a challenge, is that the president must tell the Greeks things they want to hear—namely, that their cause will be taken up with Germany—while at the same time saying nothing that risks rubbing Angela Merkel the wrong way. When I share this fledgling idea with him, he deflects the question. (Okay, I didn't exactly expect him to say, "Hey, bull's-eye.") Nevertheless, he doesn't mince his words: "The Greek crisis was a European crisis, a European failure even. Instead of punishing its leaders for their lies, we punished the people of Greece, whose only mistake was to listen to these lies. The rifts produced in Europe by this crisis are deep, and that's why I have to go to Athens: to return to the source, to talk about democracy."

Talking about democracy is what he did on the Pnyx, the hill in the center of Athens where in ancient times the assembly of citizens raised their hands to vote on the city's laws and budget. From there you can see over to the Acropolis, and in the early-evening light it was a scene of stunning beauty. Almost sixty years earlier, André Malraux, a great writer and minister of culture under General de Gaulle, delivered on the Pnyx one of the memorable and nebulous speeches that were his trademark, and you can't help feeling that Macron intends to situate himself in this tradition—that of the visionaries and not the managers, the philosophers and not the bureaucrats.

He started by breaking the ice in a particularly effective way with a two-minute preamble in Greek, learned phonetically. Speaking as someone with a smattering of modern Greek, I can tell you that's no mean feat. Then he launched into his favorite topic: Europe, and the sovereignty of the European peoples, which he doesn't want to leave, he says, to the fainthearted, fearful clan known as sovereigntists—those right-wing populists who want to shut out the world and retreat into splendid isolation.

Half an hour of fine rhetoric leads up to the oratorical climax: "Look at the time that we are living in: it is the moment of which Hegel spoke, the moment when the owl of Minerva takes flight." Macron doesn't explain the metaphor; no doubt he overestimates his audience's philosophical sophistication. Minerva is the goddess of wisdom, and the owl is her symbol; this owl, Hegel says, waits for night to fall before flying over the battlefield of history. In other words, philosophy can't keep pace with events. "The owl of Minerva," Macron continues, "provides wisdom but it continues to look back. It looks back because it is always so easy and so comforting to look at what we have, what we know, rather than at the unknown . . ."

Later that evening I told Macron that I'd liked his speech, and he looked at me with intense gratitude, as if no one's opinion could mean more to him. Then I said, without meaning any harm, that I'd also liked the speech given by his host, the Greek prime minister Alexis Tsipras. In a flash, Macron's blue eyes clouded over and he turned away: other, more pressing matters called. Still, I'd been sincere. I thought his speech was fine indeed. What's more, it's not every day that you hear a head of state appealing to the authority of Hegel. Macron did it not like someone who'd been handed a draft by a speechwriter, but like someone who knows what he's talking about. He believes in the Hegelian notion of the "cunning of reason," which is to history what the "invisible hand" is to the market, and which explains how, in serving their personal interests and desires, without knowing it great men help bring about what the time intrinsically demands.

When it's not Hegel he's quoting, it's Spinoza, whom he loves for his struggle against the "sad passions," such as bitterness, resentment, and defeatism—to which Macron himself seems to have had remarkably little exposure. Today in interviews he has a dialogue with the German thinker Peter Sloterdijk, and while still in his twenties Macron served as assistant to Paul Ricoeur, an immensely respected, octogenarian humanist philosopher. Since Mitterrand, we've forgotten what it's like to have a culti-vated president. The day after Macron's speech on the Pnyx, he had a lunch with Greek intellectuals. These Greek intellectuals were ardently Francophile and quoted one great French poet after the next. With each poem Macron was able to pick up where the other person had left off, reciting the next verses without missing a beat. Baudelaire, Rimbaud, all by heart: it's hard not to believe that this man really likes poetry.

•

Such mastery is intriguing: you start looking for the flaw, the chink in his armor. Macron has political enemies, but not much gossip circulates about his personal life. According to one rumor, he's gay. His wife and he denied it with elegance and good humor, and with-out making a big thing of it. Nevertheless, at least one somewhat screwy anecdote is in his unofficial biography, a bungle that puts him in a more human light: the *Le Monde* takeover affair. In 2010, *Le Monde*, the most venerable French newspaper, was put up for sale. Unusually, the newspaper's statutes allow its journalists to choose the buyer. The bids come in and the journalists are having a tough time keeping them straight when the young and dapper Macron, then a banker at Rothschild, appears and proposes his services as an adviser. Pro bono, he says, because he likes *Le Monde*, and the press, and freedom of the press, and that kind of thing. The people at *Le Monde* find him supernice, and they get a kick out of going to see him at Rothschild & Co. late in the eve-ning after the offices have closed.

Two powerful groups are lining up to buy the paper. The journalists favor one group, but Macron isn't thrilled with this because that group includes a banker whom he hates. The rival group is being advised by Alain Minc, the éminence grise behind a good many French politicians for the past forty years. Minc has a reputation for devious clairvoyance, even if the candidates he has backed have generally been defeated at the ballot box. By chance, a journalist working with *Le Monde*, Adrien de Tricornot, has some business near the Champs-Élysées in the building where Minc's luxurious offices are situated. When he gets there, he sees Minc coming out, accompanied by . . . Emmanuel Macron.

In what follows, Tricornot has to be taken at his word, but he's a respectable journalist, and crucially, the story has never been denied. In a fit of panic at being caught playing a double game—advising both *Le Monde* and Minc—Macron rushes back into the building, runs over to the staircase, and disappears. Tricornot follows in hot pursuit and finally catches up with Macron on the top floor, trapped and with no way out, ridiculously pretending to be talking on the phone: a child caught with his hand in the cookie jar. The journalist takes cruel pleasure in saying to the Jupiter-to-be, "Well, Emmanuel, we no longer say hi to our friends?"

•

Macron hates nothing more than being caught out. In the election campaign, he stated that French Guiana, a French overseas department, was an island—which it isn't. As the gaffe was picked up everywhere by the media, he defended his remark by saying that he knew French Guiana wasn't an island, but that, stuck between the Atlantic and the Amazon, it was nonetheless a sort of island—more an island than not an island. I observed this poker player's preternatural self-assurance in person earlier this month, when I saw him briefly once again at the Frankfurt Book Fair, where France was the guest of honor. Macron gave a sparkling opening address; Angela Merkel, following, spoke in her more down-to-earth way. Then Macron swept off to shake the hands of authors and editors.

It's all going well until the Franco-Congolese author Alain Mabanckou pushes his way through the crowd to say that he heard Macron's speech and has one criticism. "Yes?" Macron asks, seizing the writer's hand. Mabanckou explains that the president didn't say a word about La Francophonie (that is, the entire French-speaking world, particularly the former French colonies). It would be easy to answer that, in a speech celebrating Franco-German relations, that wasn't the heart of the matter. But Macron says something else, eye to eye: "Talk about Francophonie? I did nothing else."

Somewhat exasperated, Mabanckou insists, "You didn't mention a single great francophone author. At the very least I'd have liked to hear the name Léopold Sédar Senghor."

"You didn't listen closely enough to what I said. I did talk about him!"

The situation becomes embarrassing. Hundreds of people are there, and none of them heard the name of the great Senegalese poet and statesman any more than Mabanckou or I did. As it becomes clear that the incident could blow up and go viral, Macron understands he's got to back down, and his way of backing down is to say that while he didn't actually pronounce Senghor's name, his name is understood as soon as you say "Francophonie," so it's clear to all that you're also talking about Senghor. (As a former math teacher of Macron's said in an interview for a documentary: "In my discipline, things are fairly simple: either you know the answer or you don't. But I discovered that there's a third possibility: the young Macron." Even if he doesn't know, he'll string you along until you're convinced he does.)

•

When I asked the president's office for permission to accompany and interview Macron, it went without saying that he would not read the piece prior to publication. The one condition: that I send them the sentences I quote Macron as saying. This is customary in the press and protects the person being interviewed from journalistic extrapolations. But it also protects the journalist against the interviewee's bad faith: once he's approved the sentences, the interviewee can't then turn around and say he didn't say them, or that they were misrepresented. In theory, I had no problem with such an arrangement, but in practice, I do. I've got several dozen pages of notes in front of me, jotted down during a half-hour interview on the flight to Athens, and an hour-long one on the way back from the Caribbean. In all of my notes, in my view, there's only one strong, beautiful sentence—and this strong, beautiful sentence, this sentence that rings true, was off-the-record. In its place I was given permission to use a perfectly dull, perfectly formatted variant, which I will spare you.

By default, then, here are some samples of the president's words: "I believe our country is on a cliff edge; I even think it's in danger of falling. If we weren't at a tragic moment in our history, I would never have been elected. I'm not made to lead in calm weather. My predecessor was, but I'm made for storms." And: "If you want to take a country somewhere, you have to advance at all costs. You can't give in, you can't fall into a routine. But at the same time, you have to be willing to listen. Listening to people means recognizing their share of anger and suffering. And that's something that will always belong to them. I'm not here to promise happiness, but I can recognize this constant, this uniqueness: it's the only way to respect them." Finally: "France isn't cynical, but the elites think it is. France isn't made to be a postmodern country."

I listen to him saying such things—they're quite interesting and he says them well. His voice is youthful and smooth, his sentences fluid, natural, persuasive. Sometimes I can't help smiling to myself, for example when he says he's a "metic"—the ancient Greek word for a foreigner accorded some of the privileges of citizenship—in the world of politics and the media. That's the word he uses, *metic*, and you can see why it gives rise to smiles when it's used to describe Emmanuel Macron. Why not *pariah* while we're at it? So I listen, half under his spell—okay, let's say three-quarters. And I remember the comment made by my fellow writer Michel Houellebecq: "I tried to do an interview with him . . . Frankly, getting people who talk very well to say something real, something true, is like pulling teeth . . ."

I continue to look for the flaw. Everyone has one—a place of shadow and secrecy, a melancholic zone—and as a writer, my job is to see it. With Macron, the flaws don't exactly jump out at you. Nonetheless, I'm sure they exist, or rather, I hope they exist. So I ask him what he thinks. The question throws him off a bit. He reflects, hesitates, then: "My flaw? Maybe that I'm claustrophobic." He remains pensive, and for the first time I hear something like three dots between the words that file from his mouth in battle formation. ". . . Not in the physical sense: I don't have any listed phobias, but I'm claustrophobic about life. I can't stand being shut in, I have to get out, that's why I can't have a normal life. Deep down, my flaw is no doubt that I don't love normal life."

To an extent, that's a good thing: the life of someone who wants to—and does—become president of the republic cannot be normal. And the interaction you have with him can't be normal either. But I don't let up and go at the question from another angle. Philippe Besson, a French writer who knows him well, wrote a book about him, aptly called *Un personnage de roman*, or "a character from a novel," which contains the following description: "This man, so warm, so physical, who knows so many people and whom so many people know, has no friends." Is that true? I ask. Macron will go on to answer that it's not exactly true, that although he has few real friends, he does have some, and that his private life is absolutely essential for him. But before he says these reasonable things, before reflecting at all, he blurts out, "My best friend is my wife!"

•

It's tempting to see Macron as a cyborg, a seducing machine completely void of emotion. It's tempting, but no sooner has it occurred to you than you're obliged to think the opposite. Because there's no getting around that the young, ambitious technocrat, the man who tells everyone what he or she wants to hear, is also the hero of a grand love story. I think this story is what the French like most about him, particularly Frenchwomen. It's a kind of revenge for centuries of patriarchy during which everyone found it normal for a man to be twenty-four years older than his wife, but not the other way around. Taking this breach of convention to the extreme, the woman who is twenty-four years older than him seems perfectly at ease, and her husband loves her as much as he did when they first met.

Let's go over the file once again, from this almost mythological angle: Brigitte Auzière is from a solid, provincial, upper-middle-class background; she's married to a banker (not an investment banker) and is the mother of three children. A French teacher, she's just been assigned to the Lycée la Providence, a Catholic school run by Jesuits in Amiens. In the staff room, all talk focuses on one pupil who dazzles everyone with his knowledge and intelligence: the young Macron. He's fifteen, he, too, comes from a well-established, upper-middle-class household, both his parents are doctors. He's good-looking, with a pleasant manner and longish hair, and he's more comfortable in the company of his elders than he is with his classmates.

Madame Auzière teaches a theater class. He enrolls and falls head over heels in love with her. It takes him two years to win her heart. "You're not serious when you're seventeen," runs a poem by Rimbaud. Quoting the poet as she tells the story, she says with a laugh, "He was very serious when he was seventeen." He was very serious when he convinced her that this was the love of their lives, and that she should leave her family to be with him. A high school student who falls in love with his pretty teacher and ardently pledges his love to her isn't all that rare. What's rarer is when, twenty-two years later, the high school student and his former teacher are still together, and the high school student is president of France.

I observe them on the flight to Athens. They're in the central block of the Falcon 7X jet, and from what I can see from where I'm sitting three yards away, they touch each other nonstop. If he gets up to go to the toilet, he squeezes her shoulder in passing. He smiles at her; she lifts her head and smiles back. Their eyes seek each other out, find each other, often they hold hands. It's remarkable, moving even. But still: they display this intense closeness, this insatiable need for each other, as if they were forever posing for celebrity magazines. So you wonder: Is some of this for show? Carefully staged storytelling? Maybe, but what would it be masking? What truth? What pact? When everything looks so harmonious on the surface, you can't help looking for the catch. Yet it seems clear that you can't fake this sort of thing—not for that long, not all the time. You can go back and forth endlessly about how much of Macron's personality is authentic and how much is cooked up, but you need only see him and his wife together for half an hour to know that part of him is as true as can be, and that this element of truth is her.

I sat with Brigitte Macron on the way back from Athens and started off our discussion on quite a bad note because I was still puzzling over the question of flaws and melancholy. Clearly her husband views his life in terms of destiny, I said. That's true, she confirmed. But since any real destiny must imply adversity and even defeat, I went on, I wondered what form adversity and defeat could take in the life of someone such as Emmanuel

Macron, and how she, his wife, imagined the proverbial retreat from Russia that necessarily awaited him—because if such a fate didn't await him, he would not be a great man, not a hero. The more I proceeded with my gloomy, interminable question, the more Brigitte's face, usually so open and buoyant, showed signs of dismay. But she's not someone to succumb to a passing mood for long. Glasses of champagne arrived just in time: it was the birthday of Tristan, one of her young staffers. At her prompting everyone burst into a chorus of "Happy birthday to you!" After that she said to Tristan, with a laugh and a shake of her blond hair, "We're your present!," and it struck me that must have gone down just as well in her classes in Amiens.

She had been a teacher loved by her students, who would hang around after class to talk about Stendhal or Flaubert. Even though she's retired, she remains a teacher and accepts with a smile that she's a bit of a pedant. Where others would say, "I don't want to talk in my husband's place," she said something I've never heard anyone else say: "I don't like prosopopoeia." (In case you don't know, prosopopoeia is a figure of speech in which an absent person, or even an abstract thing, speaks.) Coming back to my question, she let me know kindly that both she and her husband had faced their share of adversity. "I can't honestly say we've had to deal with defeat. But adversity, yes. To live a love like ours, we've had to harden ourselves against malicious remarks, mockery, and gossip. We've had to stand shoulder to shoulder, be courageous and joyful." She was joyful when she said it, just as joyful—and likable—as everyone told me she would be. (Everyone loves her.)

To wind up our conversation, she told me a charming story about her theater class. She and the young Macron are looking for a play to stage together. There's one they like, by the Neapolitan playwright Eduardo De Filippo—already quite a demanding choice. But the play only has five characters, and the class has twenty-five students. No problem: the young Macron rewrites it, inventing the twenty missing roles. They still have a video of the performance that Brigitte would like to watch one day—but, she says, her husband has asked her to wait so they can view it together.

•

Like many people I know, I've witnessed three phases with Macron. During the campaign, I thought, "Something's happening." When the elections rolled around, I thought, "I'd like to see him win." Yet I knew that my vote was a class vote: it was normal for privileged people to vote for Macron. Now that he's in power, I think, "It would be good if he succeeds." But what would that entail? That he make history? That he transform France? That he turn it into a country of start-ups where everyone is an entrepreneur, and the only thing that matters is efficiency? And after that, that he transform Europe, because France is going to seem too small for him?

All of that is possible. Or rather, not impossible. He could also go crazy—that's a risk you run when you get so much power so fast. Or, quite simply, he could fail and join the crowd of ambitious politicians who sought the "third way," stumbled over messy reality, and wound up administrating like everyone else. That's his big worry, I believe. That's what makes him say, "If I don't radically transform France, it'll be worse than if I did nothing at all." In the meantime, he is ready to write roles for the whole country, provided Brigitte and he will be directing the play.

Published in "The Long Read," *The Guardian*, October 2017